Every Day With a King

by Dale Best

Daily Devotions with King David

PREFACE

There is hardly a mood or feeling one experiences that King David or the Psalmist doesn't mention in the Book of Psalms. Each of us has feelings ranging from desperation to anger to gratitude to peace. King David and succeeding holy men express daily distress while living in their world. Age old situations correlate to life in our fast paced society.

God produced the Psalms to inspire us. These lessons teach us. Many verses provide us with the essential rules for living a life pleasing to Almighty God. Each devotion is written for introspective Christians whose aim is to be Christ-like. The conclusion of many of the Psalms instructs us in achieving that goal.

These devotions are written from the Wesleyan perspective that we have a free will to sin or not to sin. God has mercy and will forgive us from any and every sin.

It is assumed that King David wrote the first seventy two Psalms, while holy men called Psalmists wrote the remaining chapters. The devotions attribute credit to each respectively.

Another book written by the author is Gems for the Day at Amazon.com.

The cover was created by
imagesbybest@mac.com

All scriptures quoted are from the New King James Version, The New Possibility Thinkers Bible by Paul David Dunn and Robert H, Schuller, Ed., Copyright 1996, Thomas Nelson Inc. unless otherwise noted.

©2009 by Dale E. Best

INTRODUCTION

Every Day with a King is a devotional centered on the book of Psalms. Since December 1976, I have read five chapters of Psalms and one chapter of Proverbs each morning. As you read the book of Psalms, notice that Chapter one and 150 each have six verses, which are short, powerful, and distinctly different in their application to our lives.

The Psalms begin with How blessed is the man who does not walk in the counsel of the wicked, nor stand in the path of sinners, nor sit in the seat of scoffers! But his delight is in the law of the Lord, and in His law he meditates day and night. Psalms 1:1-2.

It seems very appropriate to read more of the Psalms living in a world teetering on eternity's death row. A prayerful reading of Psalms and Proverbs gives what is needed for life and godliness.

At times when I have wanted to share salvation with someone, and the time frame was a few seconds, I simply encouraged them to read Psalms 51, which is a prayer of repentance followed by praise. Jesus is the center of the universe; *all things were made by Him and for Him.* His wisdom framed the world and our existence; *He established the earth upon its foundation, so that it will not totter forever and ever.* Psalms 104:5. The wisdom of Christ is found throughout the Bible, and everyone who professes to be a believer should endeavor to be marinated in God's Word.

In today's world, there is much uncertainty and a need for peace. *Those who love Thy law have great peace and nothing causes them to stumble.* Psalms 119:165. C.H. Spurgeon, author of an expository and devotional commentary on the Psalms, refers to it as the "Treasury of David." This "Treasury" covers years of history, gives us hope, joy, and a sense of peace and belonging. The Psalmist writes, *Thou doest open Thy hand, and doest satisfy the desire of every living thing.* Psalm 145:16. There is a place of refreshment for a thirsty soul. *O God Thou art my God; I shall seek Thee earnestly; my soul thirsts for Thee, my flesh yearns for Thee, in a dry and weary land where there is no water. Thus I have beheld Thee in the sanctuary, to see Thy power and Thy glory. Because Thy lovingkindness is better than life, my lips will praise Thee. So I will bless Thee as long as I live; I will lift up my hands unto Thy name.* Psalms 63:1-4.

Psalms 150 closes the book with adoration fitting for our Lord. This praise for the Lord comes from a heart filled with holy love and delight, and a heart filled with great confidence that the Lord is who he says He is. As you read *Every Day with a King*, may you be encouraged in your faith.

A prisoner of Hope,

Warren Hardig
Men For Missions International Executive Director

January 1

"But his delight is in the law of the Lord, and in His law he meditates day and night." Ps. 1:2

Jerome, one of the saints of the past observed that meditating day and night is a continual type communion. This is a far cry from our short morning secular devotion and an evening prayer with table grace thrown-in which many of us practice. I recall a time when our pastor encouraged us to spend an hour each day in prayer for our coming evangelistic services. I readily took him up on the challenge thinking that would be 'no problem'. So that night as I prepared for bed I arbitrarily decided now is the time to start. Arrayed in my pajamas I ceremoniously knelt beside the bed. I began by confessing my sins and then moved on to praying for others. My prayer encompassed my family, friends, all government officials, and ending with all leaders of the world. Satisfied I had prayed my hour, I raised my head. Only five minutes had elapsed on the clock. What in the world was I going to do for the next fifty-five minutes? Maybe, just maybe, I was a pygmy Christian.

To possess the delight or joy King David had, we must practice the presence of Christ every moment we are not concentrating on a task. We receive a pleasure similar to talking to a friend. This sensation seeps in as we keep our mind focused on Him. This pleasant feeling comes slowly almost imperceptibly as we consciously spend more and more time with Christ, our Savior. After walking with God on a moment by moment basis, we will be able to say the joy of the Lord is our strength (Neh. 8:10).

January 2

"I will declare the decree: The Lord has said to me, 'You are my Son, today I have begotten you.'" Ps. 2:7

If it were possible, how would you like to be the child of a king? You would have a genuine feeling of security with the secret service men always close by. At your call would be abundance of pleasures, conveniences, and exotic foods to eat. The king provides his children with the best of everything. Wouldn't it be truly enjoyable to be a son/daughter of a really wealthy king?

The only thing better than being the pampered child of the king is to be the king. The king could have anything his heart desired; a new speedboat, a fancy car, or the latest designer clothes. You would only have to answer to your conscience because you are the highest authority in the land.

Our scripture gives us a situation that exceeds being a child of a king and even superior to being a king. The status, that can not be surpassed, is being a child of Almighty God, the Creator of the Universe. As a parent desires good things for their child, God wants the best for his children even as humans. We are on equal terms with the inheritance that Jesus Christ gets. We can always gain an audience with God, our Father. He only requires us to ask in faith, then we shall receive that our joy may be full (John 16:24). God is presently preparing a mansion for each of his adopted sons and daughters. Eyes have never seen nor have ears heard all the things God has ready for his kids (I Cor. 2:6). So each of us can live each day in the joyful anticipation of our eternal destiny.

Today, let's open our heart to the cleansing

blood of our Savior, Jesus Christ. We, at that moment, become a child of the Prince of Peace. We will then be entitled to all the riches of heaven.

January 3

"But You, O Lord, are a shield for me, my glory and the One who lifts up my head. I cried to the Lord with my voice, and He heard me from His holy hill." Ps. 3:3-4

When danger is near, I will trust in You, O Lord. Why should we ever fear when Almighty God will be our constant shield and protection? Do we often act as though God is nowhere in sight, when we are criticized for doing good, passed over for promotion because of our Christian stand, or a financial crunch squeezed us? The Psalmist brings to our attention that we must recognize that God is always nearby to help and/or to save us from disaster.

God promises to lift our head when we are in the terrible throes of depression. What an awesome thought! God cares for us when we are blue, in a bad mood, or in depth of despair. We, mere humans, receive individualized personal attention from an infinite God. Wow! God takes his precious hands and gently lifts the face of every believer. Then we can look upon Jesus rather than stare at our immediate problem. Who but our God has the unlimited capabilities to give every Christian personal time and attention? Our Savior is alive and well as evidenced by his resurrection. Since he is alive forever more, he still hears our prayers. He is not an idol made of stone or any such thing that cannot hear and respond.

God answers in marvelous ways! One time He turned the sun backward. Our Omnipotent God sent rain after two and a half years of drought. On another occasion, He calmed stormy seas. Jesus personally healed the sick daughter and through the Holy Spirit does the same even today. He made the Russian iron curtain to fall in the 1980's after seventy years of atheism. He leads our loved ones to the point of salvation.

God performed the miracle of answering our prayer of confession and saved us from sin. How He is fitting our lives for a glorious mansion in that magnificent place called heaven. Praise the Lord! He hears needs and answers from heaven.

January 4

"Hear me when I call, O God of my righteousness! You have relieved me in my distress; have mercy on me, and hear my prayer. Be angry, and do not sin. Meditate within your heart on your bed and be still." Ps. 4:1, 4

David begins by stating that he, a man after God's own heart, endured trouble and distress. He begs God to hear him. In that very next sentence, he lets us know that God has listened in the past. Could it be that we forget how many times God has helped us out when we prayed? David admitted that God had relieved him in his earlier times of distress. Isaiah concurs that God hears, "...and while they are still praying, I will hear" (65:24b).

David continues by invoking the mercy of God. The king knew that he was in a no bargaining position. Therefore, mercy, undeserved help, was desperately needed. Do we humble ourselves or do we rationalize? We say, "Everyone else does it, so it must not be too bad." Or do we say,"My cousin does it all the time and he's a Christian." All I need mercy for is the little white lies or inconsequential sins. King David knew that sin was sin, no matter how gigantic or trivial. Mercy is invariably needed from our compassionate God.

King David says, "Be angry and sin not." So there is an anger that is a sin. When we get mad, are we so upset that we lose control of our body or mind? This is when we sin! When anger rises within, we need to carefully guard our mouth and be cautious of our actions. When we are mad, we may blurt out things that later we are so sorry for. In anger, we may even abuse our family or injure our body. It is sin to damage the temple of the Lord, our bodies. The way to be angry and sin not is to permit God to help us control our impulses.

A normal remedy for getting rid of pent up anger may be to punch a pillow or go outside and give a primeval scream. King David suggests another way. Hold that anger until night when we can in the quiet of the bedroom, consider the causes and possible alternatives to revenge. In that stillness, think about permitting God to minister to our distressed mental and emotional state. If we call upon God in confession and depend upon His mercy, our prayers will be answered for God hears!

January 5

"For you are not a God who takes pleasure in wickedness, nor shall evil dwell with you." Ps. 5:4

Has wickedness, murdering, abuse, or drugs stalked your neighborhood recently? King David proclaims our God does not condone nor take pleasure in sin and evil. So if God does not approve of that kind of behavior, guess who is the sole blame for initiating it? You're right! Satan! So let's not accuse God of the trouble, but praise and bless His holy name.

If Satan, that fallen angel of light, is responsible, let us not be a part or participant in any evil. If we follow Satan and his ways, we will suffer in hell while the ages roll on. One version of the Bible translates the last half of the verse as God will not tolerate the least sin in heaven. If that is the case, we better check our lives for the least sin in our lives; gossip, favoritism, resentment, cheating, white lies, or insincere flattery. If we ask God, he will cleanse our soul entirely of all evil (1 John 1:9).

There is a place that is without all strife, bitterness, and hatred. It is heaven! The scripture states our life can be white as snow and blameless before men (Eph. 5:27). So today we need to shun the very appearance of evil (I Thess. 5:22). We must cling to our Savior for protection. If God takes no pleasure in sin and evil, neither should we, as blood-bought Christians.

January 6

"You shall destroy those who speak falsehood; the Lord abhors the bloodthirsty and deceitful man." Ps 5:6

What is the truth? It is telling the facts, as we know them to be, right? Then any shade of change tends to be a lie. If it is not the whole truth, then it is not the truth.

King David writes here that, "God will destroy all who tell lies." That person, who lies to get out of being punished, is in trouble. Watch out for people who lie to their friends or enemies. Keep your eyes peeled for the punishment those who say they were at one place and weren't or vice versa. God is aware when we lie about the amount of change we receive, the speed we were driving, or the extent of our relationship with a certain person. God's desire is to do away with those who are a gushing fountain of lies.

One reason God is so strongly against lies and

liars, is that Satan is the father of lies (John 8:44). The Devil is the archenemy of God. Satan only wants bad and harm to come to us. God warns us in order to save us from punishment. He keeps us on the road to heaven, where blessings and everlasting happiness are. Satan's goal is to trip us up, spoil anything good we are doing, and herd us toward hell. Thirst, heat, and torture are the final end for all who don't watch out for Satan's temptations.

God hates it when we break His law. He still loves us but not our actions. Some parents can't seem to separate these two, but our Heavenly Father does. Remember God **always** loves you. Lying and breaking His laws **always** leads to trouble and punishment.

Since we don't do things that displeases our parents, similarly let's not do things that make our Heavenly Father unhappy.

January 7

"Depart from me, all you workers of iniquity; for the Lord has heard the voice of my weeping." Ps. 6:8

Have you ever had a good friend who for some reason or other turned cold toward you? They treated you with indifference after all you had been through together. Oh! How that hurts your feelings! You did a lot of soul searching in an attempt to unearth a good reason for the change in their behavior.

In our scripture, God is saying to all who do evil, a lot or a little, you are departing from my commandments. What if the King or Queen of England said, "You can not come into my presence? Go away."? What a gigantic sense of rejection! Let us refrain from evil, so God will welcome us into his presence, when we pray and when life is over.

Most often evil accumulates in our lives by littles. One day we over-ride the urgings of the Holy Spirit to visit a sick friend or church member. Most likely the next time the voice of God will be less distinct and harder to distinguish. This process is called hardening our hearts to God. When we turn from God, we automatically consent to following Satan and his evil schemes. Yes, doing our own thing is actually doing what Satan desires for us.

Did you ever pray fervently for something and God did not bring it to pass? After that experience, you took for granted God never hears our prayers. King David emphatically states that God does hear our cries and moans if we are sinner. When you seek me with all your heart, I will be found. Our God is never deaf to the calls of his children! So let us take courage and renew our efforts to converse frequently with God Almighty, who definitely hears our fervent pleas.

January 8

"O Lord, our Lord, how excellent is your name in all the earth, who have set your glory above the heaven! .... What is man that you are mindful of him and the son of man that you visit him?"

Ps. 8:1, 4

How excellent is your name, O Lord, even though multitudes of people are habitually cursing your name! Mankind's defaming your name does not keep you from being omnipotent, omniscient, nor omnipresent! It is similar to the old saying. "Sticks and stones may break my bones but words can never hurt me." Jesus' name is known and used in every major country on the earth. What a statement to your majesty and divinity!

The universe was created by You, O Lord. So you rightfully own every planet and star. There is galaxy upon galaxy and they all belong to you. Mankind has inhabited the earth for centuries yet You have known each individual, every aborted baby, and all the starving children by name with all their potentialities. The universe is so vast and all of it declares Your magnificence. Lord God, you know the name of each microbe and germ that is invading human bodies around the globe.

We, like King David, ask in wonder, "What is man that You are mindful of him?" As a shepherd lays out a course for sheep, the Lord pampers and cares for each of us? How can we possibly wrap our arms around such an immense idea?

King David personally experienced a visit from God. Have you and I ever been in a prayer group where two or three came together in the name of Jesus (Matt 18:20)? Christ's presence appeared among you. How can God afford the time off from running the laws of nature and hearing others' prayers to be in our prayer meeting? But isn't it marvelous that the Holy Spirit comes to guide us, visit us, and live within each of us (I Cor. 3:16)? I revel in the fact that Jesus loves us and wants to walk and talk with us!

January 9

"Arise, O Lord, do not let men prevail; let the nations be judged in Your sight. Put them in fear, O Lord that the nations may know themselves to be but men." Ps. 9:19-20

This morning a group of men called the 'Power Team' flew out of the local airport. These men gave a powerful Christian message as they bent steel rods around their neck, crushed concrete blocks, and blew up hot water bottles until they exploded.

They indeed are strong but some day the arm of flesh will fail them.

We have and serve an all powerful God! When we pray for protection for missionaries on the other side of the world, God hears and answers the request. One time an intercessor felt the urge to pray. She knelt on her knees in her bedroom. Soon the urgency left. She marked the day and hour on the calendar. When the missionary returned to her homeland, the prayer warrior inquired about that specific day. The missionary calculated the time difference and recounted how God sent a group of angels to protect her. She couldn't see them but the natives saw people dressed in white guarding her.

There was a tavern at the edge of town called the Wagon Wheel. It was a rough place. Once a gun fight occurred injuring one of the combatants. In time, they went out of business and a church started in that once evil place. God did it! The communist party was strong with its Berlin wall which controlled the flow of people. God in a period of seventy years crushed the regime. For several years they were asking missionaries to come teach classes on morals and ethics using the Bible as a basic text.

Our God is the only power that can forgive us of our sins. Today trust the almighty and all-powerful God of Israel to wash our sins away and use his righteous right arm to protect us.

January 10

"But you have seen, for you observe trouble and grief, to repay it by Your hand. The helpless commits himself to you. You are the helper of the fatherless." Ps. 10:14

If Satan walks to and fro upon the earth seeking whom he may devour, how much more God marches up and down our world looking for ways to help? "For the eyes of the Lord run to and fro throughout the whole earth, to show Himself strong in the behalf of them whose heart is perfect towards Him" (II Chron. 16:9). Our heavenly Father knows our needs before we ask, yet we must ask. While we are praying He is in the process of answering our prayers. He knows we are dust and succumb to the ravages of germs and viruses. Jesus physically walked this earth so He would be acquainted with our pains and troubles. Every victim of cancer, heart trouble, broken heart, broken home, or war ravaged villagers can seek God and know Him.

Our heavenly Father not only observes hurt and injustice but does something. He comes to our rescue. Many fast-paced individuals must be crippled by a crisis before they realize God is ever-present to hear and aid them.

The Lord has caused Christians to establish hospitals, other saints to start up food banks, to found used-clothing stores, to raise up crises centers, to build houses for wayward girls, and to establish orphanages to reach out to the helpless children. In some countries, the church people furnish a school where the helpless and hopeless can break the poverty cycle in their family. The Salvation Army and Red Cross have disaster teams to help those overtaken by natural disasters. Goodwill was founded to help the physically challenged to make a living and be productive citizens.

The key ingredient for the helpless, fatherless, homeless, and hopeless is to commit themselves to Jesus Christ. He directs His children in the way of truth and life. God does hear and answers the cries of the needy!

January 11

"Consider and hear me, O Lord my God; enlighten my eyes, lest I sleep the sleep of death; lest my enemy say, 'I have prevailed against him'; lest those who trouble me rejoice when I am moved. But I have trusted in your mercy; my heart shall rejoice in your salvation. I will sing to the Lord because He has dealt bountifully with me. " Ps. 13:3-6

King David unconsciously knew that mankind and himself, in particular, was not worthy of Paradise. So he asked the Almighty to enlighten his spirit and mind. There were times of guilt even though King David was attempting to keep the commandments of Moses. When these times came, he pleaded with God to show him the error of his ways before death came and it was too late. After he confessed his sin and shortcomings, life continued on with its temptations, various trials, and sometimes severe sufferings. Evil almost seems to bombard us as though the enemy were at war with us. So King David cried out to God to support and strengthen him so his adversaries could not gloat when he fell into their schemes. He understood how trials seem to all come at once and they almost overwhelm us spiritually! It is then that each of us instinctively knows we must trust in God. King David openly stated his dependence upon God. His mercy is from everlasting to everlasting and can be depended on in our time of need.

After the spiritual storms are over, we ought to remember who saved us from disaster. Lifting our voices in song and praise would be in order. I don't know if King David had Sunday church but that is an excellent time for us to recall all the victories Christ helped us with. Praise from a thankful spirit should flow, like an artesian well. This Sunday remember how bountifully God has dealt with us.

January 12

"The fool has said in his heart, 'There is no God.' They are corrupt, they have done abominable works, there is none who does good." Ps. 14:1

In the 1970's a professor loudly proclaimed "God is dead!" All the atheists and some of the agnostics joined in his rallying cry. Have you or I ever meditated in our heart that God must be dead because he didn't answer our prayer nor extricate us from the trouble we were knee deep in?

There are those who would never ever say, 'God is dead' but their actions shout it. They use God's name in vain, cheat others, abuse their family, neglect their friends, flaunt their arrogant attitude and lie as if it would never boomerang. They don't seem to fear God or man. Some of these are even corrupt, taking bribes, taking kick backs, killing, murdering, and stealing. These corrupt persons will have their place in the lake of fire.

To offset their evil, many of us strive to be righteous. Our efforts at being good morally, even if we succeed, are as filthy rags. So we must humble ourselves at the foot of the cross and say, "All I am and try to be I owe to God." Without God, we could do nothing. Without Him we'd surely fail. Without Him life would be hopeless. With Him everything works just as it should. Trust in God! Let us continue throughout the day asking, looking for, and expecting God's help in living at home or at work. May our eyes see only Jesus and our lips continuously pour forth a never-ending stream of praise.

January 13

"You have tested my heart; You have visited me in the night; You have tried me and have found nothing; I have purposed that my mouth shall not transgress." Ps. 17:3

Often the world tests our heart. Sometimes it might come as a decision of whether to put in tithe from our overtime. Our actions tell if extra money or God's wishes are our priority. At other times, we have a chance to go to the river boating or the lake swimming instead of attending church. Once in a while we are so tired and run down from the week's activities that we are tempted to sleep in on Sunday morning. Sometimes during the summer, our cousins drop in on their vacation. Do we stay home with them or say, "Come go to church with us"? If they give a negative reply, do we let them stay, while we go? It is rare that any of us can declare with King David, 'Lord, you have found nothing, wrong in my heart and life.'

Is our life in tune with God to the point He can speak to us in our dreams? Have we had visions of God blessings for the future? Maybe God has visited us as we lay awake in bed praying for friends and family needs. How wonderful to experience a visitation of the Holy Spirit! We, at that moment, know for sure we are a child of the Almighty Creator of the Universe. What a sweet sweet spirit washes over us leaving us feeling spotless and clean. Oh, Lord, we yearn for You to do it again!

Since this happened, King David declared that he was going to guard all the words that passed across his lips. To accomplish this, one must keep a defense against dwelling on evil and negative thoughts. Once in a while, we have unclean thoughts, so what we think often unintentionally slips out of our mouth.

The following verse is a step of action. Let's use the formula printed in Psalm 19:14, "Let the words of my mouth and the mediation of my heart be acceptable in Your sight, O Lord, my strength and my Redeemer."

January 14

"Concerning the works of men, by the word of your lips, I have kept away from the paths of the destroyer." Ps. 17:4

There is the temptation to do drugs or cut the edge with alcohol because of the extreme stress of life. It is easy to let the anger of road rage fly into us, when someone cuts in front of us. How simple, when hurt, to let feelings surge through our being until it spills out in curse words. If we don't make a deliberate effort to purge ourselves of grudges, they can smolder and at the wrong time burst into a conflagration of a raging forest fire. How easy to let a little resentment stick in our craw until it turns into hatred and malice which is a sin according to the Word of God.

King David discovered or unearthed the secret to keeping away from sin and evil. He was able to obey God rather than do the will of old Lucifer, the Destroyer by following the voice of the Lord. When we know what God says, we must follow it. A few examples are: Let the words of my mouth and the meditations of my heart be acceptable in your sight, O Lord my strength and my Redeemer (Ps. 19:14). I will keep him in perfect peace whose mind is stayed on Thee (Isaiah 26:3). We have fellowship with Jesus, if we walk in the light as he is in the light (I John 1:7). Shun the very appearance of evil (I Thess. 5:22). In all your ways acknowledge Him and He shall direct your paths (Prov. 3:6). If God be for us who of any consequence can be against us (Rom. 8:31b). Never will I leave you nor forsake you (Heb. 13:5). With all these precious promises we need not sin against God by following Satan. God bless you today in your Christian walk.

January 15

"As for me, I will see your face in righteousness; I shall be satisfied when I awake in your likeness."
Ps. 17:15

The first question that pops into my mind after reading that verse is, who is worthy to ascend into the hill of the Lord (Ps.24:3)? How can a person such as me with all the imperfections and shortcoming dare look into the righteous face of Almighty God? Most of my prayers include a time of confession for sins committed. Is there a chance that as we continue to be more Christ-like, we will be able to look upon Jesus and His righteousness?

Moses, the great prophet went up on Mt. Sinai. As he returned with the stone tablets of the Ten Commandments, his face shone. He was unaware of this radiant glory. The Hebrew congregation begged him to put on a veil. The point was that Moses was unaware of his personal brilliance. As we daily walk and talk with Jesus, we will acquire a glory like the Son of God. The transference comes gradually. A good example is of a husband and wife. After living together for nearly fifty years, they seem to look alike. Even so, if we spend days and nights with our Lord, we become more like him. Some day a person will comment, "There goes a saintly couple." Continue to focus on the Word and stay engaged in the work of the Lord then you will be 'blessed' by God.

How many of us would desire to awake in heaven viewing ourselves as saints? We will then know God has shaped and molded us into an exemplary Child of God. How great to know our life and all its labors are over! Also how satisfying it is to realize that we resemble our brother, Jesus. It will be worth it all, when we get over there!

January 16

"They comforted me in the day of my calamity, but the Lord was my support."   Ps. 18:18

Have you, like me, stood next to the casket, and heard words like: "I'm so sorry." "They look so nice." "You have my sympathies"? These words seemed to float in one ear and right out the other. Their words didn't ease the pain. I didn't feel a bit better, after they had taken their seat in the funeral home. The loneliness continued to haunt me. I continued to stand there in a daze. My hurt feelings were impenetrable. If only someone could bring me true comfort!

I know that death comes to all families but do my comforters understand the hurt that goes deep into my psyche. It seems like dark deep troubled waters that can not be reached. Everyone's rope of sympathies is way too short. I understood that my friends were making a genuine effort to comfort me but their efforts did not bring any relief to my emotional hurt.

Maybe this area of me is what Augustine called the 'spiritual vacuum.' He said we all have it. **Real** support can only be given and applied by God. Our Creator fathomed the depth of this need and only He can impart genuine relief.

Have you had a tickle in your throat? You sucked on cough drops but that didn't seem to touch it. The only way you ended the coughing spell was to take an internal medicine that brought relief to the cough center. Our only relief for internal grief is to call on God, and invite the Holy Spirit to live in our heart. This is when each of us finally experience comfort from the pain. The throat tickle or the pain of grief then disappears. It is then, that we realize God has been our support all those long weeks of recovery from painful grief.

January 17

"As for God, his way is perfect; the word of the Lord is proven; He is a shield to all who trust Him."
Ps. 18:30

When you were a kid, do you recall some of the gems of wisdom your grandfather or grandmother gave out? Here King David tells his readers some wisdom he had learned.

First, he states that God's way is perfect. As he listened to and followed the leading of God, all went well. As he aged this statement became a solid undisputable fact.

Later he learned that God's words could truly be trusted. Maybe if we reject unstable words, current thought, and conventional wisdom of the world, we will have more blessings and successes.

Second, King David stated that not only had he proven this true but others had too. Daniel lived a righteous life. At God's urging during his teenage years, he trusted God to make him healthy on vegetable soup instead of eating the rich food of the king. Daniel won the contest. Later he became a C.P.A. When his enemies combed though his books, they could find no discrepancies. Following God's way is the winning way! Even though they threw him in a lion's den (hard times), God saved him for following him faithfully.

Thirdly, God is a shield. King David knew about this first hand. When he and his small band of soldiers were skirting King Saul's army, God was his shield. One time, to escape the pursuing army, he took his men to the back of a cave. They all breathed very shallowly because King Saul, himself choose to sleep at the mouth of that very cave. Can't you just visualize the invisible shield God placed halfway up the cave to protect David and his entire army? On a different occasion, a different king set the men's temple choir in front of the army as they marched into battle. They were sure God was their shield. They won without a spear or death of one man.

Let's remember today that God's way is perfect. His word through the centuries has been proven. God will be our protection. You can confidently depend on this wisdom.

January 18

"The judgments of the Lord are true and righteous altogether. More to be desired are they than gold, yea, than much fine gold; sweeter also than honey and the honeycomb. Moreover by them your servant is warned, and in keeping them there is great reward." Ps 19:9b-11

What are the real guidelines to life on earth? The teenagers might say, "Whatever the rules are, let it be success." The young adult might put forward the idea, "Whatever brings me wealth is right." The middle aged person might project, "Whatever works is right." The older person could give the rule, "Whatever doesn't hurt anyone in the short term or down the road is the rule to live by."

King David lays out this life creed for youth to hold to throughout life. The only sure guide is found in the Scriptures. We call it the Bible. Only these rules and principles are true and righteous. He is advising us to obey God's word. These are more important than pounds of gold and tons of silver. That is very important. Following these are far better than food from the finest restaurant of the world. If and when we keep these rules, there is great reward. Even so, King David warns us! Don't follow the rules of society. Follow God's rules for they yield benefits in this world and the next.

January 19

"Who can understand his errors? Cleanse me from secret faults. Keep back your servant also from presumptuous sins; let them not have dominion over me. Then I shall be blameless, and I shall be innocent of great transgression." Ps. 19:12-13

It is often difficult for us to arrive at a true evaluation of ourselves. Anorexic people believe they are too fat. There are others who think they are smart enough to assume they are boss everywhere they are. Some are very talented but so timid they never put it to use.

One man attended church every Sunday morning, Sunday night, plus Wednesday evening Bible Study. He would encourage the preacher with 'Amen's and 'That's Right.' This man faithfully gave of his tithe to the church. With his extra offering, he supported a preacher on the local radio station. His faith was so strong that he canceled his insurance policy saying, "God will take care of me." All the while he was sleeping with a lady, who was not his wife. The lady came with him to all the church services. He could not see his sin until the church barred him from attending their services.

The conditions for his return were to marry the lady. Up to this point, he could not see his own secret sin. The fellowship of Christians forced him to face God's Word.

Another area King David mentioned was sin that had control of him. This could be an emotional addiction such as sex. There are mental addictions such as gambling and pornography. Physical control over us might be alcohol, nicotine, and drugs. God's desire is that nothing He created should have control over us. Only devotion to Almighty God should control our actions, emotions, and thinking. If we do this, God will spare us of ever committing gross transgressions such as King David feared.

January 20

"Yea though I walk through the valley of the shadow of death, I will fear no evil; for you are with me; your rod and your staff, they comfort me." Ps. 23:4

King David had a confidence in God that whatever crisis came, he would not be afraid. Wow! Oh, that we could make such a confession like that before God, before our family, or even to our self.

How comforting to walk in the presence of God! What a blessing to know He is as close as our elbow bringing peace!

The shepherd's rod was his protection, his '44 magnum. He drove off the invaders with it. Some of the sheep's enemies were good-sized, like bears and lions. Some of our spiritual enemies are much bigger than us like: undue pride, envy, uninvited lust, or consuming greed. Be careful, least these assailants overpower us. We need a reliable weapon, like the shepherd club in our lives. If we use God's rod, the name and power of Jesus, we can win -- every time!

The shepherd's staff was used to comfort the sheep. The crook on the top was used to hook under the front legs to lift it off the dangerous side of a cliff. What a consolation to know God can rescue us, when we fall into sin or stray.

The staff was also used to bring connectedness between the shepherd and the sheep. He would lay the staff across the shoulder of a sheep as they walked. Contentment flowed from the shepherd to the sheep through the staff. In a moment or two, the sheep would leave to graze assured that the shepherd was close and present. This happens for us while in church or at Bible study, and prayer time. Then we go back out into the world to live for Him. We no longer fear death or its fear-inspiring shadow.

January 21

"Surely goodness and mercy shall follow me all the days of my life; and I will dwell in the house of the Lord forever." Ps. 23:6

God's love will accompany us all the days of our lives. When we were born, each of us was showered with love from our mother, father, and grandparents. As toddlers, the people at church made over us and told us how cute we were. As adolescents and teenagers, God began to uncover the love he has for us. At that early age some of us accepted Christ into our heart, so the love of God began to reside within us. Then we experienced and began to realize the devotedness and genuineness of our love for God. Sometimes due to immaturity, the display of our love was inconsistent. God placed in our heart a love for someone else that would endure through sixty or sixty-five years of marriage. In God's show of love, He permitted us to create a family. At that time we transferred the love that God gave us on to our children. As the children began to leave the nest, our love went with them as does God's love for us as we struggle to live for him in a wicked world. God's love continues to reside in us as we mature into senior citizens. It is at this point in life, we take time to review the many times God blessed us. We marvel at the number of times, the various occasions, and crises God's love ministered to us.

People enjoy being with others in the Christian fellowship! How much better will it all be when we celebrate around the throne in heaven! Like King David, we bask in the glory of the Lord while in the house of worship. Sometimes in a worship service, we dream of staying on forever in the house of the Lord.

January 22

"Lift your head, O you gates! Lift up, you everlasting doors! And the King of glory shall come in. Who is this King of glory? The Lord of Hosts, He is the King of glory." Ps. 24:9-10

Can you figure out how one of Jerusalem's enormous gates can lift up its head? Can't you visualize a gate, if it were a person, could open both arms and let people or vehicles in and out? The big gates at Kentucky Dam locks open and let a ship down a step or shut and fill up to lift a huge ship.

King David longed to see the city gates open and permit Jesus to ride in on a donkey. In that triumphal parade the people shouted blessings to the King of Glory. Surely the gate must have been so glad to open her arms and let the Messiah ride through. One terrible Thursday night though, it had to open and let some hate-filled priests, temple soldiers, and Roman soldiers out to capture Jesus. That led to the crucifixion of God's son.

Surely King David was dreaming of the time, when humans would open the doors of their hearts. The Lord of Glory could then humbly ride into their life. When that happened they would feel like joining other saints in praising the Lord of Host, the King of Glory.

Even if a gate can't lift its head, we can! We can keep our eyes on Jesus. Unlike Peter who took his sight off Jesus and began to sink, we can keep our eyes fastened on Jesus who is our perpetual helper. Bless you as you lift your head and focus your attention on the Lord of Glory, the King of Kings.

January 23

"Do not remember the sins of my youth, nor my transgressions; according to your mercy remember me, for your goodness' sake, O Lord."   Ps. 25:7

Do you remember the dating days of high school? God, please don't recall the indiscretion of that night. Please don't remember the lies I told, while dating three at one time. Forget the rule I broke, when I got home extra late and worried my parents nearly to death. Do not bring to your mind the times I took the dare: ...to drag at the stop sign in the middle of town.   ...to steal or shop lift when they called me chicken. ...to do drugs that left me with noticeable damage to my body.   ...to take apples from someone else's orchard. ...to go with the gang into in a "X" rated movie.   ...to steal money out of mom's purse or dad's wallet to go somewhere.   ...to sneak out of church to have a puff on a cigarette which was against mom's command.

King David writes that he is sufficiently ashamed of his sin! How about us? King David was! If all our sins were plain to the world, would we spend time in a county jail, state prison, or even a federal penitentiary? I'm admitting, that if prosecuted I would spend time in one of these human holding facilities.

Praise the Lord! Unfailing love is ours in Christ Jesus. Our heavenly Father is not eagerly searching through our lives for sins committed. He is looking for a humble and repentant spirit so our sins can be eradicated by the precious blood of his Son, our Savior Jesus Christ. Rest assured, He will look upon our lives and reward us according to his goodness and mercy. Hallelujah, What a Savior!

January 24

"Give them according to their deeds, and according to the wickedness of their endeavors; give them according to the work of their hands; render to them what they deserve." Ps. 28:4

Dear Lord, may I always come to you for help? I have had so much wrong committed against me. May I dump my burden on You? Thanks!

Lord, you remember how I trusted my boss? went to him with my problems. After helping, he went directly to the board of directors and told them how poorly I was doing.

Lord, do you recall the time I paid to have some work done? They never came over to do it. When I ask them for the money back, they vouched that I never paid them.

Lord, bring to your mind the instance where I was humping to please the boss, and I might say, making the company some money. When promotion time came, they passed me over. That hurt then and still pains when I remember, Father!

Lord, please recollect the time when that evil person had a higher prestige than me. It seemed as if the people doing the wrong were getting all the breaks. My self-esteem scraped bottom.

O Lord, our Father we join King David and ask you to render to them what they so richly deserve. Along with this request, assist me in not rejoicing when they have to eat their just desserts. Also, Lord, give me strength to pray that they turn to You and seek forgiveness so they may also live in Paradise some day.

It felt good to express my hurt. Thanks Lord, for letting me tell you of my painful mental hurts.

January 25

"O Lord my God, I cried out to You, and You healed me. O Lord, You brought my soul up from the grave; You have kept me alive, that I should not go down to the pit." Ps. 30:2-3

Have you ever had a serious accident? I mean one that took you to the gates of, was it heaven or hell? The last thing you could recall was the impending collision or your body temperature was so high you were out of your head? The next thing you recalled was the nurses and doctor commenting how close they were to losing you on the operating table. You were still unconscious while all of this was registering. As your mental capacities returned, you mulled over the nearness to eternity you were. Then you were transferred to a room from the ICU. Like King David, you thought how close to the grave you were and near to being away from your family forever!

Again you can repeat the words of our King and say, "O Lord my God, I cried to You, and You healed me." When you look back at your rapid recovery and therapy, you are extremely grateful to

God for His watchful care over you. How blessed you are to still be on planet earth and loved by your family and friends.

When you get down in the dumps or tend to complain, do like King David recall the day you almost died. True values then return and joy reappears in your heart.

January 26

"....Weeping may endure for a night, but joy comes in the morning." Ps. 30:5b

"Can you say you have raised your children in the nurture and admonition of the Lord, but one of your children has slipped into drugs? There are nights you cry yourself to sleep searching for things you might have done wrong to cause them to get addicted. Nothing ever comes to your mind. Faint rays of joy burst upon your despondent heart when you remember you bought him up hearing God's mighty Word (Prov. 22:6).

Has your daughter wandered off into prostitution? You worry and fret about diseases she may acquire or the abuse that she may receive. Your desperation often throws you into a crying jag. The tears flow like a river and your husband just can't comprehend your thinking. Remember your daughter has an angel of God observing her, plus God Almighty loves her no matter what she does (I John 4:10).

Has financial devastation wreaked havoc with your family budget? Some nights and some days you weep saying, "If one more creditor or bill collector comes, I'll fall apart. Lord, oh Lord, hear and answer my prayers. Supply my every need as You promised" (Phil. 4:19).

Has your spouse been unfaithful? You feel as worthless as pair of old worn out penny loafers.

You yearn for things to return to what they used to be. Tears soak your pillow while the children are soundly sleeping in the other room. God will avenge His children (Luke 18:6-8). You can rest assured that God will work all things out for your good and God's glory, even if we flub up royally (Rom. 8:28).

King David was forcibly run out of his palace by his son, Adonijah. He cried over his son, Absalom. On another occasion he cried because his infant was going to die. God blessed King David with the best kingdom in the entire history of the Hebrew children. So King David's life proved that joy will come when the morning breaks. Look forward to that time in your life, my friend.

January 27

"I will be glad and rejoice in your mercy, for you have considered my trouble; you have known my soul in adversities." (Ps. 31:7)

How long has it been since you have been happy? Did something good happen to make you that way? Or were circumstances just right so you were happy?

The way the Psalmist states this declaration, it seems that he personally determines to be cheerful. It appears to be mind over matter. In one place, Solomon says that as a man thinks so is he (Prov. 23:7). In another place, King David starts off the day by saying, "This is a day the Lord has made, I WILL rejoice and be glad in it" (Ps. 118:24).

King David had reason to be glad. It was not physical circumstances because he had lots of enemies. People were trying to get him off the throne. Gladness always came from thinking about and rejoicing in the mercy of God. King David was delighted in the personal attention of the Creator of the Universe. God looked down when he was going through difficulties and rescued him from them all.

Where would we have been, if God had not come to our aid? God guards our souls! He assists us in resisting temptation and remaining a true child of God. Being an authentic Christian entitles us to a precious spot of real estate in that eternal city. We should be jumping for joy. Let us decide to rejoice and to be glad for all God has done for us.

January 28

"For I hear the slander of many; fear is on every side; while they take counsel together against me, they scheme to take away my life. But as for me, I trust in you, O Lord; I say 'You are my God.' My times are in your hand; deliver me from the hand of my enemies, and from those who persecute me. Make your face shine upon your servant; save me for your mercies' sake." Ps. 31:13-16

Has your life been dinged, dented, or damaged by rumors? Some were completely unfounded, right? Others were outright lies! Many were concocted with the intent to hurt or put you in a bad light. Lots were started because someone thought out loud or imagined what might have happened.

For King David, his enemies tried every way to dethrone him. Some rumors were calculated to create dissatisfaction among his subjects. Almost all of the ones he heard, hurt him down to the bottom of his gentle heart. He learned not to dwell on the pain and inequity of their actions.

King David looked and trusted in God to even the score. He knew that God was in control. The time of his kingly reign was in God's hands. No matter what harm his enemies intended to do, it would not shorten God's appointed time for him to serve as king.

When it comes to our welfare, God is so gentle and generous. He will take revenge on the gossip monger who caused us hurt. He will take care of those who try to upset us.

Lastly, King David made a request of God. Please, O Lord, make your divine face shine upon your children. Extend your mercy and grace upon us. Heal the wounds we have received from the rumor mill.

January 29

"My times are in your hand; deliver me from the hand of my enemies, and from those who persecute me." Ps. 31:15

As a child we pray, "Oh, Heavenly Father up in heaven you have our future in your hands. While in school, we ask God to select our play-mates to help us grow up to be more like You. Help us be obedient children to You and to our parents. Amen."

As a teenager we pray, "O Master of All Life, walk into our future and prepare a road for us. You are aware of possible temptation to do drugs, to lose our virginity, and to break the law. Guide me in paths of righteousness for your name's sake. Amen."

As a young adult we pray, "O Creator, be our hero. You are well aware of our promotions, job changes, and tribulations in raising a family. Provide us with wisdom to wisely lead our children and be successful in your eyes. Thanks Lord, in advance for guiding us into the future. Amen."

As a middle aged adult we pray, "O Loving Protector, slip into my being. You know my past and love me still. You love me enough to guide my life into my retirement years. Keep me loving and compassionate yet stern enough to mold my children for your divine use. Put within me a discerning spirit when my children try to pull the wool over my eyes. Amen." What a comfort to know that You, O Lord, know and will be in our future.

As a senior citizen we pray, "Thanks, Heavenly Father, for loving each of us with an everlasting love. It is very difficult to realize how strong your love is or the length you will go to love us. You love us more than we can possibly love ourselves. You displayed your love in such a marvelous way when you died for us over there in Judea. Your love for us is further displayed as you continue to prepare us heaven, our final destination. Amen."

January 30

"Blessed be the Lord, for He has shown me His marvelous kindness in a strong city!" Ps. 31:21

Lord, when I was a spiritual stranger, You thought of and cared for me. I was only concerned about me and mine but you reached out and touched me and took me in as a child of yours. What marvelous kindness!

There have been times in my life when I felt the sting of indifference from my close friends. At other times, I experienced the pain of rejection from my enemies. But what a warm feeling, when you expressed your marvelous kindness to me!

On one occasion I was sick in bed in the hospital. I was blue, depressed, and lonesome. The pain was so intense that I didn't care whether I lived or died. Then in compassion you enfolded me with your muscular arms of marvelous kindness.

I recall the time when one of my parents died. I was grief stricken and emotionally numb. I walked in a daze for days. It was then you visited my heart and imparted your gentle spirit of kindness down deep where my hurt had been festering.

Once when our children were teenagers, they rebelled against our every wish. We were pushed to the end of our proverbial rope. We contemplated leaving them to their own way, when you came along side us with your long-suffering kindness.

Lastly, Lord, when I was away from you, you came into my sinful life. You carefully excavated the evil from my life and replaced it with your loving-kindness. Now each day I revel in your marvelous love!

January 31

"I acknowledge my sin to you, and my iniquity I have not hidden. I said, 'I will confess my transgressions to the Lord,' and you forgave the iniquity of my sin."   Ps. 32:5

It is often difficult to concede that we have sinned. King David openly acknowledged his sin. He openly confessed! To hide a sin, it requires self-deception on our part. Satan or our human nature helps us to succeed in this deception. Confession is to verbally acknowledge our wrong doing or breaking God's commands. Somehow hearing our own selves say this releases us. We at that time trust God for pardon.

After confession or acknowledgment comes repentance. To repent means to stop doing what is wrong and do what is right in the eyes of God. In this 180 degree turn around, we forsake our former ways of evil.

The forgiveness comes at a cost. Acts of contrition or punishments are not required. It is through faith in Jesus Christ alone that consummates the spiritual transaction.

John in his first letter chapter one and verse nine states that if we confess our sin He is faithful and just and will forgive us our sins and cleanse us from all unrighteousness. The first half of the verse is our responsibility. We, like King David, must confess our sins. God's part is to forgive us and cleanse us from all evil. When we fulfill our part, God invariably does His.

When this transaction occurs, you will experience the joy of guilt-free living. This is why Christians go around smiling, whistling, or singing. Christ has control of their lives.

February 1

"....Surely in a flood of great waters they shall not come near him." Ps. 32:6b

Floods are devastating and thoroughly destructive. A tornado may take two or more city blocks but a flood is more comprehensive and inclusive. The American Midwest experienced a disastrous flood in 1993. It covered millions of acres and hundreds of towns. The flood waters became contaminated from the waste treatment plants, floating caskets and butane gas tanks. The real danger was the whirlpools that could pull rowboats down to the bottom in the five mile wide river at flood stage.

The sin and filth of this world does not need to cover us like a flood. Through prayer and Bible study, we can build a levee against its onslaught. Even the tiny leaks can be plugged by listening closely and obeying the urging of the Holy Spirit. If a flood of worldly temptation or a menacing whirlpool does come near us, it can not cause spiritual death nor harm us.

Houses that have flood damage must be gutted and all the insulation and wall board removed and replaced. When any sin enters our life, an awful stink rises to the nostrils of God. Like the flood damaged house, our souls must be gutted, cleansed, and renewed.

Implied in the Psalmist's statement is that God will not be far from each of us. He will protect us from waters that might harm us. When God does not remove the flood water or perform miracles to divert the water, he will show us some high ground. God is the only one who can be our solid rock, our high ground, and our refuge. All else we might trust in is doomed to fail.

If waves of sin are presently lapping at your feet, lift your eyes and look to our scriptural Rock of Gibraltar. King David says God will be your everlasting rock of salvation.

February 2

"Rejoice in the Lord, O you righteous! For praise from the upright is beautiful. Praise the Lord with the harp; make melody to Him with an instrument of ten strings. Sing to Him a new song; play skillfully with a shout of joy."
Ps. 33:1-3

How inspiring are the hymns our church sings each Sunday morning? Does the tempo drag as slow as funeral dirge? I pray your pastor or minister of music makes the songs ones of praise and adoration. If they do a good job yet the music lacks life, maybe the cause is sinners are doing the singing. There is seldom a time in a sinner's life when they have any cause to praise God. Trouble and sorrow plague those who follow Satan, like trouble followed Jonah.

The founder of the Methodist Church, John Wesley, wrote an instruction list of how to worship. One of these suggestions was to sing 'lustily'.

Would that drastically change or maybe even transform your Sunday morning worship service?

King David was naturally musically inclined. So it was his inclination to have musical instruments in worship. He designated a family called Koran to be in charge of the choir and band. Would you enjoy having a band backing you as you sing "Amazing Grace"? You definitely wouldn't have to worry about every one hearing you. I believe God would think that kind of praise was beautiful.

The Psalmist urges us to sing a new song. We seldom enjoy learning a new song. We wander up and down the scale trying to find the note the pianist is playing. The struggle continues, 'do I watch the words or follow the notes'? When it is over you're feeling like a beginning clarinetist squawking off key. How pleasant and comfortable to sing songs like: "The Old Rugged Cross," "O How Great Thou Art"! It will be different in heaven, when we sing a new song written by God. The melody will come to us naturally as if we composed it. When we finally are finished, we will suddenly realize it was song of praise to our precious Lord and Savior.

February 3

"He fashions their hearts individually; He considers all their works."   Ps. 33:15

Was today a wonderful spring morning with the shaft of sunlight pouring down though the trees, similar to the day when God took a lump of clay and created Adam? A few days later God realized Adam was not happy so he created Eve. God is still creating. When you were a fetus, God was creating you to be whom He wanted you to be. After Adam and Eve, God didn't just leave the DNA to do its thing. You are more than a blob. He still creates every child that's being born this day.

God placed a soul in our great grandparents. It was uniquely theirs. Believe it or not, God has done the same for you. Your soul is special, unique, and one of a kind! Your soul is not one from an assembly line. God loves you and your soul so much that if you were the only one who needed salvation, He would have permitted his Son to die to redeem your soul.

God, being efficient with the labor of his hands, did not create us then leave us to find our way for ourselves. He created each of us a specific individual suited for the gifts in us. The Psalmist stated that God considers all the works we do. If these works are evil, they would be added up against us. If we labored in the Lord's vineyard, he will reward us according to our labors. If we do nothing or present a neutral influence, how can God bless us? God continually searches the earth keeping watch over the works of His children.

Each of us truly enjoys a physical hug from our spouse, relative, or friend. It is a stupendous feeling of assurance and affirmation of our personhood! Today, God is waiting to give our soul a gentle hug. You are His child. Remember He loves you without limit! Look for a hug from God today.

February 4

"Our soul waits for the Lord; He is our help and our shield. Our hearts shall rejoice in him, because we have trusted in his holy name. Let your mercy, O Lord, be upon us, just as we hope in you."   Ps. 33:20-22

'Troubles, troubles, troubles! All I have are troubles.' Sometimes these troubles crash upon us and collapse our lives like a house of cards. At other times, these troubles stay at bay, so we can see them coming. Then suddenly they all bounce upon us like Tigger, the tiger does to Pooh, the bear.

Other troubles come like a thunderstorm. We see the trouble coming like a car in the wrong lane of traffic. Often there is no way to avoid the trouble. The front fender and driver's door end up in terrible shape. The aftermath of the wreck is worst. Even when our life and health are okay, we have the inconvenience while it is in the shop.

Our finances seem to be doing pretty well. All at once the phone rings and they ask, "Where is the balloon payment on the house?" It came down on you as fast as a spacecraft re-entering the atmosphere.

When these troubles come, trust in God! At first we are numb from the shock of the news. But as soon as we can, set it at Jesus' feet and wait. Wait! What do you mean 'Wait!' I have to solve this problem! The Psalmist said he had learned to wait for God's help because only He knows the best way to handle it. When God imparts to our mind the answer, we can then move toward resolution. Speak of waiting; George Mueller of Bristol, England had to wait fifty years for one of the parishioners in his first pastoral appointment to accept Christ as Savior.

If you can, go to prayer and wait on the Lord to direct you. You will eventually rejoice with exceeding great joy. Our God shall supply all your needs according to His riches in glory (Phil. 4:19).

February 5

"Oh, magnify the Lord with me, and let us exalt His name together. I sought the Lord, and He heard and saved him out of all his troubles. The angel of the Lord encamps all around those who fear Him, and delivers them. Ps. 34:3-4, 6b-7

One day the preacher presented a challenge to me. "I would like you to praise the Lord for ten minutes." Like a sucker at a circus, I took him up on it. Later in the day, I decided I am not doing anything so I'll do this easy thing right now. My praise and adoration lasted about three sentences and then came to an abrupt halt. My problem was that I was not accustomed to using that kind of vocabulary. I had far too few words to express my love for God. Do you think you would have a similar problem? Since that rude awakening, I have worked more diligently at magnifying the Lord.

Next King David sought the Lord in prayer and was pleased to find Him. The Old Testament prophet in Deut. 4:29 assures us that we will find God when we seek him with **all** our heart. When our soul is right with God, He will hear our prayer (Ps. 66:18).

God promises to deliver us from all our troubles or divert them from us. Angels, messengers of God, will continually set up a defensive perimeter around those who love and fear God. Can you recall the number of times God has already guided you around defeat before you arrived? We ought to create and initiate a daily routine for magnifying the Lord. How we enjoy hearing compliments and words of encouragement! Let us determine to please God with words of endearment and actions of affection each day of our earthly life.

February 6

"Who is the man who desires life, and loves many days, that he may see good?" Ps. 34:12

You may ask, "What is the secret to a good and long life?" King David reveals some hidden principles we need to incorporate in our daily life to achieve this satisfying life.

One job is to keep our lips from speaking evil or deceiving others. The words that exit our mouth originate in our mind. What we continually think is what we wind up saying and doing, whether flattery or murder.

Departing from evil is mandatory. This is true whether we initiate the deeds or follow the lead of other corrupt people. Evil faithfully and consistently rewards us with grief, sorrow, and trouble, but never the good life with accompanying pleasure.

Look everywhere for peace. Follow that path; even strive with all your strength to achieve peace within and without. Jesus said blessed or happy are the peace makers, for personal and internal peace shall be theirs. Isaiah (26:3) suggests that we keep our gaze fixed upon God, not our problems nor the world, and then perfect peace will be ours.

God provides the good life. God is continually watching us. His ears are attentive to every one of our prayers. God is against the evil doers. When we call on God in our need, He will deliver us out of all our trouble (v.17). If our heart is broken, no matter the cause, God promises to stay near us. How close? He will be closer than your hands and feet. God saves us from all evil. What a Lord and Savior!

February 7

"...Seek peace and pursue it." Ps. 34:14b

Do bickering, fussing, and arguing follow us like our shadow? This kind of negative and upsetting feeling need not be a part of our life. Some astute observer said, "Change our direction from being right to a life of peace." This is the shortest distance from strife to peace.

One's life usually moves toward our most predominant thoughts. To move toward peace, we need to seek out the Prince of Peace. That Prince can cleanse our life of all sin, as well as, all negativity. We must continue to concentrate on Jesus Christ and follow His example. When this is accomplished, peace will begin to come between us and our brothers and sisters. When peace is flowing in our family, it is such a wonderful life! This may require apologizing for some of our former actions.

Next, we need to pursue peace in the small groups to which we belong like; scouts, sorority, fraternity, lodge, or a board or committee at the church. When hotly contested subjects arise, we need to search for areas of compromise instead of joining one side or the other.

Lastly, God may call on us to bring peace on the community level or possibly on the international level, such as a crisis or hostage negotiator, marriage counselor, or national peace arbitrator.

It is to our advantage to look for peace and even run after it.

February 8

"All my bones shall say, 'Lord, who is like you, delivering the poor from him who is too strong for him, yes, the poor and needy from him who plunders him?'"   Ps. 35:10

King David is exclaiming that God sure is good! He uniquely expresses his praise, 'with all my bones'. We would say 'with my entire being' or 'from the bottom of my heart.' I will proclaim to my world that God is a marvelous Redeemer. Can you recall a time in your life, when an evil person kept you in debt and subservient? In time, God caused a change to come about to relieve you.

King David had witnessed many times, when God rescued the poor. God is the same yesterday, today, and forever. So the abundant mercy of God continues to rescue in our day and our time. Have you had times when there were too many bills and too few dollars? There appears to be no groceries in the house, the car seemed to run out of gas, and there was no money for lunch while at work. Can you recall how God made it stretch? Personally, I can't tell you how, but I do know that we made it. Even though greed or lack of sales resistance got us into the mess, God saw us through.

King David knew for sure the poor were not left defenseless. God is their guardian and protector. God provides. The local church pantry, the nearby clothing center, or the food kitchen are available. The hardest thing to let go of is our pride, so we can receive from others instead of us donating. The Lord begins protecting the poor long before their day in court. He touches the heart of others even while Satan has hardening the landlord's heart.

What a comfort that God rescues and protects the poor!

February 9

"Fierce witnesses rise up; they ask me things that I do not know ....But as for me, when they were sick, my clothing was sackcloth; I humbled myself with fasting; and my prayer would return to my own heart. ....Lord, how long will you look on? Rescue me from their destructions, my precious life from the lions. I will give you thanks in the great assembly; I will praise you among many people." Ps. 35:11, 13-14, 17-18

Although King David had the greatest variety and the richest of food to eat, he fasted. Have you fasted to lose a mere ten pounds? Hope you were successful. The best way to fast for a spiritual blessing is to do it with the idea of achieving a closer relation with God. During the time you would have eaten, meditate and converse with God. If that doesn't fill the lunch hour, open God's word to learn His thoughts.

King David included in his time of fasting a session of humble confession. Humility begins with a mental searching for any moral rebellion, physical disobedience, or spiritual indifference. It is a difficult task to open the door of one's ego. We guard it very closely to keep others from hurting it. As we open the curtain to our inner self, we feel free to confess our shortcomings to our precious Lord. When we pray the prayer of confession, God ALWAYS hears our petition. As we pray in a serious and fervent way, God answers our prayers (James 4:16). Aren't we often surprised in the way in which God answers our prayers?

St. Paul in Colossians (4:2 TLB) says that when God answers, don't forget to give him thanks. King David promised that he would express his thanks in church and public meetings. Are we ashamed to publicly admit that we had to lean on God in prayer and how graciously He answered? Also let us always praise God. We can praise Him by using phrases like, "What a day the Lord has made!" "God bless you." "With God's help..." or "God loves you and so do I." Praising God brings a renewed sense of belonging to the great heavenly family!

February 10

"Stir up yourself, and awake to my vindication, to my cause, my God and my Lord." Ps. 35:23

Are you feeling hassled and harried? Is your boss overloading you while giving light assignments to their pet or is it that you get the entire load of menial and 'go-fer' jobs instead of anything meaningful. Maybe your boss is a micromanager, sticklers for details instead of a macro-managing and seeing the entire picture. Your burden is heavy the entire time at work. When will the stress ever let up?

Maybe you are frazzled because of a continuous barrage of lay offs. You no sooner get back to work and the bills and collection agencies stop hounding you, when a cut back comes or the contract wasn't renewed. You are so weary of the financial struggle. Lord, when will our family get on our monetary feet?

Could it be that since you went to work for this company, you feel intentionally excluded? It feels like you are exempt from any social interaction even at the water bottle or at break time. It hurts to be ostracized. Lord, when will I be accepted for who I am?

Others due to birth or handicapping conditions have felt the sting and hurt of prejudice. Just because you are not like others, you feel down graded in their eyes. Even though you realize that the public is the ones who have a problem, this stress still stretches your nerves and emotions to the breaking point. When will it ever stop?

Let's join King David and say aloud, "Please, Lord Jesus, come to my aid." I plead,
"Vindicate my cause, my God and my Lord."

February 11

"An oracle within my heart concerning the transgression of the wicked: there is no fear of God before his eyes. He flatters himself in his own eyes, when he finds out his iniquity and when he hates. The words of his mouth are wickedness and deceit; he has ceased to be wise and to do good. He devises wickedness on his bed; he sets himself in a way that is not good; he does not abhor evil." Ps. 36:1-4

The evil people of this world forget completely about God or the idea that there even is one. Their universe revolves around themselves. The consequences of any of their actions are not even thought about. There is no higher authority than themselves.

Corrupt people glorify themselves; consequently they never brag on or lift up God. Our spiritual nature is to lift up God. When He is not considered, we elevate the opinion of ourselves to fill that position.

After a while, we begin bragging on how smart we are. Our world shrinks until we are the only thing of importance. The wickedness, which people should be ashamed of, seems to be what they lift up as worthwhile. Stop a second and think of how many things in our life are backwards to God's rules. Surprising, isn't it?

When God is omitted from life's equation, we cease to be wise and begin failing to do good and right. When evil people continue accumulating money and gathering friends, they are gathering punishment for eternity. Evil people are not stupid people. They take time to meditate on how to scheme to their advantage. Their sinister plans are even hatched, while they lay awake at night. So be careful!

In contrast, God is good all the time. One, who sincerely loves God, abhors evil and wrong. A Christian brags on what God is doing and has done for them. Along with divine reverence, usually comes a desire to do only the right thing. Their motivation is to please God, not follow Satan and evil. Christians hold God in awe, not glorify themselves.

February 12

"Your mercy, O Lord, is in the heavens; your faithfulness reaches to the clouds. Your righteousness is like the great mountains; your judgments are a great deep; O Lord, You preserve man and beast. How precious is your loving kindness, O God! Therefore the children of men put their trust under the shadow of your wings."
Ps. 36:5-7

Heaven has a foil-proof safe for the mercies of God! All of God's mercy is stored in the high heavens. As knowledgeable as we think we are, we seem to foul up everything we touch. Take a look at the earth's ecological system, for example.

Can you visualize coins stacked as high as the tallest cloud? If you can, then maybe you can imagine God's faithfulness that thick? In other words, God runs on the principle of abundance, not scarcity.

There is an abandoned coal mine pond where kids swim. In the middle of the pond is the mine shaft that is almost a mile down. God's judgment is that deep. There is no chance of a superficial decision from God.

What an insight to say that God's righteousness exceeds the height of Mt. McKinley or Mt. Everest! Solid as granite and miles thick is the rightness of Almighty God. The loving aspect of God can not be equaled. Since we are His children, He will preserve humans, as well as animals.

With the vastness of God, who would want to put their trust in money, stocks, material things, or other human beings? King David boldly urges us to place our trust in God, who can safely cover us like a mother hen does her chicks. The razors sharp talons of the mighty eagle, nor Satan's arrows can never get under God's wings, where you are securely sheltered. Let's take time and praise the Lord.

February 13

"Your mercy, O Lord, is in the heavens; Your faithfulness reaches to the clouds. Your righteousness is like the great mountains; Your judgments are a great deep; O Lord, You preserve man and beast. How precious is your loving kindness, O God? Therefore the children of men put their trust under the shadow of your wings." Ps. 36:5-7

King David began his soliloquy by describing the mercy of God in the heaven. There the vast amount of his mercy is stored and dispensed as our Lord sees fit. Haven't we appealed to God to pour some of it on the tight situations we get ourselves into?

After experiencing the frailties of his advisors, leaders, and subjects, King David stresses the faithfulness of God. How often have we come to the place where we are tempted to throw up our hands and QUIT! We need to remember that the Lord faithfully walks with us.

The enemies of King David were always nipping at his heels. It appears that he never did any thing right. When he made an edict, decree, or decision, his adversaries were always on the other side the table. We, like him, wish at times for God to squash our enemies like the bugs they are. After thinking such a judgmental statement, we should intuitively know we are not capable of judging fairly. So King David extols the fairness of all of God's judgments. God's thinking is so vast and so deep.

Finally, David mentions God's loving-kindness. If we were in control and a person had messed up like we have, would we still treat them with loving kindness?

Isn't God wonderful? How nice to squat down and slip under the wing of our protecting Savior. While hearing the heartbeat of God, feeling the warmth of his love, and living in the shadow of his loving-kindness, we can live a glorious life, even in this sinful world.

February 14

"For with You is the fountain of life; in your light we see light." Ps. 36:9

The fountain of life brings to mind the water fountains of Europe with the fresh smelling spray. When the sun shines on the mist, it produces a rainbow. Their fountains are always spraying? That is like the ever flowing love and blessings of God. Closer to home, I was shown an artesian fountain in the side of a hill near Cumberland Gap, Maryland. The family piped the water, gravity flow into their house. They had only to open the faucet to get very cold, sparkling refreshing water. It produced so much water that the excess had to flow down the hillside. God's love and blessings are like that. It flows continually, so even after we drink all we can hold, it splashes on others.

Its influence is like a light. It is nothing like the Boy Scout flashlight I used to find my way to the latrine in the middle of the night. It was one spot just one step ahead of me. God's light is more like the searchlights of World War II with a million candlepower or more. These searchlights could spot an airplane at 18,000 feet in the air. God's loving kindness chases all the fear right out of our life. It feels so good to be able to see all around us.

St. John (I John 1:7) tells us what happens when we can walk in the light of Christ. We can have fellowship with Him. We must be a born again child of God to commune and stroll down the road together. Later (Ps. 119:105) the Psalmist mentions that God's word will be lamp unto our path way and light unto own feet. We would then agree with King David that God's love is a fountain of life and that as we walk with Him, God shines through our lives to brighten other's paths.

February 15

"Do not fret because of evildoers, nor be envious of the workers of iniquity. For they shall soon be cut down like grass, and wither as the green herb. ....Rest in the Lord, and wait patiently for Him; do not fret because of him who prospers in his way, because of the man who brings wicked schemes to pass." Ps. 37:1-2, 7

Don't worry about the evil family that is making a mint, while your daddy is barely eking out a living. Let's not brood at night about the lazy co-worker who got the promotion, when they only looked good because of the hard work you had done. God doesn't want us to whine or gripe to our co-workers about inequalities in the office.

God is not pleased when we are jealous or resentful of the drug dealer or loan shark who has the best of clothes and finest of vehicles. Don't be covetous or envious of the politicians who are getting filthy rich from kick-backs.

King David encourages us not to lose sleep or mope over the person who hatches and brings evil schemes to pass for their advantage. These people are headed on a collision course with a just God. This is a certainty. They may seem to go unpunished, but God is watching every evil move they make.

If God is going to give them the punishment they deserve, why don't we see it happening? God's timing is not the same as our timing. His justice may be slow but it grinds exceedingly fine.

Our task is to wait patiently on the Lord. You can rest assured that not one promise of God has ever failed to be fulfilled. In short, focus on the omnipotence of Almighty God and do not keep score of the evil and inequity in our world.

February 16

"Trust in the Lord, and do good; dwell in the land, and feed on his faithfulness. Delight yourself also in the Lord, and He shall give you the desires of your heart. Commit your way to the Lord, trust also in him, and He shall bring it to pass. He shall bring forth your righteousness as the light, and your justice as the noonday." Ps. 37:3-6

In preceding verses, the Psalmist began by urging us to trust God and do good. It sounds like the promise in this verse pertains to one who has already given themselves to Christ or to any bone fide Child of God. Such a person is adverse to evil but looks for, finds, and actively does good things for others. With this frame of mind, a Christian exudes joy, pursues peace, helps others, and lives confidently for God.

The succeeding verse urges us to commit everything to God. Everything includes all our past, all our present, and all our future. Quite a tall order, huh? If we fulfill this tall order, God promises to help us! Surely you wouldn't say, "No help wanted -- I can do this job all by myself." As for this writer, I could use the assistance!

As we commit more and more of ourselves into God's care, verse six states God will make us more Christ-like. Isn't that marvelous? After we have done wrong, evil, or something against God, He is always willing to forgive us. Permit me a shout, "Hallelujah!" What a loving Savior, who cares for us so much!

Our verse today states this enriching promise! 'If we delight in the Lord, He will give us the desires of our heart.' As a child of God, we naturally only want what God wants for us. He graciously answers our prayers. No matter how God decides to fulfill our desires, you can stand firm on this verse. It is a promise of our infinite God!

February 17

"Rest in the Lord, and wait patiently for him; do not fret because of him who prospers in his way, because of the man who brings wicked schemes to pass." Ps. 37:7

Have we ever said, "Why does that evil person get rich and I, a Christian, can't get all my bills paid?" I guess it is alright to question God. King David didn't question, worry, or fret, when Satan's people prospered. We aren't to let prosperity of evil people neither upset our stomach nor lose any sleep over.

Our scripture suggests that we are not to envy that rich family because envy only leads to harm. The harm comes to us, who envy another's good fortune.

Also, we are not to worry over a wicked person who plots evil, schemes to rob, or does harm to others. My father-in-law used to remorsefully lament, "The store robbed me and I didn't even have my hands up." My father-in-law would be angry for a week. Every time he would think about it, the smoldering hurt would burst into a flame of anger. Often it is very difficult to refrain from anger, rage, envy, worrying, and fretting. The Psalmist suggests in verse eight to stop our anger. He insinuated that we turn from the grudge that is pawing in our heart like a mad bull in a packed arena.

The key to success is found in the first four words of the verse 'rest in the Lord'. After you rest awhile and nothing happens, then wait patiently. God chooses his own time and particular circumstance before he answers. If God wants us to wait patiently, then it must be possible. Okay, Lord, I'll try to wait on your divine timing.

February 18

"A little that a righteous has is better than the riches of many wicked." Ps. 37:16

If I had a little bigger paycheck, we could afford a new car. Oh! how I wish I had some of that rich perfume at the upscale department store. If only I had a higher spending limit on my credit card, I would have that pretty outfit in the store window. If our business had not fallen through, we would have had a new Lexus sitting in the driveway. Our house has 5,000 square feet in it, but we don't have a swimming pool in the backyard. I would go to Acapulco on vacation, but my busy schedule won't allow me. You wouldn't believe what it costs to be a member of the country club! The stock market is such a worry. Yesterday it took a 600 point plunge in one day. We lost 30% of our retirement that day.

Oh, what will we ever do? How will we be able to send our kids to college?

How many of you can remember the depression of 1929? Those were hard but happy days. I can remember many saying, "Because we were all poor and didn't feel sorry for ourselves."

Grandma was never rich in things of this world. I recall her spending evening hours with her Bible and sometimes with her eyes closed in prayers. So with her little of this world's goods she was blessed. Oh, that we could acquire such an attitude about riches!

February 19

"The Lord knows the days of the upright, and their inheritance shall be forever." Ps. 37:18

The Lord knows when you are enduring pain, sickness, or disease.

The Lord also your enjoyable days. He takes note of your smile and witnesses your good deeds.

The Lord notices the many times you were helpful to that person or family in need. He genuinely understands the hurt, when they don't say so much as, "Thank you."

The Lord is cognizant of the days your body starts out depleted emotionally. The battery only gets lower throughout the day. He watched while that person verbally kicked you the day you were already down.

The Lord is aware of the hours and nights you cried out in prayer for your wandering child. He actually feels the hurt and measures the love you are exercising for their salvation from sin.

The Lord knows when the check book and the budget seem to be separate entities. Instead of working harmoniously, one spends more and more on mandatory things while the budget seems to get deeper in the hole.

The Lord knew the exact time you spoke up for Him. He knew the frustration, when they tried to make you look foolish. Your motive was pleasing to God.

King David wants to assure you that your eternal inheritance is not lost. It lies in the safest safe deposit box in the universe. The terms are: it will be there forever or until you die and claim it. Stand firm against evil and filthy-minded people. Your payday is not on this side of death. God is guarding your reward until He personally presents it to you in heaven.

February 20

"The wicked borrows and does not repay, but the righteous shows mercy and gives." Ps 37:21

The wicked borrows much from you and promptly forgets how much and to whom they owe. An acquaintance of ours just got another new credit card. Their first card was max-ed out. When the new credit card company didn't get a payment, they called her. She blamed the new credit card company and said, "You should have known I couldn't pay, when they issued me a card through the mail." When we max out our credit cards and don't pay them off is that evil? According to King David it sounds like we are doing wrong to the card company.

If that is the case, how does God view filing for bankruptcy? When we have enjoyed the rug, boat, or fancy restaurant meals and we don't pay them for services rendered, is that a form of robbery? Would it be different, if one filed for and got bankruptcy but then retained the bills and after getting a promotion paying all that was owed? The righteous of even the younger generation are concerned about the debt they incur. A Christian makes faithful payments to eliminate the debt.

Christians are givers, while sinners are takers. Using that criterion what does our financial ledger say about our generosity. It is usually the children of God, who come forward and truly assist when there is a natural disaster. Our giving could be encouraging words to someone who is depressed or discouraged. God **can** loosen the strings on our money, so we can be generous when the Holy Spirit shows us a need.

February 21

"The steps of a good man are ordered by the Lord, and He delights in his way. Though he falls, he shall not be utterly cast down; for the Lord upholds him with his hand. I have been young, and now am old; yet I have not seen the righteous forsaken, nor his descendants begging bread." Ps. 37:23-5

Can you even imagine a God who controls the tide, regulates the effect of viruses, and keeps the sun on time, but still orders your personal steps? How can such a busy God be interested or concerned about little old us? King David is convinced that God gives individualized personal attention to each human. He knows every dialect, language, ebonics and slang! Oh, to have a God that takes time out and who genuinely cares for each of us.

The tense of the verse shows that He is doing all of this as you read. God is doing this for you; guiding your steps, delighting himself in things you are doing, and ordering how your day is going to be. Even when you slip and laugh at a bad joke, think a devious thought, or act unkind, God says he will not let you fall. It is similar to when a baby holds our finger and begins those first steps. We put our other fingers around theirs to hold them when they get off balance. His kind hands are ever there to hold you up. He not only cares in the present, God will continue to watch over and protect you in the future.

Here is a testimony from our esteemed King David. He says that in all his life, he had not seen people of God (born again Christians) forsaken or begging for bread. Isn't that marvelous! Many older citizens remember during the depression how God seemed to miraculously supply food for their table. Can you and I lean as confidently on those everlasting arms of Jesus? Let's try it for the rest of the day.

February 22

"The mouth of the righteous speaks wisdom, and his tongue talks of justice. The law of his God is in his heart; none of his steps shall slide." Ps. 37:30-1

God, the Creator through the Holy Spirit inspired faithful persons to write the scripture. In other words, they wrote down God's wisdom for humankind to use for guidance.

When judges of a nation weaken or disobey the commands of God, the people of that nation suffer. When the legislative branch passes laws that contradict the principles in the Bible, that society will sink into depravity. The law officers, who take a bribe from the rich, cause the poor to become oppressed. Those who foolishly practice immorality will suffer the consequences in their body.

If you want to go through this life with a minimum of pain and/or stressful consequences, consult the righteous. The righteous people, Christians, continually search the Word of God. In the Bible, they find the words of light and life.

Christians hide these truths in their hearts, so when someone seeks advice from a Christian, the truth bubbles up from the depth of God's wisdom. Their advice is much more profound than what their own intelligence could produce.

St. James speaks of justice. He considers being partial to one person over another is unjust or a sin (James 2:9). In the same vain, the Christian speaks of genuine justice. He does not lean one way or the other but weighs evidence they have and renders a just verdict.

So if you ever get in a difficult spot in life where you need advice pray to God. Secondarily you can seek out a Christian. If they are truly your friend and an authentic Christian, they will search for the unvarnished facts. They will dispense wisdom based on what they have gleaned from God's Word.

February 23

"The mouth of the righteous speaks wisdom, and his tongue talks of justice. The law of his God is in his heart; none of his steps shall slide." Ps. 37:30-31

How many times have you spoken and afterwards thought about what you should have said? Join an illustrious crowd. Peter when he was on the Mount of Transfiguration said, "Let's make three booths." The scriptures inferred that Peter said that because he didn't know what else to say. In other words, he put his mouth in gear before he engaged his brain. This should not be true of the righteous or a Christian person. The word of a Christian should be wisdom, not evil schemes, gossip, or slander. The best source of wisdom is found in God's Holy Word. A great method of placing wisdom in our life is memorizing verses of scripture.

A Christian will talk about justice. Our thoughts will not be on greed such as 'what is mine is mine and what is yours is mine'. Nor will we concentrate on vengeance, be partial because of them being a friend, or things that hurt others. Our thoughts and words will be on what is right and fair.

Had you noticed that King David of Old Testament times meditated on the law of God? That's not exactly right. It says the law of **his** God. Do you and I have a meaningful relationship with Jesus Christ? If we do, we can call Him, **our** Father as in the Lord's Prayer. When we have this relationship, God will take care of our tongue, our heart, and our steps. He will keep our tongue from speaking evil. Our hearts will exalt the Lord Almighty. God promises that our steps will not slip or slide into sin.

February 24

"O Lord, do not rebuke me in your wrath, nor chasten me in your hot displeasure! For your arrows pierce me deeply, and your hand presses me down." Ps. 38:1-2

Has your father or mother ever punished you? The next question is, "Were they ever really mad, when they paddled you?" In the latter case, the swats were much harder and hotter. In our scripture, King David is pleading with God to count to infinity before he gives him his rightful punishment. Our Lord can punish us down in our heart, like where an arrow would pierce. Our heavenly Father, instead of using his hand to smack us or hit us in the face, pushes us down until we calm down. The Almighty does not physically abuse his children, like some humans do. What a marvelous example for us to follow!

Did you notice in our scripture that not once did King David proclaim his innocence? He was aware that the consequences of his willful action were due him. None of us can claim we are sinless. So, we can look forward to our punishment. As a kid, many of us had a long wait until Dad came home from work for our paddling. The Heavenly Father, likewise, doesn't punish immediately.

As sure as the tide rises and falls, so we will receive the consequences of our rebellion of God's law, breaking one of the commandments, or just doing our own thing. One of the churches in Revelation made God mad. They said, they were Christians but only served God half-heartedly. These church members when around the people at work would act just like them. Actions like these might cause God to spew us out of His mouth, as well.

Let us entreat God to not be too hard on us for our sins against Him. Definitely, the Lord never chastises us when He is angry. Thank you, Lord, for being gentle but just with us.

February 25

"Thus I am like a man who does not hear, and in whose mouth is no response. For in You, O Lord, I hope; You will hear, O Lord my God." Ps. 38:14-15

How often have you really wondered if God was hearing your prayers? Your faith was small, the ceiling seemed the distance your prayers traveled and God seemed to be answering none of your requests.

In the preceding verse, King David complained about God being silent. Was it that God had selective hearing or did He have laryngitis? In all King David's looking, God seemed noticeably absent nor was there any sign of his blessings evident.

King David had so many political snipers taking bead on him that he felt like he was before the firing squad. God knew his enemies. God knows those who at taking verbal pot shots at you and your religious stand at work. We can rest in that comfort that God keeps watch over his own. He knows all the devious and evil plots of the wicked. God does not slumber nor sleep. You are the apple of his eye! I'm talking about you. You are unique! You are precious! You are of great value to God!

While you stand with Christ, you are automatically subject to ridicule, alienation, and discrimination. While you are estranged from the world, God is walking by your side. Just reach out and take God's hand. Let your motto be as our American coins, "In God we trust". No matter what may come, put your hope in Jesus Christ, the only begotten Son of Almighty God.

February 26

"I was mute with silence, I held my peace even from good; and my sorrow was stirred up. My heart was hot within me; while I was musing, the fire burned. Then I spoke with my tongue: .... And now, Lord, what do I wait for? My hope is in You." Ps. 39:2, 3, 7

Most of us know what stirs up resentment in us. Does it come when we have to do someone else's job? Does picking up or cleaning up after someone, who is entirely capable of doing it themselves, trip your switch? Do you, like King David, hold your temper but the resentment is still unresolved.

He describes his anger while his emotions were stirred. Can you imagine for God the internal cauldron with all the foul smells of past grudges, hatreds, and wounded pride in King David or us? Do you vividly remember the time someone made fun of you in front of your close friend? It still remains like a boil on the back of your neck where the collar chafes at it constantly. Or was it the girl in high school who stole your boy friend? Even now when you see or think of her, you are hurt all over again. Maybe it was a competitor who by crooked means got the bid?

King David kept it sealed up inside. He referred to this hidden anger as red hot coals smoldering inside. At times, it burst into a roaring fire within. Through a gigantic effort, however, he kept his life on even keel. He refrained from doing anything, even from doing something good when he was angry. But the time came when King David unlatched the lid to the festering resentment and anger. He did it in a sociably acceptable way by talking. Abusing others in any manner was and is unacceptable.

After venting all this to God in prayer, the King asks, 'Now what am I waiting for'? It didn't take him long to come to the conclusion. The answer was, "The Lord!" Who but God can keep us from getting in that shape? We can praise God, who gives us victory over our resentment, anger, and hatred!

February 27

"Deliver me from all my transgressions; ..." Ps. 39:8a

If it wasn't for irritating people, I wouldn't have to confess my sins so often. The frustrating fact is that we are people.

Is it the temptations or our sinful nature that causes us to fall from grace and sin against God? King David wants God to deliver us from all sins.

Wouldn't that be marvelous! Come to think of it, he says that if we confess our sin before Him, He will cleanse us from ALL unrighteousness (I John 1:9).

God progressively reveals the sin and hindrances to our spiritual growth. For me, He started with the large and noticeable sins such as: cheating, lying, and stealing. He didn't have to work on me about murder. Next, it is sins of attitude of the heart and mind. Resentment was one of those. Envy of other's good fortune was another.

Like King David, I admitted that I had sinned. We only fool or deceive ourselves when we think we are perfect and have not sinned. Oh, how I would hate to get to heaven's gate and go through the sin scanner and find out there were sins I had not been delivered of. If we only are willing to confess our sin, our soul can be white as snow off a blizzard. So today, we need to join the wise King David and say, "Lord, deliver me from all my sins and transgressions."

February 28

"He also brought me up out of a horrible pit, out of the miry clay, and set my feet upon a rock, and established my steps. He has put a new song in my mouth – Praise to our God; many will see it and fear, and will trust in the Lord." Ps. 40:2-3

It sounds like King David was in a slough of despond or bog of depression. Sometimes our emotional problems can be described as a horrible pit. When caught in one of the webs of despair, it is hard to imagine that God is our sole salvation. Because as hard as you try to extricate yourself, you get nowhere. By the time you get one boot out of the mud, the other is in real deep almost ready to pour into your boot. The exhausting task has you down. We need to look up, up to God who is our Strong Deliverer. His almighty hand can hoist us up and sit us on the Solid Rock, Christ Jesus. He can guide our steps, even when we are wandering to no place in particular. In my life of seven decades, God has guided me through circumstances to places and positions I thought were adverse to my advancement. In the end and with hindsight, I plainly see He was leading me all the way.

At one point, God put a new song in King David's heart to sing. He sang of his blessed Redeemer and His wonderful love for him. Everyday with Jesus seemed sweeter than the day before. This kind of song is a vital and effective testimony to the world of what God can do. King David says when we witness like this; many will fear and put their trust in God. God places the song on our lips, not a 'put-on' show of religion. Surely you have witnessed a person who was saved at a revival or returned from a Walk to Emmaeus, who had the light of God shining in their eyes and the song of praise on their lips. Let's join them in their jubilant hymn of praise.

February 29

"I delight to do your will, O My God, and your law is within my heart." Ps. 40:8

What a joy to sit in a porch swing on a clear evening and watch the sky display its kaleidoscope of colors! Oh! how we wish we were in a nice boat with our fishing pole over the side. Or would your greatest pleasure be to have the wind whistling by your ears on a bike or motorcycle. Our King David could have had any pleasure he wanted. His greatest joy was, when he was able to do the will of Almighty God.

A later Psalmist says that they hid God's words

in their hearts so they might not sin against God (Ps. 119:11). He tried to store God's commandments, principles, and desires in his heart. This way he could be more like God. There is a joy that comes from pleasing God. In modern terms, King David was training his heart to keep "WWJD" in the forefront (**W**hat **W**ould **J**esus **D**o?). He wanted the laws of God to become second nature, as natural as, washing his hands and saying grace before he ate. This nature should be as common and consistent as saying "Yes, Madam" or "No, Sir."

King David got his kicks from doing right things not evil or bad things. Some serial murderers get their charge out of killing, especially when it is worse and more diabolical than the last one. Some sinners enjoy calling wrong things right such as abortion, alternate lifestyle and legalized gambling. Let's make a sincere effort to get our exhilaration from doing the things that please God. We can love Him, praise Him, and thank Him for saving us from sin and showering us with his continual blessings. Then we will do good because our hearts are pure.

March 1

"I have proclaimed the good news of righteousness in the great assembly; indeed, I do not restrain my lips, O Lord, You yourself know. I have not hidden your righteousness within my heart; I have declared your faithfulness and your salvation; I have not concealed your loving kindness and your truth from the great assembly." Ps. 40:9, 10

Can we, like King David, brag to all that we have freely spread the Word of God everywhere we've been? Even as a preacher, have we spread the spiritual table each week with the luscious fruits of truth directly from the Bible? For the pastor, the fear is that the church will ask them to move, if they are honest in their delivery. Many of us are afraid to speak up at work for fear our chances at a promotion will be nipped in the bud. Another deterrent to witnessing may be that we will be classified as a religious freak.

Although we haven't consistently spoken for Christ, have we lived a life so our light shone? When we were unjustly criticized, did we return it with love? Or when we were treated with indifference, did we treat them as a friend. Or when one of our co-workers spewed poison all over the office with their sharp acid tongue, did we have the ability to forgive and forget? Hopefully, we have not hidden our righteousness under bushel at work, at the sports club, or at our church.

Have we bragged on Jesus, our Savior and Lord? When good times happen to us, do we give credit to coincidence or luck? Let us begin to declare to all, it was the power and glory of God. Join King David in praising and glorifying our Lord and Savior Jesus Christ. Open my mouth and let me gladly spread Thy warm truth everywhere.

March 2

"Do not withhold your tender mercies from me, O Lord; let your loving kindness and your truth continually preserve me. For innumerable evils have surrounded me; my iniquities have overtaken me, so that I am not able to look up; they are more than the hairs of my head; therefore my heart fails me." Ps. 40:11, 12

You can almost feel the pathos of our Psalmist? The number of his troubles matches the number of beans in a barrel of Jelly Belly jelly beans. They are so numerous that they overwhelm him, like being under the spout of an elevator's wheat silo. If they don't stop, they will bury him. King David's troubles had him at such a low ebb that depression had taken control of his thinking. In such a case, it is nearly impossible to look up to the Lord.

In desperation, King David implores God to permit his tender mercies to tickle down from heaven and touch his mind. His plea is for God to extend His loving kindness. Come to his mental state that is on a level with a snake. No kingly credentials, no precious gift, nor huge offering could he bring – only the cry of a desperately needy person.

Let us pray, "Lord, You are my only hope! All else is as a broken crutch that will not hold me up. Take my hand and lift me. Only You can save me. Only You can be my glorious liberator. Free me from my severe mental state. Cut the bonds of opposition, so I can joyously serve and please You. Only You, Lord, are the all-victorious defender who has never lost a battle with Satan, his angels, or his multitude of followers. You are always bigger than any and all my problems. Praise your holy name! Amen."

March 3

"Blessed is he who considers the poor; the Lord will deliver him in time of trouble. The Lord will preserve him and keep him alive, and he will be blessed on the earth; You will not deliver him to the will of his enemies. The Lord will strengthen him on his bed of illness; You will sustain him on his sickbed." Ps. 41:1-3

Today's rule in society is "Take care of old #1. If you don't, nobody else will." When the prime interest rests on self, others are neglected. If a person is successful in the eyes of the world, that is all that seems to count.

In the eyes of the Lord according to King David, the person who forgets the needy will not be rescued out of trouble when it comes their way. Your enemy, who is trying for your job, will bring you down. During illness the tight wad will continue to mourn and endure pain, because God makes the promise He will not come to their aid.

The promise of God is: If you feel sorry and assist the needy, God will pour blessings upon you. God will fill you with happiness for your actions. When trouble overtakes you, God promises to deliver you. When others are dying, the Lord will preserve and keep you alive. God also vows to strengthen you, when calamity comes your way. When all else of this world fails to help, God will protect you from the evil tidal wave of trouble.

So don't listen to the wisdom of the world but obey God. He can and will reward you and strengthen as you live each day.

March 4

"But You, O Lord, be merciful to me, and raise me up, that I may repay them. By this I know that You are well pleased with me, because my enemy does not triumph over me." Ps. 41:10-11

How did you know that you pleased mother? Was there a pat on the head? Did she cook your favorite meal? Could you tell when you made Dad happy? Did he smile instead of criticize how you did something? Were you able to have the keys to the family car the next time you really needed them? It was usually easier to tell that you did a good job for the teacher. Not only was there an "A" on the top of the paper but a sticker or stamp of a smiley face. She complimented you in front of the class. Boy! Did that ever make you feel good down deep inside!

Father Abraham knew he did well. Instead of having to plunge that knife down into his precious Isaac, God provided a ram (Gen.22:13). What a confirmation that was! Can't you visualize him shouting, "Bless You, God!" over and over.

In another case, a young man prayed almost constantly. His enemies searched his ledgers and couldn't find one mistake with their audit. So they wrote a law and had the King sign it. They trapped him and had him thrown into a pit with hungry lions. Daniel knew his life was well pleasing to God. The Almighty caused the lions to go over against the wall and take a nap. I don't suppose he shouted "Hallelujah" but inside he was singing "How Great Thou Art" to the top of his internal voice. What a validation of his religious devotion. God saved him from certain death.

The evidence of your daily Christian walk and close association with God will be that your enemy will not triumph over you. When others fall, you will still be standing for God.

March 5

"As the deer pants for the water brooks, so pants my soul for You, O God. My soul thirsts for God, for the living God. When shall I come and appear before God?" Ps 42:1, 2

Do you recall when you were madly in love? You were out of your mind with nothing on it but that person with whom you were deeply in love. As soon as you left their presence, you wondered if they were already missing you as much as you were missing them. You were always tempted to use your phone and call them just to hear their voice. As soon as you got off work, you looked them up because it was more important than supper. It was agony just to be separated! The only way to solve that problem was to buy a set of rings and get down on one knee and ask her to marry you.

The King David had a similar malady. He was in dire circumstances, because he always wanted to be near or in the presence of God. His emotions longed for God's presence, as a deer yearned for a tongue full of crystal cool clear water from that mountain-fed stream. No other substitute would do for the deer. No substitute for the presence of God would do for the soul of King David. Pleasures and conveniences of this world couldn't touch that insatiable desire. Only the presence of the LIVING God can erase our pain and make it disappear. Neither fame, fortune, or good health can calm the craving for God's spirit. As the negative and a positive ends of the magnet attract each other, the presence of God invisibly draws our soul to the Creator. All others things of the world act like two like poles, repelling.

King David ended this verse by saying,"When shall I come and appear before God?" That would be the ultimate satisfaction. Just like when you were madly in love, only the continual presence of that other person gave you peace.

March 6

"Why are you cast down, O my soul? And why are you disquieted within me? Hope in God, for I shall yet praise him for the help of his countenance." Ps. 42:5

What is your life like? Does it compare to a dreary day where the sun fails to shine? Or is your life more like the dismal grey and black clouds blanketing the sky? Your body feels sluggish, while your feelings resemble a damp rag. The brightness of the day is hidden so deep you can not decide how to feel.

King David asks God why his spirit feels so washed out. Why does his soul feel down and experiencing anxiety instead of the usual peace of God? Could it be a lack of communing with the Mighty Creator? In jest, one once asked, "Why pray when you can worry?" Is it possible we guilty of not spending time in prayer?

Finally, King David realizes his plight. He looks beyond the feelings of the moment into the future. As he imagines himself in the care of God, his spirit sheds those bleak and drizzly feelings. He places his hopes in God, who always cares for him. The King summons to his mind all the happy times of the past. Since God is the same yesterday, today, and tomorrow, the King focuses on a day in the future when God will again bless him with all kinds of joy and bushels of tranquil peace.

A preacher friend of mine says this calls for an 'attitude adjustment'. Are you and I often in need of a change in perception of our present circumstance? Is this your present circumstance? If so, look to Jesus, who can and will change our dismal feelings or give us endurance until the storm of life is past. Like King David, if we can't rejoice now, we can anticipate the time when we will again praise Him.

March 7

"Then I will go to the altar of God, to God my exceeding joy; and on the harp I will praise you, O God, my God." Ps 43:4

Do we seek the advice of friends first? Is our second line of defense, our parents? Do we try to cover over our sorrow with work, or blanket over our grief with busyness? Do we attempt to drown our problems in alcohol?

King David often said he had enemies that were always on his case. They were wearing him down. He had learned over a life of experience that nothing helped but God. He headed straight to the altar at church, when things were overwhelming. He went to the Source. This is a valuable lesson of life!

After going to God with his problems, King David offered a sacrifice of praise. We can start our praise with scriptural choruses. The Holy Spirit comes, Oh! So close! It feels somewhat like being near the magnetic field of a 40,600 volt electric line. But instead of fear, there is an inexpressible joy in every fiber of your body, mind, and soul.

The piano produces the same calming affect on my sister, as a harp did for King David. The stress flows out of her fingers as they fly over the piano keys. The fullness of God then flows in. The spiritual in-filling is so precious. We almost feel like the three disciples on the Mount of Transfiguration. Let's just stay here and if we need to, we'll even build a church right here.

Did you notice in the scripture that King David claimed God as his God? If God affirms we are His children, isn't it proper for us to profess him as our own God. That doesn't exclude others spiritual brothers and sisters from asserting that God is their Heavenly Father too.

Let us start a new ritual. When life get overbearing, let's follow King David to the altar where our Source is.

March 8

"For they did not gain possession of the land by their own sword, nor did their own arm save them;

but it was your right hand, your arm, and the light of your countenance, because You favored them." Ps 44:3

Did God smile on you and cause the stock market to change from bear to bull? Your stock went up. Now you have enough dividends coming in to pay your monthly bills or live comfortably later.

Did He look graciously on you and heal you from the disastrous affects of the car accident? You were soon back walking and talking. How much better it was than lying flat on your back!

Did the glory of God shine your direction and a promotion was granted you. For so long you thought all your hard work was going unnoticed. Oh, how much better your self-esteem is in this new position of responsibility!

Did God's goodness beam down on you so that the dark depression that used to plague you is gone? It is so wonderful to feel good and greet people because you want to.

Did God finally trust you with a real live human being? He favored you with a child. This fulfilled your heart's desire. What a marvelous blessing from God!

In God's good grace He sent loyal friends. Many others are still friendless. God has sent several your way. What an overflow of God's blessing on your life!

God's countenance upon your life created a new peace and serenity in your life. This makes you different from the world. It is all because God bestowed this upon your life.

How can you thank or show your appreciation for His blessings and heavenly benediction upon your life? Let us search today for ways to show or tell others how much we love God.

March 9

"For they did not gain possession of the land by their own sword, nor did their arm save them; but it was your right hand, your arm, and the light of your countenance, because You favored them." Ps. 44:3

Some days we feel strong enough to fight our weight in bumble bees. Just let us get the start of a cold or flu, and then we realize the limitations of our capabilities. The Psalmist is stating an indisputable fact. We are of little consequence on the large or small scale of things.

The children of Israel were going about from coffee shop to coffee shop recounting how strong their father and forefathers were when they fought the Canaanites. Even King David could recount in vivid detail how he used the sword to decapitate old Goliath. In all cases, God had to be on their side to have succeeded.

Although there were many valiant and strong men among the Hebrews, the victory was not gained by physical strength. In our own strength, Satan will surely trip us with temptations. Could it be that God knew our human thinking? We might get egotistical, or brag on our success. In reality, it is the right arm of Christ who always gives us the victory.

King David put it this way, "... because You favored them". This clearly sets things in the right perspective. God desires to receive all the glory.

When God lifts His eyes and looks upon us, we feel drenched in his wonderful love. If God loves us that much, shouldn't we love in the same fashion?

March 10

"My heart is overflowing with a good theme; I recite my composition concerning the King; my tongue is the pen of a ready writer."   Ps. 45:1
In the morning I arise and greet each new day,
This fortifies me to walk the spiritual way.
Guide me safely throughout this day by your hand,
I look always to You, not put my head in the sand.

At breakfast, I dwell on your kindness,
Thank You for hours of refreshing rest.
On restless nights upon You I call,
I meditate on You or on the rosary my hands do fall.

Energetically and enthusiastically each morning I begin,
Work, play, and leisure is fun until the day ends,
Mentally, physically, or emotionally at work I start out with glee.
Labor I enjoy because that is how You created me.
Some circumstances or obstacles by Satan does cram,

Drives my life askew, but flee to Thee I always can.
Other days God is merciful and I can sing all day long,
Whether in my heart, in my mind, or on my lips, I sing an assuring song.
A pattern has usually established itself by noon,

Praise, glory, and honor to God has become my tune,
When things go well, I praise Thee.
In all things give thanks, this is
Thy will for you and me.

After lunch my body takes a nap for a short time,

But my spirit relaxes as into your arms I climb.
Then it's off to work in the Lord's vineyard,
But vigilantly I keep my spiritual guard.

When the day's work is over and the whistle blows,
Again praise, honor and glory from me to You does flow.
Graciously, You provide food for my table of love,
Therefore, my tongue speaks of your love from above.

Evening brings lower levels of stress and tension.
After dinner, the family receives my attention.
Precious time and activities create memories,
Enjoyment is found in these for remembering.

As darkness covers the earth, I think of sleep.
Into my prayer guide for missionaries and friends I peek
Then say "Good Night" to my lovely spouse,
Things become quiet in the house.

From daybreak to the setting of the sun,
I sing hymns of praise to your Son.
Each day may this be true,
So in heaven I will see You.

March 11

"You love righteousness and hate wickedness; therefore God, your God, has anointed you with the oil of gladness more than your companions." Ps. 45:7

    Do we participate in the sins of gossip or extortion? No! Do we put up with or tolerate sin as inevitable? No! The politician who takes the pay-off or the policeman takes the bribe and says, "What can I do?" Are we like King David who thinks God believes that we ought to hate evil and work to eradicate it? It is alright to hate, ...evil that is!

Do we love righteousness? Being totally honest is an enjoyable challenge! How great a feeling when you look for and find an opportunity to show love or help someone in need! What a sense of serenity overlays our psyche or spirit, as we sit quietly in church or participate in the wonderful worship service! We really feel proud of ourselves, when others say, "Oh so and so can't be guilty of going that, because they are a Christian." We are even willing to take the heat, when others pick on us because of our clean and pure life. We realize they are dealing with their feelings of guilt or ashamed of their behavior. It is a real pleasure to be around other righteous or Christian people. You don't have to keep up your mental guard. You can sense the kinship of like minds.

Since you love right and love to do right, God wants to anoint you. A divine anointing is a sign that spiritual and physical blessings will begin to come to you. With these blessings comes gladness. This gladness remains in your heart through sorrow, physical pain and mental stress. This gladness will come in such abundance, that like King David you will think God is blessing you more than any of your Christian friends.

March 12

"Listen, O daughter, consider and incline your ear; forget your own people also, and your father's house; so the King will greatly desire your beauty; because He is my Lord, worship Him." Ps. 45:10-11

So many trials, temptations, and hard knocks spin out from life's potter's wheel. Our physical bodies take on many shapes throughout a lifetime but God greatly admires our beauty. We may even consider ourselves so much trash, but God considers us a thing of beauty.

When salvation comes to our soul, God enhances our beauty and increases our face value. It is then that we will follow King David's admonition to open our ears and listen to the Word of Lord.

With Jesus as Lord of our life, things begin to happen. This new life in Christ generates energy, instills a strong moral backbone, and assists us in helping others in need in our neighborhood. The new heart of flesh puts a song on our lips or a blessing in our soul. The plight of the needy around us now seems to tug on our heart strings for us to initiate relief. The new attitude of Christ decreases with the on set of negativity in our thinking. Christ places positive and constructive ideas in our mind. This born-again experience produces a new compassionate sense of love.

March 13

"God is our refuge and strength, a very present help in trouble. Therefore, we will not fear even though the earth be removed, and though the mountains be carried into the midst of the sea; though its waters roar and be troubled, though the mountains shake with its swelling." Ps. 46:1-3

A sudden thunderstorm came upon me while out walking the dog. The miniature poodle and I ran to the nearest place to get out of the rain. He shook his fur and was dry in just a few minutes. I felt secure because I had located refuge from the sudden downpour. How like Christ the shelter was?

When troubles and trials sweep down upon us, we immediately go to God in prayer.

Before our relationship becomes strong, we try to figure it all out on my own. We attempt to confront and overcome our problems. Seldom are we able to solve our problem. Most of the time we are like the Negro spiritual, "It's a me. It's a me. It's a me, O Lord. Stand'in in the need of prayer."

King David's problems were multiples of ours and acutely more life-threatening. He proclaimed to the world through this Psalm that since he had a relationship with God, he would not fear. King David's problems were unstable as Jell-O on a plate. All of his faith was in God to fill his being with love replacing the fear! God is substantially more powerful than any possible havoc in his life.

Even as people roared at him and circumstances stared him in the face, David did not fear! His mind was focused on God so peace reigned instead of fear permeating his heart (Is.26:3). Our lives can resemble King David's! The exterior may be filled with monstrous problems, but internally, we can be confidently trusting God without fear.

March 14

"Be still, and know that I am God; I will be exalted among the nations, I will be exalted in the earth! The Lord of hosts is with us; the God of Jacob is our refuge." Ps. 46:10-11

How in the world can we ever get still? The television is always blaring. Even when we try to get still, we play our favorite CD or listen to the local radio station. If ever we should try to sit motionless and be silent, the refrigerator continues to hum and the horns loudly honking out front. Once when I tried, and all the above were silent, I was then disturbed by a ringing in my ears. At this point, my mind was still thinking of many things: irritations, incidences, jobs that needed doing, and wondering about the family. The only way to truly concentrate is to focus on the attributes of Jesus, quote scriptures from memory, or praise him with the thoughts of our mind, while our mouth remains motionless. When we stop our hurrying, we realize it is God who is our all in all. We exalt God. We praise Him. We glorify Him. We lift up His name. Our Lord says that some time in the future all people shall praise Him.

God is with us, what a comforting thought! Why then do we fear? Why are we upset? Why worry about today or tomorrow? Why do we let troubles annoy us? God is in our midst. He is standing at our elbow! Where is our faith for the next step?

When spiritual or economic storms come, God said he would be our safe retreat. God could cup his immense hands around us, fold his gigantic wings around us, or touch our upset feelings with his little finger. O what a joy to work each day realizing He is with us and provides safety when a storm comes our way!

March 15

"Oh clap your hands, all you peoples! Shout to God with the voice of triumph! Sing praises to God, sing praises! Sing praises to our King, sing praises! For God is the King of all the earth; sing praises with understanding." Ps. 47:1, 6-7

These exclamatory sentences presuppose that you have come to God and dropped your distractions of family, work, or harried life. When one finally enters the presence of God, a new sensation invades and permeates our life. It is no longer the same old six and seven, but a life of joy.

When joy enters our spirit, our physical body is activated. It seems natural to clap our hands. Has the church you have been attending ever experienced the intense Spirit of God so that clapping the hands has occurred or people raised their hands in praise to God?

In our verse, the Psalmist urges us to use the human instrument, our voice. We are to shout. The last shouting I recall hearing was in 1952, when my Aunt May and Aunt Eulala shouted around the church waving their hankies.

Later in the verse King David urges us to sing. We should join the congregation in singing. Surveys say that 15% of an average congregation is capable of singing in the church choir. Are you and I one of that specific group that should be up in the choir loft?

Praise the Lord all you his people (v.7). Rejoice with a clean heart and clear conscience. Some may rejoice in the same manner as my grandfather. When blessed, he shed tears of joy and mopped them with his big white handkerchief.

In King David's day, the culmination of praise was to dance before the Lord. This was done individually not a slow close waltz with your spouse or friend. The gratification then went to the Lord, not the partner.

Instead of being sensible and sedate, King David urges us to praise God by clapping our hands, shouting amens and hallelujahs, singing songs of adoration, and praising our Almighty God. If the Holy Spirit presented the right occasion would we take up King David's challenge?

March 16

"For this is God, our God forever and ever; He will be our guide even to death." Ps 48:14

King David was confident in this declaration about his God. There was not a glimmer of doubt even in the back of his mind that God was only temporal. It is a concrete fact, that God will personally guide us every step of our life, not something abstract. Where are we on the spectrum?

God is unmovable and as enduring as the Swiss Alps. They were there when we were born. In our old age, they still look the same. Our God is forever and ever.

King David was convinced of another thing. God was not only the Creator of universes but was also a compassionate God, who was vitally concerned about his creatures on planet earth. King David was totally unwavering that his God would and did guide him each day. God directed King David around the traps and schemes of his enemies so he would not fall in or get caught in them. He'll do the same for you and me, if we will only let him. Eliminate the thought that we have to travel this life on our own.

Wouldn't it have been great to know and apply this truth when we were kids? Through all those youthful temptations, God could have assisted us to avoid, reject, or overcome. God is trying to get us to walk by his side. King David in his old age was still firm in his belief that God was still there. God was going to continue to guide him right to his royal tomb. If God did it for King David, He will do the same for you and me!

March 17

"For this is God, our God forever and ever; He will be our guide even to death." Ps. 48:14

Can you claim that God is **your** God? You experienced a cleansing called 'born again", after which you become a child of God. In time this personal relationship kept getting sweeter and sweeter. At a point, you proclaimed that God is y<u>our</u> Father. You cried out "Abba, Father!" God continually guides the events of our lives whether we live in Jerusalem, Canada, or Washington, D.C. We might be born into a Jewish home, Muslim home, a Catholic home or a Protestant home. The truth is that God can be our personal God.

God can keep us from temptation that would cause us to sin. These temptations are like land mines. We never know where they are or when they'll explode. In the army, only the planter knew where the land mines were. Our Lord is infinite in knowledge. God knows where every temptation is and how to defuse it. Only if we follow in the footprints of the Great Shepherd, can we be safe from all outside destructive influence. God is capable of and promised to lead you in the way eternal.

Can we say that God is **our** God? When Christ comes into our heart, He promises to hear our prayers and in an instant forgive us.

Whether we are on the battlefront facing the enemy with land mines or we are living our daily lives facing Satan with his secretly hidden temptations, God will guide us safely through life and beyond death to heaven.

March 18

"For He sees wise men die; likewise the fool and the senseless person perish, and leave their wealth to others. Their inner thought is that their houses will last forever, their dwelling places to all generations; they call their lands after their own names. Nevertheless man, though in honor, does not remain; he is like the beasts that perish. This is the way of those who are foolish, and of their posterity who approve their sayings." Ps. 49:10-13

Do you remember when grandma and grandpa died? Did you stop to think how much knowledge was lost at their death? How to make home-made lye soap, construct a log cabin, who was married to your great uncle, and when great grandpa passed away. As you have noticed, sooner or later all people die.

The Lord compares the intellectual view of death with the strange ideas that the foolish propagate. They may be smart in the economic world and still be foolish. The man who builds his family business at the expense of his children cannot expect them to run it after he dies just to keep his name before the world. That too is foolish thinking.

Another foolish person is the one who builds a hundred thousand dollar house or even a million dollar house and expects it to last four generations. These persons may be rich in money but not blessed with wisdom.

In a negative way, the King is attempting to show us that riches, a good name or even life does not last forever.

Only our soul endures through all ages. The wise man chooses that! So if we would be declared wise by others, we need to be ready to die at any moment. Acquiring material things and getting people's honor should not be our sole goal. It is our choice. What will it be? Be ready for eternity now or act like you will live forever?

March 19

"I will not rebuke you for your sacrifices or your burnt offerings, which are continually before Me. I will not take a bull from your house, nor goats out of your folds. For every beast of the forest is mine, and the cattle on a thousand hills. I know all the birds of the mountains, and the wild beast of the field are mine. 'If I were hungry, I would not tell you; for the world is mine, and all its fullness. Will I eat flesh of bulls, or drink the blood of goats? Offer to God thanksgiving, and pay your vows to the Most High. Call upon me in the day of trouble; I will deliver you, and you shall glorify Me.'" Ps 50:8-15

Here God says that He is not unhappy with our faithful Sunday attendance. God is actually pleased with all the tithes, gifts, and offerings we have given to the church over the years.

The first recommendation to us is to offer up thanksgiving. It is simple to verbalize all the good things that have happened to us, our family, and our friends. You might think that it is silly to mention these to God, who gave them to us in the first place. The exercise of offering up to God a litany of benefits is for **our** good. The same thing is true of tithing. Our giving God back one tenth serves to remind us, who provided the income. It also serves as an antidote to greed. See, it is for our good!

God promises to deliver us from evil. Only God has the power to retrieve us from sin and evil. Out of gratitude we ought to glorify the Lord. Each Sunday it should be a pleasure to thank and praise him for keeping us from evil. God doesn't need what we give him. He owns the world. He knows the location and condition of every bird and beast of the forest. If he needed anything, he says he would not oblige us. He just wants us to thank him, praise him so he can continue bless us.

March 20

"'Now consider this, you who forget God, lest I tear you in pieces, and there be none to deliver:

whoever offers praise glorifies me; and to him who orders his conduct aright I will show the salvation of God.'" Ps. 50:22-23

Often the rascal or scoundrel in the church knows and publicly recites the scripture more than the genuine Christian. King David is asking, "God, what right do they have to do that" (V. 16)? These same people hate the commands of God and disobey the rules of the congregation (v. 17). Who gave them permission to spout God's Word to us? Instead of heeding the admonition of the Lord, they toss it aside, as over their shoulder, like one would who spills salt (v.17). Often this crowd joins in with a thief or a person committing adultery although they serve on a church committee (v.18). The King decries their twisting the Word of God for deceit and treachery instead of following the unaltered commands of God in preparation for heaven (v.19). They replace blessing others with slanderous and deceitful words and actions, which are designed to separate them from God.

King David says something like this; listen up you insincere people who forget God. Watch out! God may tear you to pieces. There will be no one who will come to your rescue. They will not be able to get you away from God's hot anger.

Listen up, real Christians; when we offer up true praise at church then during the week we can authentically look for a blessing from God. The person, who follows God's Word to the letter and loves to live for him, will see the joy of God's salvation now and also life in heaven.

The choice is ours! Do evil -- then we catch God's wrath. Live for Christ -- then we enjoy the glorious blessings of God then later enjoy the riches of heaven.

March 21

"Behold, You desire truth in the inward parts, and in the hidden part You will make me to know wisdom." Ps 51:6

See no evil, hear no evil, nor speak no evil are the three monkeys. Here King David is adding another just like many American add an eleventh commandment, "Think no evil (dishonesty)".

God expects us to be 'perfectly' honest. We are to be truthful through and through. Would it be fair to compare it to "pure" chocolate? A choc-a-lohic can not only visualize but smell how delicious "pure' chocolate would be. God dreams that his children will be completely honest to the bottom of their toes. Every muscle would scream, if they tried to stretch the truth or utter a lie.

This truthfulness reaches the hidden parts, that is to say, our subconscious. Instead of dreaming of schemes through our subconscious, we think of actions that will glorify God. This is the thinking pattern of the wise. The cunning and crafty person works on evil schemes, traps, and snares so they might gain wealth or advantage.

As one begins to create a lifestyle of honesty and integrity, then wisdom begins to accumulate. You begin making decisions that are advantageous to you instead detrimental to your welfare. Influential people will unconsciously notice your uncanny ability to make wise decisions, come up with simple conclusions to knotty problems, as well as, live a productive life. The foundation of this new found wisdom is an honesty that is crystal clear and transparent to all. Honesty may be the physical foundation but the Almighty gives us this wisdom because He is omniscient.

Let us praise God for the integrity and wisdom he has given us. We can humbly ask for more wisdom, when He sees fit to supply it.

March 22

"Purge me with hyssop, and I shall be clean; wash me, and I shall be whiter than snow. Make me hear joy and gladness that the bones You have broken may rejoice." Ps. 51:7-8

Nothing, I repeat, nothing we ever do, no matter how heinous or horrendous can ever be outside God's ability to forgive. This murderer, King David, sought God to perform the ritual washing ceremony and make him clean. He knew the mercy of God was limitless. After the prophet Nathan revealed that God knew all King David had done, waves of guilt splashed over his soul and mind. It was absolutely depressing. If the prophet knew, the whole kingdom surely is aware of the sin he had committed. At the realization of this fact sent a rip tide waves tumbling in and around and around King David like a pair of trousers in a washing machine. Oh! How awesome the guilt that lay on his heart that day.

King David immediately called for the mercy of God. His efforts at reconciliation were stymied as the victim, Uriah, was dead. He could not make things right on his own. The only option left was the Lord with his infinite mercy. Wash my soul, O Lord, then I will again feel clean like I did as a shepherd boy on the foothills of Judea. Lord, may I ask one more favor? May I experience joy and gladness and may my body feel like dancing as I did when we brought your Ark of the Covenant home to Jerusalem. Please, Lord, restore to me the joy I had when I wrote the psalms of joy. I want that squeaky clean feeling, knowing that you scrubbed all the sin out of my soul. When I sing with my harp, may the court know with a certainty that my life again is pure, clean, and undefiled!

May God hear our prayers. "Oh, thank you, Lord, for your power to forgive. Forgive and cleanse me **today**. You know the sins I have committed, even my thoughts. So please cleanse MY soul like you did King David's. I will be grateful and give You thanks all day long. Thanks, Lord Jesus!"

March 23

"Create in me a clean heart, O God, and renew a steadfast spirit within me. Do not cast me away from your presence, and do not take your Holy Spirit from me. Restore to me the joy of your salvation, and uphold me by your generous Spirit." Ps. 51:10-12

Each of us has had the natural urging within for a clean heart. This desire may have come after we secretly took money from Mom's purse to get something or go somewhere. Maybe this feeling surfaced after we had done something wrong and we were headed home. We knew Dad disapproved of what we just did. Maybe this desire of a clean heart occurred when we were sick and tired of a habit or addiction in our life that was getting us down.

For King David, this genuine desire climaxed as he entered the presence of God. It is like looking upon an ex-ray of your life where the naked truth is before your eyes. This revelation by Prophet Nathan to the king demanded action. One must decide! Am I going to remain in sin, which leads to death? Or am I going to ask God to give me a clean heart? The King chose the later.

When you determine to walk like Jesus walked, we can ask for and expect joy. This joy is deeper and broader than happiness. Happiness lasts for a moment, like when you first saw your birthday cake with all the candles. Joy can remain inside despite disruptive outer circumstances. King David craved that deeper joy.

To keep that joy, this wise king knew he must keep the rules of the scriptures. His primary desire was for God to renew a right or steadfast spirit within. If we have God's spirit in our heart, and follow the commands of the Bible, life will be less difficult and burdensome. You keep doing good things for your spouse because you love them, not because it is your duty. Like King David, "I love to go to church; it is not a chore for me!"

Chose today to have Christ install a new clean heart and place a genuine desire to please Him instead of gratifying ourselves. Soon the joy will automatically appear.

March 24

"For You do not desire sacrifice, or else I would give it; You do not delight in burnt offering. The sacrifices of God are a broken spirit, a broken and a contrite heart – these, O God, You will not despise." Ps. 51:16-17

Have you ever hurt someone's feelings? How did you go about making amends? Did you buy flowers, take them to a movie, or buy them jewelry? King David here was willing to sacrifice 500 sheep and 100 bulls to make amends to God for killing this woman's husband.

After much begging, King David began to realize that his ego had to be deflated. He was the richest king in the history of God's people to this point. Everywhere he went in the world at that time, people loved him. His average in battle wasn't .450 but victorious every time. So God laid an axe at the foot of his ego and said it must go. The Lord must be first in his life! Since nothing he could do would bring a clean heart, he laid his pride at his Master's feet. Can you imagine! No, I can't imagine the richest and most powerful person in the known world on his knees before God presenting his pride to God. The King was truly broken-hearted and genuinely contrite over the murder of Bathsheba's husband, an innocent man.

You know something? God did not make King David grabble and roll in the dust in front of all his subjects. He accepted the true confession of his sin right in the king's bedroom. No extra burdens or acts of penance were strapped to his back. God was happy with a complete surrender of self and all past sins. His life was made over anew. He again began to enjoy the presence of God in his life and God's help in ruling Israel. He will do the same for you and me today.

March 25

"But I am like a green olive tree in the house of God; I trust in the mercy of God forever and ever. I will praise you forever, because You have done it; and in the presence of your saints I will wait on your name, for it is good." Ps. 52:8-9

What was the largest tree you have ever seen? Were you fortunate enough to see General Sherman, a sequoia in the Redwood Forest? Or was your tree an oak tree back home on the farm? Maybe it would take three or four people holding hands to get around the trunk. We have a massive cottonwood tree on the ditch bank that is at least sixty feet tall. A squirrel looks really small on one of her upper limbs.

How do you suppose those huge trees grow so big? You're right. They had to get lots and lots of nourishment. An enormous amount of water in continuous supply is also necessary. King David was aware that palm trees in the arid country of Palestine need that endless supply. Closer to his palace he noticed the green olive trees. When God's blessings were on his life, he was just like a green olive tree in the midst of the Lord's house.

In church, King David could relish and rest in the presence of his precious Savior. All of God's children joined him in praise and worship. All of us can enjoy this awesome feeling of the aura of God.

Oh! how good it is! God can not only be around us while we are at church, but near us at home, work, and play. When Jesus ascended in heaven, he left the Holy Spirit. We have the privilege of having God's Holy Spirit dwelling within us. That's a continual presence that is closer than a twin brother or even nearer than our hands and feet. Hallelujah! For such a God that can be that close! Thank you, O Heavenly Father.

March 26

"But I am like a green olive tree in the house of God; I trust in the mercy of God forever and ever. I will praise You forever, because you have done it; and in the presence of your saints I will wait on your name, for it is good." Ps. 52:8-9

In previous verses, King David is making a contrast. The negative is presented first. He pictures the evil person, who climbs the corporate ladder by stepping on all the staff who works under them. They even use deceit to make others look bad, while elevating their image. When success and wealth do come to them, they trust in their new found wealth to take care of them. Calling on the

Lord for help, wisdom, or guidance would be the last option in their daily planner.

King David after his confession and subsequent renewal in Psalm 51 likens himself to an olive tree that flourishes in the presence of God. He is planted in the middle of the Lord's house. This sounds similar to living our lives in the center of the will of God. There are no hindrances to the flowing of grace and blessings straight from the throne of God. Instead of trusting in mankind, King David says, "It is, oh! ...so delightful to trust in the infinite love of God." This happens when one lives where God wants them. We feel like praising God continually. Blessings come so often that we never run out of reasons to lift up praises to God. With valid reasons to praise God, why would anyone be afraid or ashamed to let their friends know who has been blessing them. King David says, "I will witness to the church on Sunday morning how You have blessed me. I won't be ashamed to stand up in church and testify of God's goodness." Can we take his last statement and make it ours?

March 27

"The fool has said in his heart, 'There is not God.' They are corrupt and have done abominable iniquity; there is none who does good." Ps. 53:1

It is the **fool** who says, "There is no God." With this false premise, the fool's philosophy begins. Since there is no God, someone must make a decision. I'm handy and I think I can handle that job. So they try to make themselves indispensable. They take on the air that they are the most important. Everyone must look up to them for their decisions. I have met a boss or two like that. As time lapses, they begin to think their decisions are infallible. These men or women are lead into evil, as some of the presidents of the United States were. As they exalt themselves, God becomes angry at their insolent behavior.

King David noticed that fools, who claim to be God or equivalent to God, are all corrupt. Do you recall the abominable things that happened in cult groups that have collapsed in your life time? Fools have their moments of glory but always, every time fall ignominiously on their faces.

St. Paul, the one who had several degrees behind his name and could speak several languages rather fluently said of himself, "I am of all men most to be pitied." Why didn't he brag about all he had done for God like a stoning, beating and jailing? He knew who was important and it wasn't him. He put Christ above all.

Where do we put ourselves in relation to God?

March 28

"I will freely sacrifice to You; I will praise your name, O Lord, for it is good. For He has delivered me out of all trouble; and my eye has seen its desire upon my enemies." Ps. 54:6-7

On this particular day, King David said he would 'freely' sacrifice to God. This is opposed to those who give because they are commanded to give a tenth. His attitude was even different from those on the other extreme who are glad to offer to God a tithe of all they earn. This was one of these occasions when he told some of his servants to go round up a thousand perfectly healthy sheep and two hundred bulls that don't have so much as scratch from a rose or blackberry bush. Then herd them down to the temple and have them sacrificed to the Lord. Wonder what provoked him to such generosity?

He tells us. To begin with, it is a good thing to do. That wouldn't account for the figure of 1,000 sheep. King David goes on to say that God has delivered him out of **all** his troubles. Now that is sounding like something that would make him feel more generous. Over your lifetime has God let you stew in trouble or has your experience been like King David's? If God has always led you out of your trouble, how come you and I aren't praising our Deliver more?

He finally gets to the main point of why he was inclined to so much generosity. God had visited his wrath upon King David's enemies. Without losing one soldier in battle, God took care of the King's adversaries. Has God taken care of the bully in your life without you getting a bloody nose? Has Lord quietly and mysteriously solved your financial crisis? If you can say yes to these and dozens more, let's be generous to God in praise and in our giving. You and I might surprise ourselves how much we would do and give, if we decided to be generous with God.

March 29

"My heart is severely pained within me, and the terrors of death have fallen upon me. Fearfulness and trembling have come upon me, and horror has overwhelmed me. So I said, 'Oh that I had wings like a dove! I would fly away and be at rest.'" Ps. 55:4-6

Was there a time recently when you were severely emotionally distressed? Your whole body joined your mind in a time of despondency. Everything about you seemed to hurt or be affected by whatever or whoever caused it. Did thoughts of suicide flash like lightning through your head? That sounds similar to King David's "terror of death had fallen upon me." Maybe you were so sick, the doctors were afraid you might die.

But for most of us fear comes like water surrounding us and seeping into our thoughts at ever chance. We no sooner get the last fear conquered or at the least, replaced with a good one than here comes another. Fear hounds us like a stalker because we were emotionally upset.

King David's depressive thoughts of horror covered him like a big wet comforter blocking out any light or hope. It was an overwhelming feeling! What is more horrible than considering your own demise?

At that moment from his balcony in the palace he saw a bird. A thought from heaven bounced into his brain. He wondered about taking the wings of that little white dove and flying away from all these negative feelings. Oh! to have the burden of today left behind and we be in the thin blue air with the wind whistling passed our ears. If we could just feel the warmth of the pure sunshine upon our backs. What a rest that would be! Like King David, let's take our minds closer to God, even when our hearts are pained and hurting.

March 30

"Day and night they go around it on its walls; iniquity and trouble are also in the midst of it. ....Let death seize them; let them go down alive into hell, for wickedness is in their dwellings and among them. As for me, I will call upon God, and the Lord shall save me." Ps. 55:10, 15-16

Many of you who live in the city, hardly ever have an hour that you can't hear a siren wailing. When you go anywhere, you are so glad the car doors lock automatically as soon as you put it into drive. Every night on the evening news there has been a murder, robbery, or stabbing somewhere in town.

King David noticed that iniquity and trouble in Israel was prevalent 24-7. They were ever present, like the sentries on the walls of Jerusalem. Crookedness and harmfulness never cease. The King wishes that death would grab a hold of these evil doers. If it were possible, let them descent into hell alive so they could really feel the torture of that place.

As for King David, he put his hope in the God of Israel. He was sure that God would rescue him from the evil and wickedness of this world. The icing on the cake was that God was preparing a glorious mansion for him that would make his royal palace look like a peasant's hovel. He had a pass to go there upon his death. We can be assured of our reservation through the precious cleansing blood of Jesus Christ. The only cost to us is to confess all our sinful actions then trust God to cleanse us. At that specific point, God adopts us as one of His own precious children. What a miracle!

If it is good enough for King David, I'll trust God too.

March 31

"He has put forth his hands against those who were at peace with him; he has broken his covenant. The words of his mouth were smoother than butter, but war was in his heart; his words were softer than oil, yet they were drawn swords. Cast your burden on the Lord, and He will sustain you; He shall never permit the righteous to be moved." Ps. 55:20-22

Were you ever with a salesperson and they were telling you about all the grand advantages of their product? You began to notice that they were stretching their claims. Then they stated that their product always did something. A red light suddenly popped on in your unconscious mind. It said, "Watch Out!" When you run into one of these super slick salespersons, you could soon be signing on the dotted line and not experience one shadow of caution.

King David had met some real sharp persons. Their word spreads smoother than warm butter, the whole time they were aiming at your wallet. Their arguments were as slick as motor oil of a Formula One racing engine. After we get taken a time or two, we get pretty skittish about signing on the dotted line. We began to fear any one with a slick tongue.

King David says not to worry about these dishonest people. Concentrate on the positive. He suggests that we cast every worry and care on the Lord. When fear of getting taken again comes upon us, we should go to the Lord in prayer and leave it there at Jesus' feet. Most of the time, the hard part is that we can't leave it there. We pick it back up and worry about it some more. Remember God is more than glad to take care of our problem. He is more than capable too.

King David was sure that God would protect his own. I quote him, "He shall never permit the righteous to be moved." What an absolute or an irrevocable guarantee! So let's live an authentic Christian life through a vital personal relationship with Jesus Christ, and be eligible for that personal promise of God.

April 1

"The words of his mouth were smoother than butter, but war was in his heart; his words were softer than oil, yet they were drawn swords. Cast your burden on the Lord, and He shall sustain you; He shall never permit the righteous to be moved." Ps. 55:21-22

Watch out! Oh, please be careful! There are people in this world who can flatter you, then take advantage of you. No matter how good your defenses are or how strong your sales resistance may be, you will lose. The words of this man or woman are smoother than butter. They couch their phrases so as not to raise any red flags that cause you to resist their plea.

Others have a voice that is softer or slicker than oil and dull your defenses to sleep. When the final question is asked you agree with them. Their intentions are not for your good but their pocketbook. King David says he found some with a silver tongue but their hearts were filled with drawn swords to do him in.

How do we guard against such deceptive evil people, who are aiming at our demise whether emotionally, financially or physically? King David bids us surrender our burden to God. Be careful! If we cast all our burdens over on God, we will not worry about everything. We will be different from all our associates. They won't understand because we don't worry like them. They may put us at a distance instead of the close friend we once were.

When this slight alienation happens, God promises to sustain you. He gives us the pledge of never leaving or abandoning us to the wiles of Satan. Our Heavenly Father states emphatically that He will not permit his righteous children to be moved. Oh! What a Lord and Savior! In everyday life, trust in God to protect and sustain. We will definitely come out victorious, because God will see to it.

April 2

"Whenever I am afraid, I will trust in You. In God I have put my trust; I will not fear. What can flesh do to me?" Ps. 56:3-4

Fear! What an awesome word! What an insidious feeling! Fear can invade a person and consume their every thought. There are a host of fears or phobias. You could probably name a handful of these fears, couldn't you? Go ahead and see how many you can quickly name, if you have time.

King David made the defense simple. "Whenever I am afraid, I will trust in God." That sounds so easy. When fear comes upon us like a steamroller stop and either think positive, or meditate on the alternative to fear. How wonderful, if only we could instead train our mind to reach out to God, when fear is controlling us as an epileptic seizure!

Could we even after a fear has a toe hold on us, repeat over and over the phrase, "In God I will put my trust"? If we kept reciting it, maybe our heart would follow our mind. As we repeat those words, God would make himself known to us. When we are walking side by side with Jesus, no fear can harm us.

As a man in authority, King David had threats on his life and upon his position. At one time his son, Adonijah drove him out of the palace and took over his beloved nation of Judah. While living with evil threats, this King of Israel and Judah said he would not fear what any person could do to him. Prior to saying that, King David must have been continuing to trust God through the long years of his life. To get to the point of trust King David had, we must start today trusting God with each and every little fear that pops into our mind. It is easier said than done, but it can be done. I dare you! More civily said, "I challenge you to cast every care and fear over on Jesus, beginning NOW."

April 3

"In God (I will praise His Word), in God I have put my trust; I will not fear. What can flesh do to me?" Ps. 56:4

As this day's devotion is being written, missionaries in Indonesia are being gathered by radicals. The minimum intentions of the Taliban Muslims are to deport them. If these Muslims yielded to the least of their feelings and emotions, it will be torture. Should the missionaries resist these Moslems, they would kill them and consider it an honor to Allah? When each missionary was called by God through the Holy Spirit, they considered the price they might have to pay. Never have I personally, heard a missionary complain about the trouble they endured or death threats they received because of spreading God's word. The only sorrow is to leave their parents, relatives, and friends. They ask the question similar to King David's question, "What of any eternal consequence can the Taliban do to me?" The resounding answer echoes back "None!"

Are we as sure as the missionaries of our soul's destination? Can we praise God, when a neighbor gossips about our going to church, a co-worker makes fun of us for being scrupulously honest, or people putting us down for speaking for Jesus. Hopefully, the immediate hurt will not prevent us from keeping our trust in God, who is in control. When the catch net of God's love is under us, fear does not gain control of us. Our trust initiates God's protection around us. When our faith grows small, the way to inflate it is to praise God. Begin thanking

God for all your blessings. When you get really into that, the world grows faint. At that point, begin telling God how much you love Him. You will move into praising God for His greatness. The next step would be to converse with God. This includes a time of silence so God can talk to us. While we are with Almighty God, who can fear?

April 4

"You number my wanderings; put my tears into your bottle; are they not in your book?" Ps 56:8

Remember when Mom told you to keep your "eye" on your little brother or sister, while she went to the store? It was amazing how quickly that scamp could be into something before you noticed. It required a colossus amount of self-discipline to concentrate on them to the exclusion of everything else.

God keeps track of: every off color joke, each lustful thought, the Sunday we slept in, shady establishments we enter, every occasion when we break the law, each time a co-worker lead us to sin, when we exact revenge, thought more about accumulating money than God, read a dirty magazine, or abuse our children. What rapt attention God gives each of us! He even writes them down. Now days we would say He put these in his computer and archived them to the hard drive. How does God do that for every person living at this second? What a magnificent God we serve!

God also watches all the things we do right. We do these deeds because we love God. These Christian actions will be added up and we'll be rewarded. Good deeds will not get us into heaven.

God also cares when we are hurting or sorrowing. When the many people got killed in the World Trade Center Twin Towers, plane in

Pennsylvania field, and Pentagon, God was hurting immensely. King David visualized God caring so much that he collects all our tears in a bottle. I'm sure God had an adequate supply of bottles for all the family members and friends of all the victims plus relatives of the perpetrators. God didn't miss catching one tear from all the families around our globe. What a sovereign God we have!

One other thing he logs in that book is our name, if we have been spiritually born again. I pray, if you are not saved, that you seek a place of prayer or a saint to lead you to that saving grace. Let God print your name in bold print in the Book of Life.

April 5

"Vows made to You are binding upon me, O God; I will render praises to You,"   Ps. 56:12

"Sure, I'll be there Thursday afternoon at six." "On the 25th, let's go together and visit the people at the nursing home." How many times have we promised we would do something? What is our average 15% to 90% fulfillment? You did try! I did.

We stood at the marriage altar and we made a vow to God and to our mate that was binding on us. I remember repeating what the preacher said. Over my past fifty two years, I have tried to be faithful in every way. I was alert to feelings toward others beyond what is controllable, spent appropriate time with the family and kept my thoughts clean. Vows to our spouse are carefully monitored by God.

When we first gave our lives to God or when we were in a crisis, did we make any promises to God? Maybe it was to do something, like read the Bible every day and pray. Has there been seasons when we read the Upper Room, or Daily Bread but failed to crack open the Word of God? I confess to that. God really desires for us to get into His Word. Let's make time! Don't let our schedule in a Day Timer squeeze God out of our lives! Jesus at times got up way before dawn to spend time in prayer with his Father.

Oh, did you vow to witness for Him? Many times we miss opportunities because we aren't looking for the chance. Today set your mind to searching for a way to witness or mention how good last Sunday morning's service was. You'll find one, I'm sure.

Have you made a vow to God? If you have two minutes, stop and think before you leave for the rest of the day. Like King David, let's render to God what we promised.

April 6

"I will cry out to God Most High, to God who performs all things for me. He shall send from heaven and save me; he reproaches the one who would swallow me up. God shall send forth his mercy and his truth." Ps. 57:2-3

Do troubles boil over on you, and keep coming, like lava from a live volcano? They keep coming as fast as the lava flows down the hill. King David made advance preparation for a time like that. King David's plan at the first sight of trouble was to say, "I will call to God in earnest." Personally, I anticipate trouble and prepare for it. I live in a region where there is snow in the winter. Late each fall I mentally go though the procedure for making a quick stop on ice. I keep an imaginary egg on top of the brake pedal. If I am too nervous, then I must pump the brakes and try to get lighter with each touch. Although the car I am following gets closer and closer, don't panic. In snow, especially in a skid, keep the front wheels pointing in the direction you want to go just in case the tires find some traction.

As a leader, King David attracted the more aggressive leaders and discontented people than most. So he endured more opposition to his reign than he could personally handle. In many Psalms, he complained of this inconvenience. His pre-scheduled plan was to turn to the God of peace and tranquility. It was the same God, who helped him slay Goliath. He looked to the God, who assisted him to be a better ruler than King Saul, his predecessor. He promised himself that when circumstances overwhelmed him, he would turn to the God who directed situations to make him the greatest king of Israel. His son, Solomon became richer but not as famous as King David.

So let's begin preprogramming our mind to automatically turn to God, when the searing hot magma of trouble gets close. God is as ready to help us as He was Peter when he threw an arm out to Jesus as he began sinking into the Sea of Galilee.

April 7

"My heart is steadfast, O God, my heart is steadfast; I will sing and give praise. Awake, my glory! Awake, lute and harp! I will awaken the dawn." Ps. 57:7-8

King David was saying that his faith is as solid as the Plymouth Rock that our American forefathers' stepped on to disembark from the Mayflower.

Another man whose faith was unshakable was Mordecai. This man lived in the land of Shummen. The man, who was next in authority to the leader of the country wanted everybody to salute him. Well, each morning on the way to his executive office, he passed Mordecai. Mordecai would not so much as doff his hat or even touch the bill of his cap in recognition of his presence. This became a burr under his saddle or a berry seed under his false teeth. Haman would spend at least the first hour at work fuming to his secretary at this flagrant lack of respect for his office.

So with anger and bitterness Haman began to think of a way to do Mordecai in. The anger did not affect the heart of Mordecai, who sought to keep his heart and mind set on God. This disregard soon became an obsession for Haman. He thought he was so crafty. In planning evil for someone else, he wasn't careful enough. His scheme failed and the leader of the land had Haman killed instead of his enemy. Again God protects the person who had a heart set on pleasing and worshiping God. Haman, the evil one had lots of sleepless nights while Mordecai, the loyal child of God, didn't miss a wink the entire time.

So like the joyful King David let us set our mind on trusting and pleasing God. No sleepless nights unless we carelessly drink a pot of regular coffee before we go to bed.

April 8

"For look, they lie in wait for my life; the mighty gather against me, not for my transgressions nor for my sin, O Lord. They run and prepare themselves through no fault of mine." Ps. 59:3-4

Could you say you have lived a good life so far? You never got into heavy metal, never got into drugs, nor ever got hooked on pornographic material. Could you say you always studied pretty hard, never cheated a soul, nor socially undermined anyone's reputation?

King David answered all these in the affirmative. He had lived a life his dad and mom could be proud of. He had done no evil nor wronged anyone that he could recall. Other than the sin with Bathsheba which God forgave him, he could have been called, "an All-American Boy".

Then why, when he was innocent, did he say in our scripture others lay traps to make him look bad? Why did they network together in their golf club locker room, the local tavern, or the local beauty shop against him?

It seems a contradiction to live a clean Christian life when all of society is perpetrating evil. They aren't happy until they make us unhappy like themselves. Even though we never ever hurt them, they conspire to hurt us and to make us feel bad.

Part of the answer is that our straight life makes their crooked and evil life appear more apparent. This unconsciously gives them a guilt feeling about their life style.

So like King David, we need to keep on living for our Lord even when we feel almost overcome by evil.

April 9

"Do not slay them, lest my people forget; scatter them by your power, and bring them down, O Lord our shield. For the sin of their mouth and the words of their lips, let them even be taken in their pride, and for the cursing and lying which they speak. Consume them in wrath, consume them, that they may not be; and let them know that God rules in Jacob to the ends of the earth. And at evening they return, they growl like a dog, and go all around the city. They wander up and down for food, and howl if they are not satisfied. But I will sing of your power; yes, I will sing aloud of your mercy in the morning; for You have been my defense and refuge in the day of my trouble. To You, O my Strength, I will sing praises; for God is my defense, my God of mercy." Ps. 59:11-17

The person you helped the most didn't stand up for you. Are you mad?

People put you down. Is that your trouble, Buddy?

They lie about you. Is that what is bugging you?

Our enemy searches for ways to trip you. Is that your problem?

The guy down the street cussed you. Is that getting under your skin?

The neighbors gossip about the church people. Is that what bothering you?

King David thought about saying, "God strike them with a thunderbolt of lightning." He finally relinquished. Then he said at least scatter them far from their homeland, Lord. Could you zap them so they would disappear? Remember, God, I am asking this not to get even, but to get them to realize you are the God in control.

King David concluded that he would sing about God's power and positive actions instead using negative words. He recalled the times God poured mercy on his life. He also brought to mind times when God was his sole defense. So today, O God send your mercy upon us.

April 10

"But I will sing of your power; yes, I will sing aloud of your mercy in the morning; for You have been my defense and refuge in the day of my trouble." Ps. 59:16

While a junior in high school my younger brother, who was in the eighth grade got in a fight. He was getting beat up. One of his friends came to the other side of the playground and said, "Your little brother needs you over by the merry-go-round." A soon as I rounded the corner of the school, his adversary quit laying in on him. In a sense, I delivered him from his enemy. When God delivers us out of our trouble, do we, at least, say, "Thank, Lord"? I can't recall, if my brother did or not.

King David says he keeps remembering the day when God released him from the snare of his enemy. Like a regular morning constitutional, the king consistently practiced singing praise to God. Would it have sounded something like: Glory, Glory, Hallelujah his truth is marching on? I'm redeemed by love divine. Hallelujah! Christ is mine. All to him I now resign. I have been redeemed. Praise Him! Praise Him tell of his excellent greatness. Praise him! Strength and honor unto the Lord belong. Every day with Jesus is sweeter than the day before. Sweeter as the years go by. I walk and I talk with the King, hallelujah. He walks with me and He talks to me and He tells me I am his own. Hallelujah! Thine be the glory, Hallelujah! Amen, Hallelujah! Thine be the glory. You revive us again. We're marching upward to Zion, that beautiful city of God. Wonderful grace of Jesus, greater than all my sins. How shall my tongue describes it? Where shall my praise begin? How great Thou Art! Let there be peace on earth and let it begin with me.

Let us sing praises to God each day.

April 11

"Is it not You, O God, who cast us off? And You, O God, who did not go out with our armies? Give us help from trouble, for the help of man is useless.

Through God we will do valiantly, for it is He who shall tread down our enemies." Ps. 60:10-12

Did a friend promise to pull a string to get a loan for you and failed?

Did your parents promise you and they let you down big time?

Did the person you were going to trust your life with, fall in love with someone else and left you high and dry?

Did a mentor, whom you genuinely looked up to, fall into sin leaving you with a marred model?

Did someone you really appreciated, abuse you?

When it really counts, the help of humans is useless. Humans can not help you into heaven. Humans may help with material things but are useless with things eternal. They can not forgive sin.

King David states that he could be victorious and do valiantly only with God's help. He did not trust in armies, chariots, swords, or javelins. The King of Kings could help him overcome his mortal enemies. The Lord was almost always on his mind. This was the source for all the Psalms he wrote. That's the reason they are timeless and why we are studying them now. So we, like King David, need to ask God for help in our times of trial.

April 12

"From the end of the earth I will cry to you, when my heart is overwhelmed; lead me to the rock that is higher than I. For you have been a shelter for me, a strong tower from the enemy. I will abide in your tabernacle forever; I will trust in the shelter of your wings." Ps 61:2-4

Wherever you fly or visit, it is an excellent place to call on God. The heavenly telecommunication satellite is never in the wrong position for God to receive your prayer. No matter whether the need is trivial or overwhelming, we can readily call on God. His line is never busy. If our present communication satellites can handle all the people in New York City at one time, surely God's lines would never be busy!

King David asked God to lead him to a very secure fortress away from any and all his enemies. For us no place is more secure than Fort Knox. Our nation's gold, that used to back our paper money, resides there. No one, I repeat no one, has ever broken into this facility. God's secure place from harm is his impregnable tower.

Later in our scripture, King David switched from thinking about physical protection. He declared that he wanted live in the tabernacle. He wanted to be near the church, where God kept his presence. Oh, what a comfort to sit in the pew and soak up the precious peace of God! Haven't you felt that heavenly peace on a special Sunday or two?

You, O Lord, are the rock on which I trust. You never move. It is us, who are so wishy-washy about our allegiance to You. God will never disown or remove his protection from us. When our life is so full of confusion and we don't know which end is up, we can call on God, who always cares and understands.

April 13

"I will abide in your tabernacle forever; I will trust in the shelter of your wings." Ps. 61:4

What would be the ideal Christian life be like? Would it be to never to have troubles, trials, or temptations? It might be! King Solomon strongly suggests there will always be trouble in our lives, if we are alive. Next, it is Satan's job to see that temptations lurk at every corner of our life. Would the ideal then be victory over every circumstance that we meet in life? That may be possible but not very probable.

King David has given us the guidelines to constant victory over evil. For him, abiding or living in the tabernacle meant living in God's presence. Being in the Lord's presence will cause Satan to back off and not tempt us with certain things. Even while in the presence of Almighty God, Satan will attempt to lure us away.

Our King David knew there would be times when we stumble. When these times come, we, like him, need to hide under the protecting wings of our glorious Savior. A hen would keep her wings spread out to protect her chicks while a wolf killed her. If a hen would go that far to protect her own, can you imagine how far Jesus would go to protect you from the onslaughts of the Evil One?

So the recipe for an ideal Christian life is to abide in God's presence continually. When rough times come, confidently rest under the wings of God's loving and protecting care.

April 14

"Truly my soul silently waits for God; from him comes my salvation. ....My soul, wait silently for God alone, for my expectation is from him." Ps. 62:1, 5

Does the electric power have to go off before you are really silent? Or can you lie upon your bed at night and be in a quiet mood? Many times we are in an agitated frame of mind because of what happened or what might happen. My son experienced silence the day after the twin towers of the World Trade Center fell in 2001. He walked down the middle of Fifth Street. Not a car, bus, or even a bird was making a noise. This was a weird calm, not a peaceful quiet. I think King David was speaking of a quiet time like you might find in an abbey, monastery, or convent.

First, we must slow our body down. Our rat-race schedules keep our adrenaline flowing. All the activities of our daily lives scream for a decision. Next, we prepare our mind to receive divine messages when we are entering into meditation. In this stage, all thinking goes into slow motion. At this point, we fix our attention on God and/or his Son. Achieving this quiet may take more than a few minutes.

Now our soul is waiting in silence far away from anxiety. Our gaze focuses on God from whom all blessings and wisdom flow. There alone with our Savior, we have sweet communion. King David's faith or expectation was that God would supply all his spiritual needs from all the riches in heaven. This is the **only** place to receive the right answers for our problems or cures for our ailments. While in this receptive frame of mind and our soul is in this mood. Keep looking to God and expecting His assistance.

This is how King David did his daily devotions. Let's replicate his devotional style. Then we can have daily devotions like King David with our Lord.

April 15

"Truly my soul silently waits for God; from Him comes my salvation. He only is my rock and my salvation; He is my defense; I shall not be greatly moved." Ps. 62:1-2

King David is being completely honest when he says I continually wait on God to direct me. There was a time or two he didn't obey the Lord and it cost him dearly. He wanted so badly to take a census of all able-bodied men. His general, Joab tried unsuccessfully to persuade him to refrain. After he had taken the census, the Lord said that you, King David, have broken my wish and now you must choose.

Option one: Three years of famine.

Option two: Let your neighbor's invade your country for 3 months.

Option three: Let God punish for three days with a plague (2 Sam. 29)

King David chose option three. To explain his reasoning, he stated that God is his only hope of salvation spiritually or militarily. God is the only one who can defend him against his aggressive neighboring countries, as well as, the Evil One. He continued to reason. If God is my Defender, I will not be moved from my throne or from my spiritual ground. After those tragic days and lessons learned, he began to rest constantly in God.

So you and I can learn a valuable lesson from this illustrious king. If we silently and completely trust Jesus Christ, He will be our defender and protector. Let us not put our trust in material things but commit all our weight on the Lord. Our friends should not be surprised when they fall to the temptations of Satan, while we stand firm on the rock, Christ Jesus.

April 16

"They only consult to cast him down from his high position; they delight in lies; they bless with their mouth, but they curse inwardly. My soul, wait silently for God alone, for my expectation is from Him." Ps. 62:4-5

"You big hypocrite!" Hopefully, you have never had this statement used to describe you. Hypocrites are dangerous people. They act like sheep but inwardly they are ferocious wolves. A wolf can do much damage to a defenseless sheep. Sheep can not bite, claw or run fast. We are as defenseless as a sheep when Satan is our adversary.

King David noticed that being a hypocrite calls for pre-meditation. They consult friends and enemy for strategies to make someone fall or bring them down to their level. They used deceit in their assault on King David.

To your face and in your presence, this type of person pretends to be your friend and ally. They soak up all the details of your life to use as ammunition against you later. Then when your back is turned, they begin spreading every thing you told in confidence. They then add a twist on the truth to make you look very bad but mainly to make themselves look better. Even if they are looking you in the eye, they are thinking about a scheme to cut you down. This can be so disconcerting!

King David did not try to verbally defend his position but tried to silently put his hope in the Creator. We too can silently trust God to turn the tables around.

The king had trouble forgetting about what the hypocrites did and said. He thought about the punishment God will give them for their lies and treachery. The King trained his mind to rest in the fact that God will eventually cause all things to come out for his good and finally to God's own glory.

Instead of being a hypocrite let us so live that others and even the hypocrite will say, "There goes a child of God."

April 17

"My soul, wait silently for God alone, for my expectation is from Him." Ps. 62:5

Have you ever talked to yourself? You know like, 'Self don't let them get to you!' Or 'Self, that sure was a stupid move.' Well, the Psalmist was in a similar contemplative mood that day, when he spoke to his soul. 'Soul, calm down, cool it, and patiently wait on the Lord,' One problem modern people have is we have to be constantly talking to the Lord, when we pray. This fault was so very noticeable, when a person got their first CB radio. Having, a silent spot on the airwaves is unacceptable. We filled the air with "mercy, mercy" and phrases similar to that which had nothing to do with what we were talking about. King David is urging us to listen and not talk.

King David made a conscious decision to wait quietly for the Lord. It was more than just an exercise in being silent. Sometimes, doing that is a feat in our fast moving society with hand held computers, 3 g I-phones, e-mails and faxes. The point of silence is to enable us to hear God speak or at the least direct our path. King David was aware that sages, wizards, and intellectuals were not smart enough or dependable enough to direct his life. God is the only one who gives the right answer every time! The advice for us from the Psalmist is to not put your expectations in anyone or anything on this earth, no matter how visible and how tangible. Put your trust in God alone and rest on his word. Everything is possible with God (Matt. 9:36). So when we slow down and get quiet we are following a good example. When we pray and listen, believe that God will answer.

April 18

"He only is my rock and my salvation; He is my defense; I shall not be moved. In God is my salvation and my glory; the rock of my strength, and my refuge is in God." Ps 62:6-7

God is our salvation. Salvation involves saving us from our life of voluntary sins. Salvation places us into the family of God. We then are adopted as a true child of Almighty God. At that time God forgives and forgets all our past sins. He buries them in the Sea of Forgetfulness never to be remembered or brought up against us ever again. Then He places sign-posts "No fishing" in that sea. So if God forgives and forgets, shouldn't we forget? We need not feel guilty over sins that have been forgiven. The scripture says it is buried as deep as the East is from the West.

God has the greatest memory! He remembers to keep every promise that you can locate in the Bible. He recalls that we are created human beings and make mistakes and commit sins. God remembers to walk beside us every step we take each day. The Holy Spirit guides every decision we make, if we call on him for that help. God tenderly loves us even when we go all day or all week without thinking about him. He embraces us even when we hurt him by the things we do. God remembers that we get tired and even depressed; so He never leaves us nor abandons us. God remembers our needs everyday and supplies them according to his riches in glory.

God was King David's daily defense and is ours today. God defends us against the fiery darts and temptations of Satan. He is also our legal defense against the evil schemes of the Evil One at judgment day.

If we ask God about a sin that was forgiven, He'll ask us, "What sin are you talking about?" But

God remembers us and can call us by name. What a mighty God we serve!

April 19

"Trust in Him at all times, you people; pour out your heart before Him; God is a refuge for us." Ps. 62:8

When a terrorist strikes, where do you run for security? When death knocks on the door of your family, whom do you go to for help? When financial disaster strikes like losing your job, stock market acts like a bear, or your business goes belly up, where do you go? When your brain turns to jelly and everything, simply everything, pushes you over the edge, where do you turn? King David had wise men to check with. Personally, my wise person was my sweet mother. Today, we have psychologists and psychiatrists to go to. After years of experimenting, King David came to the conclusion that God was the best shrink. The price was right. God was the authority on mental confusion and problems. He does not consult Mr. Rogers, Mr. Freud, or Mr. Frankel to get his advice. God's record is 100% cure rate. Lastly, the confidentiality rate for God is unblemished and perfect. Your sister can't blab it nor can your cousin extort you with what you say in strictest confidence. Not even the priest need be privy to your sin or problem.

Every time you come to God you can pour out your inmost soul. Only God can and will forgive and can straighten out your soul and mind. Unconfessed sin only works like a festering sore or a cancer on the soul. Left unattended problems grow worse or larger.

God attends our confessional booth and provides a refuge from hurt and harm. He is the One to run to when sin corrupts our soul, or evil enters our lives. God is the supreme psychologist so when trouble comes, go "To the Best." Confess it to God, like our illustrious King David did!

April 20

"Surely men of low degree are a vapor, men of high degree are a lie; if they are weighed on the scales, they are altogether lighter than vapor. Do not trust in oppression, nor vainly hope in robbery; if riches increase, do not set your heart on them."
Ps. 62:9-10

Have you heard that things we can touch and feel are less important than things invisible? How important is honesty, virtue, and loyalty? Things you can touch can disappear. Your house can be hit by a tornado, your nest egg can be smashed by a stock market crash, or your luxury car can be crunched in an accident. Your ability to earn money would be more important than what you lost.

King David urges us not to trust in other humans for they can die, move, or not be around tomorrow. If you trust too much in others, they will fail you like using a rotten stick as a crutch. When you need them most, it breaks and jabs you.

Another thing to be leery of is aggressive ambition. This usually causes one to use oppression as a form of manipulation. That is effective as long as the pressure is on. It is like sticking your elbow in a bucket of water. It makes it full. As soon as you remove it, it returns to normal.

Don't trust in robbing and stealing to get ahead. Financial gains are temporary, while the more permanent reward for these evils is a long jail term.

Don't trust in riches! If God has blessed you with a sharp mind, wealth will come your way. Don't trust money to bring happiness. You will be unhappy as King David's son, Solomon. To see how unhappy he was, read Ecclesiastes. So the only hope that is secure is to put our trust in God. He is the Creator, the Rock of Ages, and our hope for all eternity. Jesus never fails!

April 21

"Because your loving kindness is better than life, my lips shall praise You. Thus I will bless You while I live; I will lift my hands in your name. My soul shall be satisfied as with marrow and fatness, and my mouth shall praise You with joyful lips." Ps. 63:3-5

Have you ever taken the time to meditate on the loving kindness of God? No! Well, let's take time and do it now. My son experienced kindness when he went to a European city. There in a hallway, he was thrown against the wall, threatened, and robbed. The hotel owner extended kindness to him. He helped him back on a plane to the United States. If I gave you the chance, you could name someone who was extra kind and helped you in your hour of distress?

God's loving kindness comes to us not only because we need help, but extends it despite our faults and weaknesses. God magnanimously bestows good upon us. Most parents extend this type of loving kindness to their children.

Instinctively King David broke forth in praise. That is, tell God how great, wonderful, gracious, and majestic He is. King David's desire was to bless the Lord. To bless someone is to pronounce good things to happen to the person. Even our soul is to bless the Lord.

Next King David said he would be brave and make a public witness by raising his hand in worship. In some denominations this action precedes a shout of "hallelujah". If we are afraid or ashamed to praise God in public, God might be ashamed of us before the angels in heaven.

In this day of materialistic accumulation, we want to be satisfied physically. How different our world would be, if all God's children had an urgent desire for spiritual satisfaction!

God, without doubt, dumped his loving kindness upon King David and is pouring his love upon all of us. These benefits should cause us to start praising, blessing, and lifting our hands and voices in praise to God.

April 22

"When I remember You upon my bed, I meditate on You in the night watches. Because You have been my help, therefore in the shadow of your wings I will rejoice. My soul follows close behind You; your right hand upholds me." Ps. 63:6-8

Do you often get into bed dead tired? When your head hits the pillow, you wake up immediately? Or do you have the habit of waking up in the middle of the night and have a dreadful time going back to sleep? Everything marches through your mind! You vividly recall the recent hurt someone inflicted on you with their tongue. You plainly recall how someone cheated you out of money that was rightfully yours. Every negative incident in the previous day marches dutifully before the screen of your mind. It seems your brain thinks more efficiently than it did at work. With a mind that's occupied, how can any relaxation go on and permit you to go back to sleep?

King David found the Unisom or Sominex pill in the form of meditation. Instead of tears in his ears from lying on his back crying over spilt milk, he thought about God. In place of the negative, he decided to accentuate the positive. There is love, joy, and peace in the Lord. The troubles of tomorrow will still be there, so why not enjoy the night and a time away from trouble?

For King David, God had been reliable and faithful to help. He thinks good thoughts in the middle of the night. There will never be a hangover from this form of sleep aid! King David rested securely in the arms of the Lord. That sounds easy. Even if is harder than it sounds to get a good night's rest, would it be worth the effort to meditate upon the Lord the next time you can't sleep?

April 23

"Hide me from the secret plots of the wicked, from the rebellion of the workers of iniquity, who sharpen their tongue like a sword, and bend their bows to shoot their arrows – bitter words, that they may shoot in secret at the blameless; suddenly they shoot at him and do not fear. They encourage themselves in an evil matter; they talk of laying snares secretly; they say 'Who will see them?'"
Ps. 64:2-5

King David entreats God for protection. Has there been a time we asked God for safety? Presently we run into the same kind of people that our scripture speaks of. People who do evil in secret commit acts of rebellion against God. Other hurt good persons with their sharp tongues.

Do you have someone in your office or club who sharpens their tongue like one would a sword. Even inadvertently the things they say hurt and penetrate your defenses. King David says these people shoot bitter words like arrows that wound our emotions. The words seem to come from "They said," so their remarks are cloaked in secrecy. When we make an honest effort to ascertain where the rumor originated, it ends at "They said".

How brazen these inflictors of pain are! Often they are promoted ahead of the persons of integrity. It is almost like they are immune to the rewards of their evil deeds, and cutting hurt they have perpetuated. It seems apparent that God has His eyes closed to the hurt they are inflicting on His children. This being the case, they boastfully continue slicing people with words and hurting others with their poisonous arrows tipped in bitterness.

Be of good cheer God has not forsaken us! He who watches us neither slumbers nor sleeps. They will receive their just desserts, if we patiently endure until judgment. Hold on, God is not short on keeping His promises. He that sins shall die, both spiritually and physically. On the other hand, do not lose heart for in due time you will reap your good rewards, if you faint not.

April 24

"Blessed is the man You choose, and cause to approach You, that he may dwell in your courts. We shall be satisfied with the goodness of your house, of your holy temple." Ps. 65:4

Do you recall recess when you were in grade school? We all lined up against the fence and the two most popular or most talented kids were captains of the softball game. If you were chosen in the first two or three picks, that was an honor. The humiliating part was, if you were in the last two or three and one captain said to the other, "You take both of them?"

It is so uplifting and gratifying to be picked early. That meant you were important to the team. Similarly, when God chooses us, we get to go stand behind him. We are part of God's winning team. What a satisfaction that is! King David was writing and remembering when God had the Prophet Samuel call him in from tending the sheep in the field to be chosen. His mind recalled the times God blessed his military campaigns so the victories came without a blood bath of his own men. King David now enjoyed the good memories that God had so lavishly poured upon his career.

The blessed time for us will be when God looks out into the sinful world and says, "I chose you!" What have we ever done to deserve it? Anyway, you sheepishly walk toward Jesus and let Him wash all your sin and rebellion away. Oh! how satisfied we are just to stop at his feet, like Mary of Bethany did. When God decides to call us to his super lovely heaven, how much more wonderful that will be!

Let's thank King David for writing this Psalm for our comfort.

April 25

"They also who dwell in the farthest parts are afraid of your signs; You make the outgoings of the morning and evening rejoice." Ps. 65:8

When was the last time through the mist of a rainy day did you see a rainbow? Or was the rainbow deflected from a drop of dew on a blade of grass? Wasn't it wonderful what God did with a million raindrops as they fall through space or with a single drop of water?

Were you ever caught in a tornado or a hurricane? What power! You witnessed the magnificence of raw power! God witnesses to us in a little ant that can carry twenty-five times it own weight, while many of us couldn't carry what we weight. How wonderfully created are the fleas who in our proportion could jump as high as a sky scraper while many of us are lucky to jump two feet off the ground. The birds cheerfully sing all morning long praising God without a sore throat. After singing fifteen minutes during church we are ready to rest our vocal chords. The lowly cricket chirps well into the night. The geese and arctic tern fly from one end of the globe to the other. How they display their endurance! Do we proudly endure persecution and ridicule for Christ's sake?

Isn't it marvelous that we can't see through clouds but airplanes fly right through without harm? Yet moments later these same clouds can release an inch of rain. How transparent are we to the world who are searching for a genuine Christian who loves them?

Wouldn't it be wonderful, if we could match nature in praising and glorifying God?

April 26

"Make a joyful shout to God, all the earth! ...'All the earth shall worship You and sing praises to You; they shall sing praises to your name.'" Ps. 66:1, 4

Do you sing in the choir? You really add to the worship service. Do you sing for your own amusement? Or are you one whom they would pay **not** to sing? King David urges us to make a joyful noise or shout to the Lord. That's an all inclusive invitation. Whether we can sing melodiously or must have a basket to carry a tune in, we can all praise God!

There are many ways to praise God.
When we are blue,
It is God we look to.
When the world gives us a steady diet of hate,
We look to the Lord who is great.
When the evil people want to fight,
We turn our backs and walk to the Light.
When the burdens of this life drag us down,

We look to the God who can always be found.
When tribulations come day after day,
We stand firm and continue to pray.
When our vision only sees a spiritual haze,
We lift our tremulous voice in praise.
When our spirits are wounded like a dove,
To You, O Lord, we look for your magnificent love.

The earth and all that is therein will lift up the name of Jesus. One woman in an uptown church said, "Amen" often as her preacher preached. The visitor preached that Sunday evening and she was strangely quiet. After the service, the visitor asked her, "What's the difference in our sermons? How come you seldom "Amen'ed" my sermon?

"Well, brother, I only Amen my preacher when he lifts up Jesus. Tonight you only told what our denomination was accomplishing."

So today people will encourage you to lift up the name of Jesus Christ, our Savior and Lord.

April 27

"All the earth shall worship You and sing praises to You; they shall sing praises to your name." Ps. 66:4

Worship! Is it worship, if we sing loudly? Must we do it with all our hearts? Maybe worship is to pray as we look at the names in the bulletin or as the preacher mentions the sick people in the pastoral prayer. Surely we are worshiping when the entire congregation helps the minister in the responsive reading.

Would we be closer to true worship, if we sat with our eyes closed while majestic strains emanate from the organ? Would it be real worship on Sunday to fervently pray to God? Is it true worship when we hold hands across the center aisle and pray in unison? Would the service be more worshipful, if we knelt in humility at the altar? In this position we would be looking to God mentally, while we are physically seeing the altar.

A friend of mine said that true worship of God is a process. Whether in church, out in the field, or in the house, start thanking God for all your blessings. It is helpful to be specific. As you get into the spirit of truly thanking God change over to praising God. This is more than specific or high level thanking. Praising is lifting up Jesus. This begins with naming His virtues. This continues until the world fades and your only thoughts are about God. At this stage in prayer, begin telling God how much and how many different ways you love Him. Express your deepest emotions to the God, who loved you enough to send His only son to save you from hell. This is one personal way to worship God. King David may have gone through a similar process.

April 28

"For You, O God, have tested us; You have refined us as silver is refined." Ps 66:10

Does it seem that trouble follows you like your childhood puppy? God uses these problems to make you a better person. Does your neighbor keep hounding you about trimming your tree on his side of the property line? The limbs keep scraping on his roof and keeping him awake. From this God teaches us the lesson of negotiation in a calm manner.

Remember the last time you foolishly bought an item on an impulse? You were months getting your budget back in line. God was teaching you self-discipline.

How painful it was when your best friend started giving you the cold shoulder. You did a lot of introspection and came up with no satisfactory explanation. God was guiding you to trust Him more and your friends less.

Oh, how awful the feeling was when you heard the fender crunch! Oh, if only I had been a little more alert. Now God is teaching you to be patient, while the parts come in from Detroit or Japan. Patience is a hard lesson to learn and often must be relearned.

How vividly do you remember your last stay in the hospital? Was the pain intense? Was the service extra slow? Was all the food they served unseasoned? God was attempting to correct your whining and griping attitude to one of attitude of joy and gratefulness.

Did a close family member die recently? The hurt was so deep you didn't know where or how to make it feel better. Every day the pain of missing them kept reoccurring. God was refining you to be cognizant of the shortness of physical life and the vast expanse of eternity.

So God in his divine wisdom was using everyday predicaments to refine you into a wonderful Christian, like sterling silver.

April 29

"I will go into your house with burnt offerings; I will pay You my vows, which my lips have uttered and my mouth has spoken when I was in trouble. I will offer You burnt sacrifices of fat animals, with the sweet aroma of rams; I will offer bulls with goats." Ps. 66:13-15

Do you remember the time you got into real deep trouble? How deep was it? Did you beg God to get you out? Was the situation in the midst of a shelling in Desert Storm in Iraq? Some in their foxholes made a promise to God: "Lord, if you'll get me home safe, I'll   ...go to church every Sunday. ....I'll become a preacher.   ....I'll quit this bad habit. .... I'll be a good person and be faithful to my spouse." I'll bet you can remember your vow verbatim!

After you were freed, emancipated, or released from your dire circumstance, did you begin to crawfish, back pedal, or try to squirm out of your promise to God? Lord, surely, you wouldn't care if I changed the condition just a little? If I attain this or that, would it be as good as my promise?

I don't see King David maneuvering out of the exact promise that he uttered with his own lips. He repeats the vow with his mouth before all the people. His honesty is a sweet smell to God. He offers his best to the Almighty.

Let us march straight into church this Sunday and begin the process of keeping our promise. It may be scary fulfilling that vow. God promises to hear our prayers for assistance. He vows never to leave our side, as we attempt to keep that solemn oath we made in our time of dire need.

April 30

"I cried to Him with my mouth, and He was extolled with my tongue." Ps 66:17

It's awful! Simply awful to feel like you are at the bottom of the barrel of life! The only way you can look is up and there you see a single shaft of light down the long dark tunnel.

This is the time of life when you feel like screaming and yelling at fate or pouring out all your frustrations to God. Emotions have to be vented before you explode some hapless victim. The good thing is that God has time to listen to every sordid or trivial detail, plus He does not blab it on to any of your associates. It stops at Jesus' feet.

How good it feels when that burden is rolled over on Jesus! It feels even better than when one unlaces their tight shoes or slip off those high heels. You gasp out an "Ah - h- h - h". Your feet stretch and take the first breath of fresh air they've had since before breakfast this morning.

This inexpressible relief should lead us to give someone credit for the pleasure we just enjoyed. We can't get to the shoe company to express your displeasure. It is improper to thank yourself for unlacing the shoes. Then the thanks and praise should rightfully go to God. In our scripture, King David said that after he cried out to God with his troubles, his tongue almost automatically began to extol or lift up praise to God. Oh, that we had our tongue trained or our mind conditioned to do that! Have weeks gone by without us uttering a syllable of praise to the Creator, who formed me in our mother' womb?

Let us start a schedule that forms a habit of praising God at the drop of a hat or after a confession session. Let's determine to start today!

May 1

"I cried to him with my mouth, and He was extolled with my tongue. If I regard iniquity in my heart, the Lord will not hear. But certainly God has heard me; He has attended to the voice of my prayer. Blessed be God, who has not turned away my prayer or his mercy from me!" Ps. 66:17-20

Sometimes we use our tongue to perpetrate evil, like spread gossip, slander, or hate. At other times, we just complain about our lot in life. Once we make promises to God, we try desperately to keep them. Today King David is employing his tongue in praise to God, telling of the Lord's wondrous work and broadcasting to all his subjects the glory of God. His statement was "God was extolled". God heard his praise!

When we sin, God doesn't regard or pay any attention to our prayers, whether flowery or sincere. One way to explain this is the similarity to your walkman radio. Tune it into your favorite station. As you walk, jog or run along and your arm hits the tuner then you can't hear that magnificent music with that steady beat. What your arm did to your radio, your sin does to the frequency of your spiritual communication to God. Our thoughts, words, and desires are being transmitted but God is not receiving. Asking God's forgiveness sets our prayers on the correct frequency.

Then God hears all the prayers of his children. Sometimes the answer is no, sometimes wait, or sometimes yes. God will answer your request. But always, I repeat always, God answers our request in accordance with His divine will.

So like King David, let's end our time with God in praise. Praise God who hears us, answers us, and in every way loves us. How fortunate we are as children of the Creator of our earth and the universe!

May 2

"O God be merciful to us and bless us, and cause His face to shine upon us, that your way may be known on earth, your salvation among all nations." Ps. 67:1-2

Today our illustrious King is entreating God. First, he asks God for mercy. Jesus was without sin and did not need mercy. We fall into the same category as our beloved king. We have all sinned and have fallen short of the glory of God (Romans 3:23). So let us bend our knees and implore our Heavenly Father to extend mercy our way, too.

We are also needy in other ways and need blessings from God. King David implored God by saying, "Bless us". Many of us are spiritually anemic because we fail to read his recipe for health. Some read a devotional but fail to smell the rich perfume of the unadulterated Word of God. Others fail to snap open their heavenly cellular telephone and have an imminent but momentary two way conversation with God.

Another of King David's requests was to ask God to look down in favor on all he does throughout the day. Could it be that he is paraphrasing what God told Moses to tell all the Israelites? It is found in Numbers 6:24-26. It goes like this. "The Lord bless you and keep you; the Lord make a his face shine upon you, and be gracious to you; the Lord lift up his countenance upon you. And give you peace." May this blessing or benediction rest upon our lives today.

May 3

"That your way may be known on earth, your salvation among all nations." Ps 67:2

King David was interested in his personal contribution of telling others about the God of Israel. He was convinced that his God was a prayer answering God. King David saw that idols were insufficient to meet daily needs.

St. Matthew ended his book by saying, "Go ye therefore and make disciples of all nations, baptizing them in the name of the Father, of the Son, and of the Holy Spirit (28:19)." So how can we today tell our world about our wonderful Savior, Jesus Christ?

First we can use our voice. Some of us can preach or sing so others can see the joy in our eyes. There are evangelists who can share the message of hope or assist in nurturing young Christians. All of us can speak to our friends and relate what God is doing in our life.

Second, we can let our daily life project the love that Christ has put in our heart. An example is often more impressive and convincing than a thousand words. Sometimes Christ-like things we do ultimately lead people to a vital relationship with Jesus.

Third, the messages we write can direct people to our Savior. There are people like me who write books, but there are many more newspaper reporters who can use words to influence and persuade men and women to trust in God. But all of us can write personal letters and sympathy cards to unbelievers we know.

Some who loan inspirational and Christian books are spreading the news about Jesus Christ. Some may even give Bibles and New Testaments to others, when the Holy Spirit urges them. Others of us could leave gospel tracts wherever we go.

So don't put down the little you can do. God uses that too.

May 4

"As smoke is driven away, so drive them away; as wax melts before the fire, so let the wicked perish at the presence of God." Ps. 68:2

Have you ever imagined how our prayers would appear to God, if they were smoke? Would God see the prayer as routine one day and warmly sincere the next? Are our prayers often depressing and tend to go down instead of raise? How many times are our smoke-filled prayers punctuated with praise, adoration, and joy so they would rise like the smoke from the 100 foot chimney of a power plant? How often had King David knelt in the temple and watched the smoke from his sacrifice drift to the top of the room and roll out the holes in the top of the temple. He imagined them continuing heavenward. Are our prayers most often like the two slender candles on our church's communion table?

King David made another analogy about wax. He wanted the courage of his enemies to melt like wax anytime they came into God's presence or God came near them. How would we hold up in the presence of Almighty God? Would we humbly kneel before him or melt all over the ground because of some sin in our lives? Or could we come boldly to the throne of God as St. Paul urges us? Could we come as a friend before God as Moses did? Hopefully, we would not melt before God as the heathen but be accepted as a child as we were by our dad when we were four, five, or six.

Let us always stay on good terms with God, the Father through prayer and may our prayers always rise because of the rich mixture of praise and thanks to God in them.

May 5

"But let the righteous be glad; let them rejoice before God; yes, let them rejoice exceedingly." Ps. 68:3

Did you ever look up at a sixty foot tall cottonwood tree? I did. Even though it was calm that day, one little leaf wiggled like a puppy dog's tail. Would you like to guess at how many times that leaf will wave before falling? Never has a stem broken off because it waved too much. The Creator of the stem was ultra intelligent. Now would you please multiply the number of shakes of that one leaf by the number of leaves on the tree? That's just one tree! God has acres of these. They change our used carbon dioxide back into useable oxygen. Hey! Let's praise God for his wonderful handiwork.

When the doctor checked your heart's beats in a resting position, was it near 72? Multiply that by an hour, then by 24, then by 366, then by how long you have lived. Oh, what a magnificent heart you have!

God sent his only Son to die for my sins and yours. Then multiply that times the number of people on the earth. Finally, calculate the numbers who have lived, since Jesus died. How can his spilt blood continue to be effective two thousand years later? It works! When I confessed my unworthiness and believed on Him, God made me a brand new creature. We should be exceedingly happy in the Lord. We don't have to worry about spending eternity in hell with the Devil. We are assured of a mansion in heaven, fully decorated and ready to move into. The Holy Spirit promises to guide us through every step of this life. Our life should be and can be overflowing with the fruits of the Spirit. (Gal. 5:22-23).

So let's be exceedingly glad and rejoice, as we walk in the presence of God today.

May 6

"God set the solitary in families; He brings out those who are bound into prosperity; but the rebellious dwell in a dry land." Ps. 68:6

God is gracious! Have you ever looked on a situation that stirred up your sympathy? If it were in your power, you would pay the rent, get them groceries, and outfit every child in the family. Since we can have compassion like that, God's compassion infinitely exceeds ours.

God looks down on our world. The slums we pass by on the interstate, God walks into each apartment. King David even in his day saw God put lonely people into families. It is as if these families adopt these with a solitary existence, so they wouldn't be lonely. This exchange is always a two way street. The lonely experience security, love, and sympathy. Those who take them in receive a sense of satisfaction. This feeling goes down to the most inner part of our psyche and expresses itself in an indescribable contentment.

God sees all the people working for minimum wage to support their family. The income is never enough to meet their basic needs. This is similar to being in bondage to the old company store or the indentured slave always owing the master so much that they can never buy their freedom. God in His big-heartedness releases them from that bondage. They are then free to prosper.

God does distinguish between being the victim of circumstances and willingly doing our own thing. In the latter case, one makes a personal decision to rebel. We intentionally refuse to obey God or to follow his rules laid down in the Bible. In this case, no relief is headed that person's way. God will let them continue to wander in the unsatisfying land of rebellion.

May 7

"Blessed be the Lord, who daily loads us with benefits, the God of our salvation! Our God is the God of salvation; and to God the Lord belong escapes from death."   Ps. 68:19, 20

Why do we praise God? Why in the world do we bless God in our prayers? For King David, it was because God loaded him with many benefits. This is why he said, "Bless the Lord, O my soul!"

Each day God gives you good eyes, strong teeth, nimble fingers, an agile mind, a smile to wear, strength in your legs, ears that hear, a stomach that works and all your nerves that feel. Another set of benefits are: your sound mind, your memory, social graces, plus friends and acquaintances.

God gives us bundles of blessings like a cozy house, a nice car or two, lots of hot and cold running water, indoor bathroom, job to support the family, garage or carport, power lawn mower, paydays, and an inclusive church fellowship. Some have extras like boats, house trailers, motor homes, and second home. Think of our heritage of wonderful grandparents, loyal mom and dad, supportive brother(s) and sister(s), kind aunt and humorous uncle and cousins who love us.

Most of us have children and others have grandchildren to raise, nurture, and enjoy. We have horses, cats, and dogs to love and to be loved by. What a blessing these relationships are!

If we were just a speck in the universe, do you think He would load you and me with all these benefits? Since we are more than an insignificant blob of plasma, we are blessed with blessings beyond what we can be thankful for. Let us bless the Lord with all our heart, mind, soul, and strength throughout this entire week.

May 8

"Ascribe strength to God; His excellence is over Israel, and His strength is in the clouds. O God, You are more awesome than your holy places. The God of Israel is He who gives strength and power to his people." Ps 68:34-5

Let's recall the mighty strength of God. He created our earth with only words he spoke, "Let there be light." Every animal, all vegetation, the birds of the air and myriad fish he also spoke into existence. According to the Bible, the only ones He created by hand was Adam and Eve. Presently he keeps count of how many hairs are in your head and every thought we think. He does that individually for how many billion on earth at this moment? He opened the Red Sea so a million and half could stir up dust as they trampled on the seabed. God also stopped the Jordan River from flowing at a particular spot during flood stage. This happened on at least three different occasions. How many times did he heal incurable diseases? He raised several from the dead. Jesus calmed a storm with three words, "Peace be still". Fed over 12,000 people with a little bit of food. God caused the sky to be dark at noon, the middle of the day. God raised his Son, Jesus from the dead and placed Him on his right hand to intercede for us.

Again we realize God is all powerful. It is easy to give God credit for his unlimited power. The good part of our scripture is that God will impart some of that strength and power to us. He gives us power to be over-comers against Satan. When we need to witness for Jesus, God, if need be, even fill our mouth. At that time God will bring to mind the scriptures we may have forgotten or never read. When we are touched with illness even to the point of death, God gives us vitality to fight our way back to health. It is God's desire to bless his children with strength, power, and love. You are one of the children.

May 9

"Save me, O God! For the waters have come up to my neck." Ps. 69:1

All those on the coast might have waded out into the ocean until they were neck keep in salt water. Most of us recall going to the city swimming pool on a hot summer afternoon. First, we kicked the water with our toe to check out the temperature. Then we went in and got our swimming suit wet. When we are accustomed to the temperature, we moved out to where it is under our armpits. Then we made the decision to go chin deep. Gingerly we moved toward the diving board. About that time someone jumped into the pool and created a small tsunami that threatened our nose.

Since the Psalmist lived in an arid country, he must have been referring to a flood of troubles. Haven't you been up to your neck in trouble? I have been! At the ball game I had this girl whom I was dating there. Suddenly my steady girl friend showed up. At other times, the trouble came in the form of finances. The refrigerator died, while the motor on one of the cars conked out, and then the credit card hit the max. How in the world can I get out of this hole?

Maybe the rising tide might be spiritual. Haven't you been tempted to miss church? Following that, your friends tried to get you to do something you knew was wrong. Then something came in sight that caused you to think sinful thoughts or brought up that grudge you just can not forgive. It seemed a succession of temptations hit you like the white cap waves. At times like these, let's call on God who can and will save us as the trusty life guard in the high stand. Thanks, Lord, for being there when we call!

May 10

"Those who hate me without a cause are more than the hairs of my head; they are mighty who would destroy me, being accused by my enemies wrongfully; though I have stolen nothing, I still must restore it." Ps. 69:4

In some countries being a Christian is a crime punishable by death. Yet these Christians continue to pray to You and praise You, O Lord. What a role model!

Here our King David is living by the Ten Commandments only to find out that everyone is against him. If he plucked one of his hairs for every enemy, he would run out of hair before he ran out of enemy. Yet nothing could dissuade him from praising and following the God of Israel. What a role model!

Many were out to actually dethrone King David. It appeared to him that although he was king of the country, the wicked enemy was stronger. It was wrong for them to be his enemy because he had done only what was right. King David in all his life had stolen only one thing, Uriah's wife. He paid for that plus God took one of his children. Although he had not stolen anything of theirs, he was being forced to make restitution. Oh, how can justice be so warped?

What kind of role model are we when we are wrongly accused? Do we still have the love light of Jesus shining while people talk about us in the break room or around the time clock? What kind of example in front of our children are we, when frustrations keep coming. Hopefully, we react as Jesus would.

Like King David, let's remember that this world is not our home. All of God's justice is not administered during our time on earth. We can depend on the fact that God will reward the righteous and punish the evil. Let's continue to be true to God so others can say, "What a role model!"

May 11

"Let not those who wait for You, O Lord God of hosts, be ashamed because of me; let not those who seek You be confounded because of me, O God of Israel."   Ps. 69:6

"Be a stepping stone and not a stumbling block," is the sage advice my mother ingrained into me. This must have been true of King David, as well.

In our verse today, King David's soliloquy is an oral expression of his inner unspoken thoughts. First of all, he asked, "Please, Lord, I pray that the life I have been living doesn't cause you to have a bad reputation." As the King looks back on his life, he wondered what his killings in war campaigns would do, who his adulterous affair with Bathsheba would affect, and what impact some of his rulings might have. Would God be ashamed of his public and private life?

Then he asks, "God, what if the life I'm living gives fellow believers an unclear picture? Did the Torah say one thing and his life say something else? Maybe this was confusing to his fellow Israelites. He would feel so bad, if he was leading people astray. So his questionings were asking for clarification and guidance to live a life acceptable in God's sight.

Is God ashamed of some of the stunts we have pulled? Or was it an embarrassing blunder but someone saw it and thought if that's what Christian can do, then I can do it too. Are we living according to the social rules of today's society instead of keeping the Ten Commandments and rules Jesus left us in the New Testament?

O Lord, test me and see if there be any wicked way in me. Lead me in the way everlasting, I pray. Amen.

May 12

"I have become a stranger to my brothers, and an alien to my mother's children." Ps. 69:8

In another translation of the Bible, the verse is interpreted as "Even my brothers pretend they don't know me; they treat me like a stranger."

This is different from the time in the high school hallway when your older brother or sister wouldn't speak because they were conversing with their friends. Here King David is bemoaning the reality that his own family was envious of his having riches, when they didn't.

Have your classmates ostracized you because you made a 100% on the exam? They were envious because **their** laziness and/or **their** procrastination caused them to get bad grades.

Some hold grudges and build iron curtains around themselves. This makes them treat you like a stranger. Some are very self-centered and obsessed with their own desires. King David's family shut him out of their lives. No communication or love was passed back and forth. It was as if a feeling of hostility existed.

If this is happening to us, we can evoke the golden rule on the situation. We can begin to treat them like we want them to treat us. This doesn't mandate a return of love on their part at any given time. Mutual love will finally occur in God's precise timing.

May 13

"Reproach has broken my heart, and I am full of heaviness; I looked for someone to take pity, but there was none;" Ps. 69:20

Have you ever felt like Charlie Brown? He kept saying, "Everybody is picking on me!" It often feels like you are the low person on the totem pole. Everyone has more power than you. This means you get all the flunky errands at work and left with menial jobs at home.

Were you raised on the wrong side of the tracks or in the wrong section of town? People looked down on you because you didn't wear up-to-date clothes. Your folks spoke with an accent or a vocal slang. Or was it that you had unusual features as a different kind of hair from others in town? During all your school days, it felt like you were under reproach.

You can easily identify with King David, when he speaks of having a heavy spirit. That's exactly how you felt, when you got depressed. It seemed like the world has laid a heavy dark blanket over your entire existence. The clouds stay over your head and keep the sunshine and laughter away.

You can also commiserate with the King David about no one taking pity on your situation. When you tell people how bad things are for you, they in turn tell how much worse theirs are than yours. So you receive no pity there. If they do listen to your problems, they don't understand you because often it sounds too far fetched.

King David says, "No one feels sorry for me." Don't you think King David turned to the Lord at his point? I do! the Lord would reply. Let's follow the King's example. The heavenly choir is never so loud that God can't hear our call. He enjoys any conversation with us. He never tires of hearing our problems or requests. Thanks, Lord, for having compassion upon us.

May 14

"I will praise the name of God with a song, and will magnify him with thanksgiving. This also shall please the Lord better than an ox or bull, which has horns and hooves. The humble shall see this and be glad, and you who seek God, your hearts shall live." Ps. 69:30-32

Let's bless God with what we have. All of us can, at least in our mind, sing a song of praise. Have you ever tried to praise God with ten different songs or choruses? I was surprised that I could recall the words to so many different songs. Doing this raised my spirit!

King David also suggests that we magnify God by naming our blessings. Name them one by one. Doing this changes our thoughts from concern, greed, and/or confusion to gratitude. How long do you suppose it would take for you to name a blessing for each of your fingers? We make God happy with our attitude of gratitude toward Him. We can all afford that, it comes free.

The King reminds us that the things we consider important, like material things, God is not concerned about. We could bring our travel trailer, new car, motor home, boat and trailer to church and God wouldn't give them a second glance. Here are the things we have sacrificed to buy and brought to Jesus. Why isn't God interested? We could even bring the title to our summer cottage because we love God.

God is impressed with our attitude, our praise, and our thanksgiving more than the sacrifice of all the rare coins we possess. So no matter how much we put in the offering our thoughts about God are what He sees. Whatever an atomic bomb could burn up is unimportant but the invisible thoughts we have are most treasured by God. So God has endowed us with what it takes to praise God. He wants us to love Him with our voice, our memory, and our attitude.

May 15

"Let all those who seek You rejoice and be glad in You; and let those who love your salvation say continually, 'Let God be magnified!'" Ps. 70:4

How in the world can anyone rejoice? ... when taxes are so high? ...when all around the globe little children are starving? ...where diseases, like cancer, are killing people daily? ...when most jobs are minimum wage? ...when murder and drive-by shootings are published everyday? Surely King David was out of his mind to expect us to be joyous and happy in a world like ours!

King David's second commendation was to be glad in the Lord. Maybe we could accomplish this feat, if we were perfect Christians. But I lose my temper. I fail to witness. I get depressed often. I have low self-esteem especially when I make a mistake everyone notices. How can I sing and be glad when death recently visited our family?

Does rejoice mean doing the Irish jig with a smile on our face? Does being glad mean we must act like it is the best of economic times? Rejoicing and being glad can be done despite physical circumstances. Our inner attitude is independent of external conditions. We can decide to praise in spite of adverse emotional distress. King David often praised and rejoiced because of what God had done for him in the past. Often He looked into the future and visualized God delivering him. Following this example, we can also magnify the Lord. Since Christ has recreated our heart, we can continually praise God.

May 16

"In You, O Lord, I put my trust; ....." Ps 71:1a

Our trust in the Lord is similar to beautiful blue diamonds from the deep mines of Africa. The brilliance shines from the many facets that light penetrates and refracts. Our trust is multi-faceted. Like the Psalmist, we put our trust in the Lord because He was near. At other times we place our confidence in God because He is mighty, all powerful, and always more than sufficient for my needs.

Occasionally we put our faith in God because He is so forgiving. We stumble and fail so often. What a great God, who always forgives when we confess our mistakes and sins!

Often we place reliance on Him because He is still kind even when we have flubbed up.

At times, we fling our entire burden over on God because God is loving. He never reminds us of the other times or makes fun of us.

From time to time we roll our troubles over on Christ because he is so compassionate. He even urges us to permit Him to make **our** burdens light.

Now and then we depend on God because He is just. God knows when the load is too heavy for us to carry. Even our enemy bents the rules, God is always fair in his judgments.

Once in a while we place our hope in God because we are assured we will always be accepted. It is a fact, that He never rejects any soul who humbly approaches Him.

Ever so often we come to God because he is always there. We know that God never naps or sleeps. On top of that, He is never too busy or preoccupied like our parents were.

At other times, we put our trust in God because

He is the eternal Creator. He knows how weak we are.

Lastly, we commit ourselves to God for only He can forgive us of our sin. He alone can retrofit us for heaven, that blissful home of our soul.

May 17

"Be my strong refuge, to which I may resort continually; You have given the commandment to save me, for You are my rock and my fortress." Ps 71:3

When terrorists cause havoc in our land, God invites us to his strong tower. There we can find stability and emotional healing.

When a tornado or hurricane sweeps through our county, God's refuge is always available. He promised to supply all our needs according to his riches in glory.

When divorce strikes, God always has the welcome mat out to come to him. There God heals our bruised ego and puts a brand new facelift on our self-esteem. When the vicious accusations continue to pelt us, God can heal us so completely that all resentment is gone.

When a drunken driver plows into us, God yells to us to turn toward him, not turn our attention and anger on the drunken person. If we mind God and enter his presence, our emotions are filled with sympathy and later love instead of hate and anger.

At times when our body is extremely fatigued and our emotions are unwound, God urges us to come to him for rejuvenation. We are always welcomed! In periods like these, it seems we, like King David, are continually going back to God's side for strength and encouragement. He is never too busy.

May 18

"For You are my hope, O Lord God; You are my trust from my youth. By You I have been upheld from birth; You are he who took me out of my mother's womb. My praise shall be continually of You." Ps 71:5-6

King David enjoyed praising God. Some people go around whistling or humming all the time. Their motivation is similar to the alcoholic, who unconsciously looks for any excuse to have a drink. King David was continually finding excuses to praise God.

On this day he was contemplating. First, he thought about how his life began. Even there God, Himself was forming him and imparting a personality. God was the One who decided when it was time to take him out of the womb. Then King David thought back to when he played his little lute and sang to his sheep on the hillsides. God stayed by him and gave him strength while he protected his dad's sheep from a bear and a lion. O how grateful he was to God for those times! Right up through his young adult life as a renegade general, God lead him. God watched out for his life when King Saul was desperately trying to kill him. It was marvelous how God set him on the throne of His chosen people. Can you just hear King David shout, "O praise the Lord!"

Today would be a good day for us to search all day long for excuses to praise the Lord. We could start at our birth where King David started. Then we could progress to the point when God cleansed us of sin and adopted us as one of his children. What a blessing to have the Holy Spirit dwelling in us. What an honor to have a divine nature within to guide us!

I have decided that today, all day I will find excuses to praise the Lord. People might even think King David was my brother. We both praise God a lot.

May 19

"For You are my hope, O Lord God; You are my trust from my youth. By You I have been upheld from birth; You are he who took me out of my mother's womb. My praise shall be continually of You." Ps. 71:5-6

Do we need a reason to praise God? King David began thinking one day while he had a little free time. He started back at the beginning of his life near Bethlehem. God took him from his mother's womb and breathed life into him. That was a miracle for him, as well as, for you and me. Whether with a midwife or at an elaborate hospital, God put his spirit in us.

As far back as he could remember, David recalled Eliab his oldest brother caring for him. If it wasn't Eliab, it was Abinadab or Shammah carrying him on their hip. His other four brothers played games with him. What an enjoyable family God blessed him with!

As he grew and began watching sheep, he became even more content. Hour upon hour he watched the cloud formations or composed words for songs he played on his little lute. Oh, how easy it was then to sing praises to the Great Creator.

It was a hard lesson for David to learn to trust God while King Saul was hunting him down like public enemy number one. A time or two he failed to trust God, like you and I have done. Take heart and praise the Almighty for the times we have trusted our lives into his care.

How could he refrain from praising God for now God had enthroned him as King of Israel and was imparting wisdom to his reign? He has been blessed with the desires of his heart. That is the reason he ends today's scripture with the statement, "My praise shall be continually of You!" Is this also true for you and me?

May 20

"Also with the lute I will praise You – and your faithfulness, O my God! To You I will sing with the harp, O Holy One of Israel." Ps. 71:22

In this passage the Shepherd David remembers being in the field in the solitude of a grassy pasture. He looks over the mountain side and down the ravine into the bubbling stream. From off to the side he hears contented sheep pulling at the blades of nourishment. His brothers, who dearly loved him but teased and picked on him, are back at the house away from him. What a feeling of peace envelopes him. At this point, he picks up his six string lute which today would be the guitar. He strums over its strings and begins singing a little ditty that he had sung many times. The lyrics tell of God's power, wisdom, and love. How natural it can be to praise God!

Let's hear what the older King David has to say. He reigns as victorious commander of Israeli forces. People have come to love him for he brought peace to their small country. All the nations he had conquered are now paying a high tax just to keep their homes, children, and their lives. As King David recounts all the victorious campaigns, his current wealth, his precious wives, Bathsheba and Abigail gratitude wells up within. What more could a person want? For him the habit of singing comes naturally. Instead of six string lute, he now has a 54 string harp with a much more melodious sound. Only such an elegant instrument is worthy to be used to sing praise to Almighty God, who continually pours blessing upon his kingdom, his people, and his family.

Do we have a habit of singing praises to God our heavenly benefactor? If not, let us be creative and find a way to praise God today. Okay? Okay!

May 21

"My lips shall greatly rejoice when I sing to You, and my soul, which You have redeemed." Ps. 71:23

Could we just stop and think? As our lips flapped today, what kinds of words were formulated and exited our mouth? Words of griping? Clean or dirty jokes? Words of criticism or praise? Words of self-depreciation? Words of gossip? Words of popular songs or hymns? Putting someone down or bragging on ourself? Of the 25,000 words men speak and up to 40,000 words women speak, how many were words of rejoicing or praising and blessing the Lord?

King David made a personal decision to continually urge his lips to be happy and rejoice. The present bad and hurtful things he was going to neglect mentioning so his tongue might soon forget them. His desire was to get an above average grade in praising. He said he wanted to greatly rejoice.

King David enjoyed expressing himself through song. If you are like me (writer), my goal is to get up to an average grade in rejoicing and praising God on a consistent basis. We need that goal of greatly rejoicing before us.

My father loved to sing specials in church. Often he would whistle on the way home from work. I believe it was more to praise God than to release the stress of his workday. When I sing, I seldom worry or realize whether others are listening. Like the King David, all praise belongs to God for redeeming our life from sin.

May 22

"He will spare the poor and needy, and will save the souls of the needy. He will redeem their life from oppression and violence; and precious shall be their blood in his sight." Ps. 72:13-14

God is not on a vacation! He is constantly watching the oppressor in your life. Does God see our trying boss, the harassing credit company, or our low wages? God is not idle! He is limitless in power, wisdom, and sympathy. He spoke to the King and said, "I will spare the poor and needy."

Not only is God noticing that your budget is consistently falling apart before each payday, but He is watching any spiritual disaster you may encounter. God promised David that He will save the souls of the needy. If we confess our sin, He is faithful and just and will forgive us our sin and cleanse us from **all** unrighteousness. There is no sin He will not forgive!

God will see that you are released from your oppression. Those who are being physically abused will rest from the pain. God delivers us emotionally, mentally, and from other bondages. God enjoys delivering his children from the hands of the Evil One. Can you visualize his gentle face as He lifts you from oppression?

King David observed people patiently enduring under tremendous struggles until they were released through death. Wouldn't it be wonderful to know that if you die at your oppressors hands, God considers your life precious, not St. Peter's life nor

St. Paul's life but YOURS! Would it be worth all the suffering just to know God Almighty calls you "Precious"? Your oppressor thinks of you as "it" but God considers **you** precious. What a mind exploding thought! Hallelujah!

May 23

"And blessed be his glorious name forever! And let the whole earth be filled with his glory. Amen and Amen." Ps. 72:19

How do you react when someone mispronounces your name? Do you get upset when your name is misspelled in the program at school? Doesn't it make you mad when they call you a derogatory name? I would probably feel like you.

The Psalmist comes at this name-calling business from the positive side. First, the name of Jehovah is a blessed name. We never think of putting this name down. It is a glorious name that is honored by God and we should too. We are creatures who live maybe a hundred years then are gone. The One who owns this blessed and glorious name lives forever. The presence of our God is so all-encompassing that the Psalmist would like for Him to fill all the space around him with his glory. Let's say this glory should stack at least as high in space as Alan Shepherd's first capsule went.

Do you believe God could put his Spirit thick as a blanket around our world? If you can visualize that, what do think would happen to the people of the world if they were under God's love? Every policeman, attorney, and judge would be out of a job, right? Christian people would not only do those things that would help themselves but others. Oh! How that stretches the imagination!

We have a great God! Let us bless the glorious name of Jesus Christ forever. That means we bless God until we take our last shallow breath. Even then we might whisper, "God, I love you."

May 24

"Whom have I in heaven but You? And there is none upon earth that I desire besides You. My flesh and my heart fail; but God is the strength of my heart and my portion forever." Ps. 73:25-26

Isn't it a sensational feeling when we accept the fact that God, the Creator is in heaven waiting for us. If we are a child of God and not a child controlled by Satan, we are assured a mansion. What a warm, fuzzy feeling floods our life just knowing He is waiting in heaven near our palace for us.

We have many people who hold a high priority in our life. One priority is to love our parents. We love them so much! Then there is our spouse. After that, comes the love you acquire for each of your children. The Psalmist says that no one on earth should top the desire to make God supreme in their life.

Humans go through so many crises, cycles of depression/exhilaration, financial feasts and famines. There are times of human pain when one doesn't care whether they live or die. The Psalmist puts it this way, 'My flesh and my heart fail."

When composure comes back after a deep crisis, we realize that our only hope is in the Lord. We need only come down with the flu and we shout, "Uncle". We give up trying to cure our self. We call on the Great Physician to heal us with His infinite power.

Why don't we humble ourselves and admit that our only hope in this world is God. The next things might be to accept God as our strength, our Savior, and our guide. He is our all in all! Our ego goes and God comes and controls. What a wise choice!

May God's richest blessing drench you today! Keep looking for it, for it is God's good pleasure to cover you with blessings, like a soda jerk covers a sundae with all kinds of rich hot fudge. Expect it soon!

May 25

"But it is good for me to draw near to God; I have put my trust in the Lord God, that I may declare all your works." Ps. 73:28

It is good to go to God in prayer especially when an eighteen wheeler is bearing down on you on your side of the road. Another excellent time to pray is when your ultra-light plane begins descending and the engine will not restart. Another good time is when your fever is spiking at 104 degree. God's ear is always receptive to your cry for help.

Another excellent time to call on the Lord is when someone asks you a question about last Sunday's sermon and/or Sunday School lesson. Maybe it would be nice to call on God when one of your children is intentionally pushing their boundaries or maybe even stomping on your emotional hot button. When you are tired after a hard day's work and one of your children begins begging you to play a game, take a walk, or do them a favor. When we call, God will answer.

When everything is going according to plan, we should also call on our Savior and bless Him with praises and adoration. On a Saturday or Sunday evening when you are viewing God's beautiful nature on our leisurely stroll, it is good and right to call upon the Lord. Maybe when we are being blessed during a worship service, devotion time, or Sunday School would be another good time to praise the Lord.

The Psalmist frequently called upon the Lord because he had placed his complete confidence in Him. Since there is joy in serving Jesus, we ought to feel free to declare to everyone what God has done for us.

May 26

"We do not see our signs; there is no longer any prophet; nor is there any among us who knows how long. O God, how long will the adversary reproach? Will the enemy blaspheme your name forever? Why do You withdraw your hand, even your right hand? Take it out of your bosom and destroy them." Ps. 74:9-11

Do you have a family member or person at work who always ribs you about your faith in God? It seems that there is always a barb of negative in every verbal exchange. You almost feel like you are a salmon swimming up the spiritual stream. To make it even worse, you don't see any other Christians taking their stand. In other words, you are the only salmon swimming up this spiritual stream at work.

Are there those who step on everyone in the office to put themselves in a better light? How long will it take for the boss to see what they are doing? They get the promotion, while we did the work to make their promotion possible.

How long will it take the Lord to see some of the backhanded smears and underhanded evil tactics some of the church leaders are using? Will God keep his hands stuffed in the hip pockets of his jeans forever? Will they ever get what's coming to them? Surely, the Lord is not blind to the lying which that board member is doing? Can't the Lord see how the pastor is cheating on his wife, or currying favor from the district superintendent?

Oh, Lord, stop looking like Napoleon with your strong right hand tucked in your vest! Please come and dish out justice to these evil doers in my life. Do something O Lord NOW! My patience with these evil people is running out. Please dispense justice on these sinners in the church, at work, and in my life! Then like the Psalmist, I will be happy.

May 27

"But I will declare forever, I will sing praises to the God of Jacob." Ps. 75:9

I will sing praises to God! Some can do a good job of humming "How Great Thou Art". If we make a mistake as we hum or are off key, many wouldn't hear. King David commanded us only to make a joyful noise to the Lord. Others can whistle while they work. It is easy for that person to stay in the same key. Whistling is easy because you don't have to recall the words of the song. Some of you could probably cut a record with your expertise in whistling.

Others have the ability to sing the melody well. Some of us can even sing a harmonizing part. Bless those who sing praise to God in the choir. We need more people to sing joyously in the pew!

There are a few who would get paid NOT to sing but they are very adept at playing a CD or programming the DVD. These praise the Lord by listening and watching.

Then the remainder of society remains silent on the outside but inside has the ability to totally enjoy and appreciate the songs of praise. They are adept at internalizing the glorious strains of the Hallelujah Chorus coming from the choir, orchestra, or pipe organ. Those, who can vocalize like the Great Singer, David have a chance to bless others in need. Those who sing in their mind are blessed but are not much of an influence on others.

To the extent of our God-given ability, let us sing praise to the God of Jacob. To this degree each of us can be like the great King David.

May 28

"All the horns of the wicked I will also cut off, but the horns of the righteous shall be exalted." Ps. 75:10

It was a pleasure for the cowboys of the Chisholm Trail to cut off the horns of the long-horned Texas cows. These horns could reach up to 30 inches across and do real damage to the horse or the cowboy's legs.

In Bible times, the length of the horn was a measurement of power. The longer the horn, the more power, the larger the area of domination one had.

Here the Psalmist is asking the Almighty to shear the horns of power of the evil persons. May they no longer be the oppressor of the poor and disenfranchised? A reduction of their power would result in bringing our opponent to their knees and down to everyone else's level. We often wonder what would happen, if God will ever intervene.

Now the Psalmist hopes God will do more than even the scales but tilt it in favor of the child of God. If Christians were permitted to rule with justice and compassion for the needy, they would surely decide with impartiality. Favoritism would not be a part of the reign of the righteous. What a practical way to rule!

When the righteous govern with wisdom and compassion, their area of control will enlarge.

When we don't cheat, lie, or steal, our area of responsibility will grow in ever widening circles. Praise from the righteous should constantly be flowing to our Master.

May 29

"You are more glorious and excellent than the mountains of prey." Ps. 76:4

Oh! How lovely is our God! God caused the earth to rotate so it would appear that the sun is rising this morning to shine on us to elevate our spirit.

Oh! How essential is God's ever-present and everlasting love to us. Without You dispensing your love to each of us, we would be bankrupt. We would have no extra love to pass along.

Oh! How lovely is your sanctuary? Each time I enter the church, I feel a divine security. Even though we are aware that God never leaves us, it is comforting to walk into the place where the Holy Spirit abides.

Oh, Lord! How thankful I am that your ear is always attentive to my prayer. How much easier it is to have faith that You are listening, when I am kneeling at the altar rail!

Oh! How excellent is the mercy You bestow on me! There are days I seem to foul up often and You are always present to extend forgiveness to me. Some days I don't need an extra portion of your mercy because I walk according to your words as recorded in the Bible.

Oh! How glorious it is when I can feel the deep relationship with You! I can sense your abiding presence within. It is like walking with our esteemed president, who has the entire armed forces of America at his disposal to protect him. Se have one better. We have a guardian angel (Ps.

34:7) and God's sweet presence around us (Heb. 13:5).

Oh! How much more glorious it will be when I parade down the golden streets of heaven! There will be no more fear, insecurity, nor any chance of not receiving my eternal reward from my gracious Savior.

Lord Jesus, help me keep this exuberant attitude all day. Amen.

May 30

"Surely the wrath of man shall praise You; with the remainder of wrath You shall gird Yourself." Ps 76:10

When people get mad and hurt others, these actions shall wind up praising God. There was a town that got up in arms about an evangelist named Stephen. Together they met outside the city and stoned him to death. A young man, who was watching, was convicted and later convinced to follow the Nazarene by Stephen's actions. We all know how great an influence that young man, St. Paul was for Christ!

God used King Pharaoh when he vented his anger on the Hebrews to turn that out for the advantage of the Israelites. God, in turn, freed them. All of this culminated in a blessed and powerful Jewish nation.

A group of preachers which included the bishop of that day took Jesus to trial. Their anger caused Jesus to die. But Almighty God caused mankind's wrath to praise Him. Because of Jesus' death, we have salvation from sin. Sometimes when people get mugged and have to be taken to the hospital, they have a chance to witness to a roommate or a nurse. This would result in another soul missing hell and able to step right into heaven.

When people at work make fun of our convictions or pressure us to do wrong, God strengthens us. We are stronger because of the persecution. It causes us to put more trust in God.

If a driver with road rage causes us to have an accident, God can use that for His glory. While we are flat on our back with lots of time, we meditate on our life. God helps us readjust our priorities.

So whether the fury and rage of man was in ancient times or now, God uses that wrath to praise Him. All of this is almost too wonderful and/or mysterious for us to comprehend. Rest assured that God is working all things in your life to his glory and **your** good.

May 31

"Make vows to the Lord your God, and pay them; let all who are around Him bring presents to Him who ought to be feared." Ps 76:11

How often do we get in predicaments and bargain with God? We then make a promise to God. To the Psalmist, that is considered a vow. Have you made any lately?

Do you remember when your child had a 104 degree fever and headed for 105. If God didn't do something quick, there was going to be brain damage. You made a vow to attend church regularly.

Your budget had been a disaster for over six months. The old car had to have repairs. So you asked God for the promotion. There was to be an opening soon, as Henry was retiring. If you give me that raise in pay, I promise to give ten percent to you.

Some mothers were praying nightly for their son/daughter in the battle zone or with the United Nations forces. Lord, if You will bring them home safely, I'll give up that little habit, I know displeases You.

Remember the time you started out late for that important meeting. Since you were in charge of it, it was imperative you be there on time. "Lord.... I'll read my Bible daily, if You'll see that no cops are watching this road."

There was a time you were flying and the captain came over the intercom and said, "Ladies and gentlemen we are having difficulties with our port engine". Right then and there you promised God that you would witness to your children, if that plane came down safely.

Immediately after the doctor gave you the bone chilling news, "You have cancer," you promised to be an all out Christian for the rest of your life, however long that was.

Keep in mind that these vows or promises were made to an awesome God. The Psalmist says it would be wise, if we fulfill what we promised our marvelous and almighty God.

June 1

"Make vows to the Lord your God, and pay them; let all who are around Him bring presents to Him who ought to be feared."   Ps. 76:11

The Psalmist urges us to make a vow unto the Lord. Is that strange? Well, we made vows to GMAC or Ford Motor Credit for sixty months to pay them several hundred dollars monthly. Long ago when we signed up with the water company, we gave a deposit and promised to pay each monthly bill. We kept this commitment by faithfully paying the bill.

Then we make other agreements with our self and others: ...promising to walk briskly for twenty minutes daily.   ...swear to abide by the law while driving. ... pledge to love, honor, and obey our spouse. How faithfully do we keep these kinds of vows?

Often we promise with hardly any resolve of fulfilling them. How often did we promise our kids we would take them fishing, to the carnival, or swimming? We made vows with little intention of fulfilling them.

The Psalmist urges us to make a vow today with the full intentions of keeping our word. It could be to daily read God's pure unadulterated Word. Our pledge could be to praise God more often throughout each day. Our promise could be to give God ten percent of our net or gross pay. Maybe we could pledge to pray each morning, each evening and at least another time throughout each day.

The final commitment of the Psalmist is to pay everything he promised God. One lady at the end of the day looked to God to see if she had pleased Him. If she perceived a smile, she rolled over and slept. If God didn't approve of her actions, she began to pray, until the burden was lifted. If you have the time, sit a few minutes, and recall how many times you pleased Him and how many times you failed? Did you try your best or do you need to put a little more effort in paying your vows to God?

June 2

"You hold my eyelids open, I am so troubled that I cannot speak." Ps. 77:4

Several times when I had parent-teacher conferences, I would drink another cup of coffee between parents coming in. When the evening was over, my eyelids were locked open. Even when my body got horizontal, the eyes lids would be stuck open. When the Psalmist had this malady, he said it was the troubles of life that had his nervous system strung as tight as a harp string. After a period of time, he asked if God had disowned him, cast him off, or forgotten all about him because of all the troubles that had flooded his daytime world.

If this frame of mind is true for you, you may think maybe God has closed the vault door on all his mercy which He usually magnanimously dispenses to you. How could a loving God like ours shut up all his kindness, empathy, and tenderness on the humans He created? Have we ever thought "Will this drought on mercy last forever?"

Didn't King David write that God would never leave us or forsake us? Surely God didn't break his promise even to someone like us. Didn't God also say He would send blessings on David's children and to his children's children to a thousand generations? Oh, Lord, please don't break that promise!

The Psalmist begins to wonder, if God has forgotten how to be gracious and bestow mercy and blessings on his overburdened children in distress. Lord, that would not be difficult for us humans to do, but inconceivable for You. We, your people, entreat you, O God, from your immense heart to generously shower us with your mercy and love. In faith, we thank you in advance from the bottom of our heart.

June 3

"We will not hide them from their children telling to the generations to come the praises of the Lord, and his strength and His wonderful works that He has done." Ps. 78:4

Has our relationship with Jesus been one of secrecy? Nicodemus came to Jesus only at night. Have we acted like a secret admirer? Have we been ashamed of Him before our business associates, our acquaintances, and friends? Surely, we haven't been afraid to let our children see us reading our Bible or lifting our morning or evening prayers.

The Psalmist was brash and brave even bold about his witness. First, he declared that he would sing the praises of His God before his family and friends. My father walked home four blocks from the Granite City Steel Co. My brother and I could hear him coming because most evenings he would be whistling a Christian song. In church, my dad was an 'Amen-er'. He urged the preacher on when what he was saying was scriptural and true.

In everyday trials have we trusted God to bring the family through? When it was easy to worry, did our children watch us lay the outcome in God's hands? The Psalmist did!

Have we related the deeds great and sometimes miracles of God in our lives to our children? When our son was a baby, he got a bad case of diarrhea. His temperature was high. We rocked him through the night until his fever broke. Or did we tell of our accident where two were killed and four were injured? God protected us! What wonderful stories of God's wonderful deeds do we have? Have you related these incidents to your children or grandchildren? If not, let's make plans to do so soon!

June 4

"They did not keep the covenant of God; they refused to walk in his law, therefore, the Lord heard this and was furious; so a fire was kindled against Jacob, and anger also came up against Israel, because they did not believe in God, and did not trust in his salvation." Ps. 78:10, 21-22

Are we or have we been under a threat of the wrath of God's displeasure? Are we carelessly living our lives by the rules of society or intentionally never inquiring about God's will for our daily decisions? Israel did just that and was about to experience God's anger. Our punishment could be as small as a reprimand or as tragic as Nadab and Abihu who were killed on the spot by God. Demas, in the New Testament, was lured back into sin and will ultimately receive what Satan has in store for him.

Can you visualize a very patient Heavenly Father's anger being kindled? Can't you just see the fuel of our disobedience, our ignitable indifference, and flammable rebellion coming before the eyes of Almighty God? Each stick of sin causes the red to rise up his neck and color his usually gentle face? It is so uncharacteristic of God that it is frightening to think about it. Can you see the meek Jesus, who joyfully held a little child, having a stern determined look toward a disobedient culprit? It is like there is a fire inside our blessed Lord that is bringing his emotion to a rolling boil. The end result could be as light as a spanking or as severe as a sentence to our final resting place with all the residents of Sodom and Gomorrah.

Let us renew our vow or commitment to keep the words of our Lord Jesus. Do we recall what we promised God at our conversion? Let us make a renew our pledge to be true to God, follow his Word, and do what a Child of God should do.

June 5

"Then they remembered that God was their rock, and the Most High God their Redeemer. Nevertheless they flattered Him with their mouth, and they lied to Him with their tongue; for their heart was not steadfast with Him, nor were they faithful to his covenant. But He, being full of compassion, forgave their iniquity, and did not destroy them. Yes, many a time He turned his anger away, and did not stir up all his wrath; for He remembered that they were but flesh, a breath that passes away and does not come again." Ps. 78:35-9

Do you enjoy being a people watcher? Well, this Psalmist must have received a distinct pleasure from that, too. Some people he was observing seemed to have their life built on the sure foundation of the God of Israel. With that mooring, they would not be moved. God was their Redeemer. He often plucked them from economic chaos. He lifted them from their mental depression. He blessed them with kindness and generosity.

Despite all the virtues they possessed, the Psalmist began to notice. With one side of their mouth they flattered and praised God but from the other side of their mouth they lied to God. In modern day terms, they were old-fashioned hypocrites. The Psalmist wondered whether God would immediately strike them dead.

The Psalmist watched God in his marvelous grace forgive them repeatedly instead of punishing them. How unlike the inclination of us human beings! Instead of venting His wrath, God was long-suffering and kind to them.

Why would God do that? After much meditation, the Psalmist came to this conclusion. God in his infinite wisdom realizes how these created humans fail, so God took that into consideration. In his great kindness and mercy, God continues to forgive our sins. God even blesses us during the interval of time that we should be serving our punishment. Hey, let's praise the Lord for his patience and mercy!

June 6

"Nevertheless they flattered Him with their mouth, and they lied to Him with their tongue; for their heart was not steadfast with Him, nor were they faithful in His covenant. But He, being full of compassion, forgave their iniquity, and did not destroy them. Yes, many a time He turned His anger away, and did not stir up all His wrath;" Ps 78:36-38

When I was a young man, I feared one man. God had recently called me into the ministry and everyone knew that fact. This man knew the Bible inside and out. When he got a little tipsy from alcohol, he enjoyed baiting any church member he could find with trick religious questions. Each time he came my way, I cringed. I knew I would lose the argument and be embarrassed before all present. He could talk gloriously about God. He knew every story and most of the genealogies of the Old Testament. It seemed he could quote whole sections of the New Testament. If he hadn't been such an obvious hypocrite, I could have envied his command of the knowledge of the Scriptures.

Many of us may be openly praising God, yet living a sinful life. The Psalmist stated matter-of-factly that God is very patient with that man and us, when we perpetuate this hypocrisy. We can hardly imagine people tormenting God for forty years in the wilderness. God never in this time lost His love and compassion. As a matter of fact, God did lose His temper a time or two but never ran out of compassion. Never was there a time then or now that if we humbly come to Him and confess our sin that He would not hear and forgive us of all our sins. Aren't you glad we serve such a marvelous God?

June 7

"Yes, again and again they tempted God, and limited the Holy One of Israel. They did not remember His power; the day when He redeemed them from the enemy," Ps. 78:41-2

How in the world do we tempt God? Oh, let me count the ways:

Often we push the speed limit when God's Word states that we should obey the commands of God and the laws of men.

Sometimes we nag and plead with God to get our way or our desire until, like a parent, God is exasperated.

Or recall the times we journeyed to a city where we were not known and did questionable or sinful things.

Maybe we tempt God to punish us when we are urged by the Holy Spirit to serve in a Christian way and we say, "No". Or even worse, we know what is right and we say, "I won't do it!"

Could it be we raise God's ire, when we gripe and complain incessantly. We keep this whining up even while He continually showers us with blessing upon blessing. We are never satisfied, like the children of Israel in the wilderness.

Have we ever been sassy or been disrespectful to God? We speak to God with contempt or demand of God to do what we want done.

How many times have we acted stupidly, when we knew right from wrong? We instinctively knew it was distasteful to God, but we zombie-like did it anyway.

Do we tempt God? Yes, we knowingly put God's kingdom and God's children in a bad light! How often do we give God's church a bad reputation by our actions?

O Lord, please forgive us, when we push your hot button and tempt You to punish us. Thanks again for Your mercy and forgiveness. Guide us, O Holy Spirit in a way pleasing to You.

June 8

"Yet they tested and provoked the Most High God, and did not keep His testimonies," Ps. 78:56

Oh, how easy it is to recall when our children were two years old! It seemed that the whole time they were awake they were testing the limits. We were afraid they would soon think their name was "No No". By three and four years of age, they asked one million questions that provoked deep yet instant and succinct answers. In the process, it truly tested our patience.

Are there ways we test God's patience? Would it provoke God when we see how close to the world we can live instead of showing how much love we have for Him? Would it test God's patience when we live like a saint on Sunday and cheat, connive, and curse like a sinner the rest of the week? Would it incense God for us to know to do right, then turn around and do wrong on purpose? Would it grate God's patience for us to spend the Lord's Day doing our pleasure and giving him no time, after he gave you a good job, a nice home, and a great family? Surely it would irritate God for us to have nothing to do with salvation that cost the life of His only Son? Wouldn't it enrage Almighty God for us to make fun of God before our friends, like we don't have any need of the salvation he offers? Would it stretch the compassionate love of

God for us to be on the fence as a lukewarm Christian?

Aren't you surprised that God hasn't vented His anger and destroyed us long before we got the age we are? Oh, we know that we would have given in to our feelings long ago, if we were God. Thanks, God, for being a patient God.

June 9

"But turned back and acted unfaithfully like their fathers; they were turned aside like a deceitful bow." Ps. 78:57

What is a deceitful bow? That is one that looks like a championship bow that could be as accurate as William Tell's bow. But looks are deceiving. This bow when pulled to its maximum twists so the arrow always goes left or right when it is released.

The Psalmist speaks for the Lord. God is saying that my people look like faithful loyal children. They attend the tabernacle as regularly as the calendars shows it is the Sabbath. God noticed that during the week lots of things took higher priority than Him. They loved personal praise, public recognition, and authority over others more than God's approval. In times of extreme stress, they forgot whom they served because curse words exited their mouth. The filthy words, that filled the air, sounded like Satan lived in their hearts. At times, their recreation had them doing activities that harm their body. They don't treat it like the temple of God. On the exterior, they look like a Christian but the rotten part is hidden in their thought life. The termite of pornography, revenge, or jealousy is chewing up their mind. This controls their mind instead of dwelling on things that are honorable, just, and of good report.

For centuries, the Heavenly Father looked down

on his chosen children of Israel and saw followers who looked like true children of Almighty God, but they walked like children of the Devil. When God takes a look today at our actions, will He decide we are His child? Do our thoughts and actions prove we really love God, and plan on going to heaven to live with Him forever?

June 10

"So that He forsook the tabernacle of Shiloh, the tent He had placed among men," Ps. 78:60

It is possible to complain loud enough and long enough to provoke God to action. Humans can tempt God continuously to the point He will withdraw.

God withdrew His favor from Israel. They began to break the Ten Commandments. They associated with evil men to the point, it corrupted their morals. Think back over time from childhood to now and tell me morals today are not loose.

The Hebrews were an unfaithful lot. They took in the gods of the Canaanites even the god of Molech, who required them to sacrifice their child.

They began doing what they thought was right instead of reading God's Word to discover and obey His statues. They did not treat their neighbors as they wanted to be treated. This favored nation did not act like genuine children of God.

God got to the place where we parents do. Can you recall when one of our kids began to act up out in public? We said, "Honey, that's your child!" Because the Children of Israel acted like the children of the Dark One, our scriptures state, "He forsook the tabernacle of Shiloh." God left the assembly of God's people. It then became a group of people at a social function, not a worship service. I have had traveling evangelists say to me,

"You might as well tack the sign 'Ichabod' over the front door of some churches. God's spirit has left that congregation."

Hopefully, each of us has not been resistant about God's commands so that His Spirit has forsaken our heart. Give me, O Lord, a heart like Thine.

June 11

"He also chose David His servant, and took him from the sheepfolds; from following the ewes that had young He brought him, to shepherd Jacob His people, and Israel His inheritance. So he shepherded them according to the integrity of his heart, and guided them by the skillfulness of his hands." Ps. 78:70-72

Even while David was a child, God was guiding him toward kingship. He was taught how to overcome fear by having him face a bear and a lion. Can you possibly believe that God is preparing you for a decisive role in your adult life? The Psalmist here is a staunch contender for that belief. The Psalmist would go so far as to say he would guarantee that God is guiding your children now for their role as responsible citizens of society. But God is presently utilizing you to help others and using you to change events, solve problems, and understand circumstances to nurture others toward total fulfillment.

God knows His personal plan for you. This distinct and individualized plan uses each of your unique talents, skills, and abilities to the fullest.

God moved David from the idyllic and simple life of a country boy on the farm to a general and on to a king. God has taken or guided you through the rebellious teenager years to parenthood and a job or profession that helps mankind. He promises to do the same for each child in the family. So don't worry!

You and your child will be skillfully guided by the hand of our all-mighty, all-powerful and all-loving God. Through untold centuries the Great I Am has skillfully shepherded and molded humans in an image like Himself. So! Relax today and let your precious Lord and Savior pat, hug, and lead your loved ones into all they can be in His sight.

June 12

"Give ear, O Shepherd of Israel, You who lead Joseph like a flock..." Ps 80:1a

Have you every been saddled for years with the presidency of a club? You were always responsible for seeing that everything was ready for the meeting. Oh! What a burden! "If only I could just come and enjoy the meeting, I would be so happy." What a relief when someone was elected to take your place!

Or are you a free spirit? It is so comforting to just wing it. You are not responsible how others feel or the amount of responsibility they wish to carry. If you run into trouble, you just handle it and go on.

The Psalmist was the most comfortable taking the part of a sheep. The shepherd is responsible for attending to the sheep's needs. He is obligated to go through the pasture and dig up all poisonous nightshade plant so their diet was safe. Our shepherd leads us into green pastures. Sheep don't have to worry or fret. Jesus gave the command, "Don't worry" (Matthew 6:31). God is in control so why stew? All the sheep need to do is keep their eyes on the Savior. If He changes directions then follow. There should never be a time when we are in a quandary as to which way to go. God's way is the only logical choice, so why question the lesser of two evil.

It is so comfortable placing ourselves in God's care. The outcome of a sheep's life is the responsibility of the Lord. God is so wise, that if we follow to the Great Shepherd closely our lives will turn out fine.

June 13

"God stands in the congregation of the mighty; He judges among the gods." Ps. 82:1

The Psalmist had recently been to court. Here he speaks of God as a just judge. If they had attorneys back then, they must have appealed to the judge for justice.

Someday in eternity we will stand before God, the Father. The prosecuting attorney will be Satan while his opponent, our brilliant defense attorney, Jesus Christ is across the room.

The first thing Satan will bring up is every one of our sins large or small. He will try to convince the Judge that we are completely unworthy of heaven. If that wasn't enough, Satan will explain to the stern Judge our motives when these sins were committed.

Then Jesus Christ will arise, who had patiently waited never raising any objections or points of order. He knew that we were rightfully guilty. Our Attorney will approach the bench in a confident manner. He will get upon His tiptoes and whisper, "Father, I died for him (her) and adopted him (her) into our family. He (she) is one of ours and their record is clean. Father, you'll have to dismiss Satan's charges and assign them to the mansion I have prepared for them on Fourth and Hallelujah Street."

The prosecuting attorney usually stomps out of

the courtroom. He keeps forgetting that Jesus Christ has an unblemished record, never lost a case. After our court session, the Judge's sentence will be, "Enter into the joys of heaven, my child"

June 14

"God stands in the congregation of the mighty; he judges among the gods. How long will you judge unjustly, and show partiality to the wicked?"   Ps. 82:1-2

Have you ever stood in the same room with the President of the United States? Did a special kind of feeling flood over you? Was it a mixture of awe, anxiety or a great honor for you to be there? As a boy scout, I was at a meeting in our high school cafeteria where a legend of my time was the speaker. It was R. G. Letourneau. He invented the wheel powered units of large earth moving equipment. He was wearing the distinguished Silver Beaver medal, a covenanted civil service award from the Boys Scouts of America. I hung on his every word. He must be wise to go from rags to riches, from a nobody to a famous personality and from defeat to victory in the business world. It was a privilege and an honor to be in his presence.

The Psalmist was overwhelmed when he realized the Wisdom of All Ages stood in the temple with him. In that divine presence, his mind immediately gravitated to his own unworthiness. The Psalmist felt the penetrating thoughts from the mind of the Almighty. Judgment came upon him and descends upon us when we contemplate on the mind of God. Do we feel guilty or uncomfortable there under the gaze of our heavenly King? If our sins are forgiven, joy and peace will be the twins in our life. If we are sinners, only fear and distress will reign in our hearts.

God will not judge us harshly but with true judgment. Some friends and enemies may judge us without cause but God knows our true heart and our intended motives. How comforting to know that God can forgive us of any and all sin and prepare us to live forever with Him!

June 15

"Let them be confounded and dismayed forever; yes, let them be put to shame and perish, that they may know that You, whose name alone is the Lord, are the Most High over all the earth." Ps 83:17-18

The Psalmist today is searching for evil doers: The employers who take unfair advantage of the poor. Maybe they are a company that cheats employees out of health benefits. Some store owners pay minimum wage, while getting filthy rich. The CEO, who shuts down a business and starts a similar business under a new name to keep from paying pensions, is evil. Many are charging twenty four percent interest on credit card balances. Maybe bribing innocent people and extracting money from them. Others are like the pimp, who is keeping young men and women as slaves. The robber lives on what others work to get. Crooked people scam elderly people out of their life's saving. The gambling casinos bilk people out of thousands of dollars every month. The alcohol and tobacco companies unsuspectingly get people ensnared with their product.

All of these people the Psalmist would like to see the Lord do a number on them. It seems as if they get richer, while we struggle to live. O Lord, if you are watching confound these shrewd people so they forget how to bilk innocent people. May depression settle down upon their personality so they won't even want to get out of bed. May the authorities catch them in their scheme, so the news media can expose them and embarrass them to tears. May those who take a life, perish themselves.

In all this punishment, O Lord, may they come to the stark reality that they are being punished by the Supreme God. You send blessings on the just and retribution on the unjust. In their anguish, may they admit that You deserve all honor and praise. Today, let's join the Psalmist in praising our Lord Jesus Christ.

June 16

"O God, behold our shield, and look upon the face of your anointed." Ps 84:9

St. Paul speaks of the shield of faith which we use to defend ourselves from the fiery darts of temptations of the Devil. The Psalmist thought of his knowledge of the Scripture as his defense against the Evil One. Recall when Jesus was tempted in the wilderness? He used the scriptures to successfully resist those temptations. If our shield is scriptures that we have memorized, how large is our shield? Is it big enough just to hide your face or is it long enough to cover you from head to foot? The Psalmist asked God to look at his shield. I hope we aren't intimidated or ashamed for God to look at the store of memorized scriptures we have.

His second request asks God to look at us from a different perspective. This time he asks God to look down upon his creation, his child. As a child yearns for the focused and uninterrupted attention of their parents, so the Psalmist is asking the same of God. When we receive this, we feel affirmed and complete in whose we are.

The Psalmist may also have been asking for God to show his favor upon their King. If God showed his favor upon their king, their country would continue to prosper and they would live in peace. Likewise, we should ask God to look kindly upon our President? Lord, give him wisdom beyond his years. Guard his personal actions so they may always glorify You and bless You. Please, Lord, make him a blessing to his nation and the world.

Lord, look upon your anointed (us) and give us peace.

June 17

"For the Lord God is a sun and shield; the Lord will give grace and glory; no good thing will He withhold from those who walk uprightly. O Lord of hosts, blessed is the man who trusts in You." Ps. 84:11-12

What images or words conjure up fear in you? Would that fear remain, if you were positive that God was your shield? You remember that Goliath had a soldier who carried his shield. How secure would you feel if the Holy Spirit shielded you twenty four hours a day seven days a week?

Since – not if – the Holy Spirit is protecting each step you take, why worry? God is lighting your path, why fear? You have the Creator of the Universe watching every footstep you take. The Psalmist's mind was overjoyed that God was his sun and shield.

Besides this, God was continually dispensing grace to the Psalmist. So anytime he erred, strayed, or broke a commandment, God was present to forgive and set his feet back on the straight road of righteousness.

In addition to grace, God passes out his glory to his children. We often experience this glory imparted by God. Moses did not realize his face was glowing. Others had to tell him to put a veil over his face so they could look at him. God used Moses and still uses us to spread his glory around. What an awesome but fantastic job!

Can you believe there's more? Yes, the Psalmist assures us that God does not withhold any good thing or blessing. The shower of unlimited blessings is ours, if we meet the qualifications. The recipients of these abundant blessings are those who walk and follow the two great commandments. Love God with all our heart and love our neighbor as ourselves.

Happy and prosperous are those persons who rely completely on the Lord. Blessed means mental, financial, emotional, and physical well being. Who could ask for anything more?

June 18

"I will hear what God the Lord will speak, for He will speak peace to his people and to his saints; but let them not turn back to folly. Surely his salvation is near to those who fear Him that glory may dwell in our land." Ps. 85:8-9

The Psalmist says that he can hear what God speaks to him. Could the reason we don't or seldom ever hear God speaking to us is because we don't listen? How many times did mother have to tell us what she wanted? Wasn't it that we were only half listening or not listening at all?

When the Psalmist directed all his attention to God, he heard God speak words of peace, not words of condemnation. Even when we are worthy of God's criticism, He speaks words of forgiveness and peace!

The people who most often heard God speak were those whose hands were clean and their hearts holy. The Psalmist states that God speaks to his children. Personally, even in the midst dribbling balls and shouts of my fellow team mates on the basketball court, I could distinguish my dad's voice of encouragement from the stands. As a born-again child of God, His voice will sound familiar.

After feeling the security of God as our Father, how in the world can we return to lying, cheating, and dishonoring God? The Psalmist noticed that some people did try to dabble in the things of sin and on Sunday try to be a happy kid of the King of Kings.

Those, who fear God and obey his commands, will have the glory of God living and daily abiding in their life. Have you noticed how pleasant it is to walk with a saint of God! The confidence and security which they have in God rubs off on us. After we are away from this delightful person, we miss that sweetness we enjoyed around them. If we obey God and love Him with all our heart, God's delightful glory will stay with us.

June 19

"Truth shall spring out of the earth, and righteousness shall look down from heaven. Yes, the Lord will give what is good; and our land will yield its increase. Righteousness will go before Him, and shall make his footsteps our pathway." Ps. 85:11-13

The Psalmist uses a metaphor. Truth will spring out of the ground like an artesian well. As we daily read the authentic Word of God, the truth will spring up from within us. These truths shall be refreshing as a cool drink from a deep well on a hot August day. Can't you almost feel the cool water on your parched throat?

Just as the sun shines on the right and the good, God shall shine on our soul, life, and family.

It will feel like the sun's warmth on our back as the March winds whip around our ears and collar. How relaxing and satisfying to know God is personally guiding us, an everyday person! God not only provides for our spirits and our emotions, but promises to supply all our physical needs according to all his riches in glory. The promise is your land (labors) will yield its increase.

Lastly, the Psalmist gives us a picture of a father and son. He visualized each of us growing more and more like our Heavenly Father. His picture is similar to each Christian trying to walk in the footprints of Jesus, God's beloved Son. I recall trying to step in the snow prints of my daddy. How much higher and holier is the attempt to step in the exact footprints of God's only son, Christ Jesus!

Today actually experience this blessing of becoming more like Jesus!

June 20

"But You, O Lord, are a God full of compassion, and gracious, longsuffering and abundant in mercy and truth." Ps. 86:15

Our God is like a milkshake that has ice cream standing higher than the top of the container. Let us compare God's compassion to this milkshake. The Lord is filled to overflowing with tenderness, love, gentleness, sympathy, kindliness, and tolerance.

Graciousness is a virtue. God is brimming with that. He is warm-hearted, friendly, sociable, pleasant, courteous, and well-mannered.

Patience flows through God's veins. It shows up as uncomplaining, tolerant, forgiving, and charitable.

Our God is abundant in mercy. Mercy today appears as unfailing love, pardon, grace, big-heartedness, soft-hearted, lenient, and kind-hearted.

Our Lord is one hundred percent truth. God is genuine, valid, honest and pure integrity.

What the Psalmist brings up are the solid basics of what God is. I would have called Him my Redeemer, Savior, Guide, Comforter, and Friend. I have made Him a permanent resident in my heart. There is never a time anymore when I wish God was a transient. My love has grown stronger and stronger. Satan will have to work overtime to separate me from God.

May God be your constant companion in your walk through life.

June 21

"And the heavens will praise your wonders, O Lord; your faithfulness also in the assembly of the saints."   Ps. 89:5

Can't you almost hear the angels of heaven singing, "Holy, holy, holy Lord God Almighty"? The tune is sweet and the harmony is delightful and easy on the ear. It comes to us as surround sound. If you think the Christmas choir of one hundred voices singing Handel's Hallelujah Chorus raised the hair on your neck, multiply that extreme enjoyment by a thousand and the number of singers by a million. Then you might experience the level of joy of hearing the angels praising God.

Can you describe the twinkle in a star? God put it there. Many things of nature are indescribable! Can you relate to me the working of stomata on the underside of leaves of every lead, flower, and weed? Each intricate design of the universe can be physically mind boggling and will always remain a wonder that praises its Maker.

Words serve inadequately to praise God in terms of what God might appreciate and enjoy. Poets and lyricist come as near to accomplishing the task of praising Almighty God as any on earth. Sometime take a morning and attempt to satisfactorily praise God with words. How subtly it changes our attitude to a positive admiration of our magnificent Lord.

The Psalmist was flabbergasted at the thought of a sinless, all-powerful, and all-knowing God ever being in his midst. Faithfully God abides with us and among us despite our blunders or sin. All praise belongs to You, O Glorious God!

June 22

"O Lord God of hosts, who is mighty like You, O Lord? Your faithfulness also surrounds You." Ps 89:8

God is faithful! Here the Psalmist was accentuating the faithfulness of God.

When we were being born, God was there with our mother. Also as we cut our teeth, God had sympathy for us when we squalled and bawled. God was there to watch over us as we took our first steps. He was as pleased as our parents were. What patience God had to endure all the times our parents said, "No! No!" That would have been an excellent time for God to be busy on the other side of the world, but he was as close as our hands and feet. God faithfully watched the day we said the pledge of allegiance in first grade. God stayed close and was present the day we broke our bone. Through all the pain God stayed near. God enjoyed the day we were chosen to be on the school team. Oh yes, the Lord was in the back seat while you and the drivers license person was in the front seat. Why did we worry? His steadfast presence was there the day we had that accident or first fender bender. God's unswerving love was with us when we fell in love and nervously had that first date. The supportive presence of God was there as we walked down the aisle to exchange vows. Nor did He leave that first five years, when we were learning to get used to the quirks in our spouse. God conscientiously stood beside us as our first child was being born. What a glorious day! Our reliable Lord was there when they said, "Lordy, Lordy guess who's turned forty!" Our trusted Heavenly Father was there, when our first grand baby was born. Never shall we forget that day. The Psalmist was truly amazed that God is there for every person on earth. He never is on break. What a wonderful and miraculous God that has that kind of capabilities! What determination to never leave us nor forsake us for a single second all our life, and for every living person!

June 23

"Righteousness and justice are the foundation of your throne; mercy and truth go before your face. Blessed are the people who know the joyful sound! They walk, O Lord, in the light of your countenance. In your name they rejoice all day long, and in your righteousness they are exalted." Ps. 89:14-16

The Psalmist walked into the light or under the gaze of the Lord. Could it be that he didn't have the distractions we have today? Maybe his schedule was dotted with free times, where ours is packed every minute with things that need to be done.

On Friday at sunset, the Psalmist began to prepare to worship God on the Sabbath. Hopefully he wasn't worn out and slept in on the Lord's Day, like we sometimes do. We are pretty sure he didn't have the soccer game scheduled on Sunday afternoon. "Lord, you know that even if we went to early church, we would be late for the game in that town far away."

In that desert country, the Psalmist was not tempted to take his boat to the lake. "Lord, this is my only day off and You do want me to spend time with my family, right?"

"I only have one hobby, that's my street rod, antique car, or motorcycle. They always have their rallies on Saturday and Sunday so I have to miss church."

St. Paul gave this advice to Timothy. 'As Christ's soldier, do not let yourself become tied up in the affairs of this life, that you cannot satisfy the one who enlisted you in His army. Let us follow the Lord's rules for doing His work.'

Since we say we are a Christian, we ought to put Christ first. If we put other things before worshiping our Savior, will God have time for us on judgment? We need to decide which is most important and resolve to do that.

June 24

"I have found my servant David; with my holy oil I have anointed him," Ps. 89:20

The Lord located Shepherd David out on the grassy hillside. God used Prophet Samuel to anoint David. Personally, I felt very honored when a bishop of the United Methodist Church anointed me as I was commissioned to preach the Word of God and administer the sacraments. I wonder how we might feel if the Creator of the World would anoint us with the oil of the Holy Spirit and lay his cool palm on our forehead.

The Psalmist said that God would strengthen the arm of David. Through him God would establish his kingdom. Not only will God strengthen his servants but the evil plans of Satan will be thwarted. God will give us wisdom as He did to David to outwit any of the Devil's schemes. God will go ahead of each of us in preparation for the defeat of our spiritual enemies. Plagues will come upon those who plan our fall.

Similar to bodyguards, faithfulness and mercy shall accompany every Christian. Our strength will increase to meet and overcome each crisis. As a genuine born-again child of God, we will be given dominion over more and more.

God made one agreement with David and he makes one with each Christian. God is the one who never has to back down or Welsh on any deal he ever made. God promises to keep all He promised. They will stand like the Rock of Gibraltar. They will endure as long as we live and beyond. What a comfort!

June 25

"'If his sons forsake my law and do not walk in my judgments, if they break my statutes and do not keep my commandments, then I will punish their transgression with the rod, and their iniquity with stripes. Nevertheless my loving-kindness I will not utterly take from him, nor allow my faithfulness to fail. My covenant I will not break, nor alter the word that has gone out of my lips.'" Ps 89:30-34

You can plant canna seeds and get a huge plant with attractive red or yellow blooms. You can take the same ground and carefully place Johnson grass seeds in it. You will raise the most prolific and insidious plant. It is almost impossible to kill this Johnson grass because it has an insatiable desire to take over the whole yard.

We can grow up taking in biblical principles and good morals. We then become upright citizens God would be proud of. Or we can learn how to cheat, get without paying, or lie to save our skin. Sin is insidious and takes over our life. We have the choice to take God's plan or follow our own plan. Remember painful consequences or joyous rewards come with either choice.

God says, "If you forget to follow the rules of the Bible, then I will punish you." If you thought your parents knew every trick in the book on punishment, you are wrong. God knows all the ways to see that you reap the penalty of what you sowed.

The part I like about our God is that the Lord's loving-kindness is always reaching out to us. Even though it was our choice, we can never go too far or too deep in sin that God will not gently pick us up and forgive us. The second part is that God made a contract with us humans to never leave us nor abandon us. In the several millennia since Adam was created, He has never broken that covenant.

Whether you have done evil or good, God is here now to cleanse you and send you out into the world to live for Him.

June 26

"If they break my statutes and do not keep my commandments, then I will punish their transgressions with the rod, and their impurity with stripes. Nevertheless my loving-kindness I will not utterly take from him, nor allow my faithfulness to fail." Ps. 89:31-33

God's consistency can not be compared to anything on earth. When we sin, punishment is due us. When Satan, formerly known as Lucifer planned to overthrow God and/or rebel at the commandments of God, he was thrown out of heaven. Other angels that followed Satan were also ousted from the presence of the Most Holy God.

When we humans knowingly commit sin, punishment should be meted out to us. When we ask, God will forgive us. Often the accompanying physical punishment must be endured whether disease, broken relationships, or prison. Our spiritual punishment was endured by Jesus Christ, while on the cross.

Often God disciplines us, as we would our children. It is always for our good and never in His wrath. It seems that humans more readily learn in times of adversity and discipline. Sometimes though, we wonder if these times will ever end.

The Psalmist assures us that God will never abandon us but in loving-kindness be near us. God's faithfulness will endure until every generation has lived their life on this physical globe. Rest assured that God's love and faithfulness is unending. He will never leave us nor forsake us in spite of all we do. Relax; knowing God's loving-kindness is waiting to cover you like a wool comforter on a cold blustery winter night.

June 27

"What man can live and not see death? Can he deliver his life from the power of the grave?" Ps. 89:48

When we are a youth, we think we are invincible. A young man named Carl just got his driver's license. One night he got a couple of kids to join him. One of the kids dared Carl to drive under this railroad tracks at full throttle. So as fast as he could, approximate 82 mph, he came up out of the dip and went airborne. The part that he didn't consider was that only ten car lengths from where he became airborne was a four way stop. This time instead of an empty intersection a car pulled across it just as he had slowed to about 70 mph. He and his friends died. They had never thought about death. They hadn't considered how terminal death was or about dealing with it.

Others of us don't tempt fate but we effectively block death out of our thinking. Even when we go to the funeral home, we think this won't happen to us. I am as healthy as a horse. Another way of not dealing with our mortality is to keep our Daytimer packed down to five minute increments. Being too busy does not negate the inevitability of our demise.

Each of us needs to prepare for eternity. Whether preparations are made or not, we will go the way of all humankind. Will our destiny be the lake of fire forever? Jesus, the only Son of God, died providing a way of escape. As far as I know, God, the Judge doesn't listen to nor consider excuses. If we take advantage of that sacrifice by confessing our sin and believing on Him, our ultimate destination is changed to heaven. There we can sing or praise God through endless ages.

Since we can't possibly avoid death, we need to prepare for it. We don't have an inkling how soon death may come for us. We need to prepare today.

June 28

"Lord, You have been our dwelling place in all generations. Before the mountains were brought forth, or ever You had formed the earth and the world, even from everlasting to everlasting, You are God." Ps. 90:1-2

When we think of a dwelling place, we don't think of a goat-haired tent. We visualize a nice cottage or farmhouse with the childhood memories that go with it. When home is mentioned, one specific house always comes to mind. Most of us think of the first home we remember as a child. What pleasure boils up into our consciousness!

The nomads had no permanent dwelling place that would come to the forefront of their mind, so this Psalmist placed the depository of his memories with the Lord. Even though he had never visited there, he knew his precious thoughts would be unmolested there.

Earlier the Hebrews used the tabernacle of God with the Ark as their bank of memories of childhood. At least, this tabernacle was something they could feel or touch.

Even later, the Israelites could draw up a mental picture of the grand temple of King Solomon. Memories of days in the synagogue with the instructors, professors, and rabbis teachings flooded into their mind. The temple was so revered and worthy of admiration that people may have thought of it as a strong box for the emotional memories of Jewish children.

Believers of today look to their church buildings as a place where God dwells. While we are there, we often feel the presence of Almighty God. Memories of precious blessings fill our mind. How delightful to stand in the presence of God!

Can you spare a moment or two to think about our heavenly dwelling place? Before God created our mountains on earth or caused our planet to be circular, God created our eternal dwelling place! How wonderful that eternal habitation will be! Thanks You, Almighty and Everlasting God for the heaven You have prepared for those who love and obey You.

June 29

"For a thousand years in your sight are like yesterday when it is past, and like a watch in the night. .... Oh, satisfy us early with your mercy that we may rejoice and be glad all our days! Make us glad according to the days in which you have afflicted us, the years in which we have seen evil. Let your work appear to your servants, and your glory to their children." Ps 90:4, 14-16

Moses is given the credit for this prayer. He prayed unto God saying I know how infinite You are. A thousand years is like a few hours to You. Our life span is to You as swift as the dream we had last night.

Our lives last only about seventy years. Some reach one hundred years. No matter how long we live, our lives are densely sprinkled with pain and trouble. Haven't you noticed how many of your high school classmates are gone?

Lord, teach us how to live one day at a time. Help us make the most of each day. The older we grow, the faster each day scoots by. They move faster than clouds ahead of a storm.

We invite you, Lord, into our days. Come in the morning with your mercy. Continue to shower us with your unfailing love. Impart your gladness in our lives in proportion to the misery we are called to endure. Open our eyes so we may see the miracles You perform about us and for us. As we finish each day, may we receive your stamp of approval. It feels so good for God to lay His hands on our head or pat us on the back and say, "Well done today, my dear child." Many of us didn't receive that from our parents because they were too busy trying to get us to improve or improve their own lifestyle.

Moses ends with one other request, "Lord, make our efforts today successful."

June 30

"You have set our iniquities before You, our secret sins in the light of your countenance." Ps 90:8

O Lord, don't make a showcase of my life. There are things I don't want the world to know. I don't want to mention the way I acted at that birthday party when I was ten or eleven. Nor the time in the locker room, they passed around some pictures. I've been trying to forget them ever since. I'm glad you don't show these on the monitor. Lord, please forget that date in high school where I learned ever so much more than I wanted to learn. You have erased the guilt of that late night so I am begging You not to lay that sin out for all to see.

As a young adult, I picked up a secret habit. You know, O Lord, how I have tried unsuccessfully to stop over the years. I have succeeded, I think, in keeping it a secret from everyone. Please don't expose that before the whole world.

As an adult, there are little indiscretions that are sprinkled throughout my life. Don't ex-ray my life and let others see these flaws.

In actuality, Lord, I know that You have seen every sin I thought or did. Extend your grace and I will extend my faith for You to apply of the blood spilled on Calvary by your precious son, Jesus Christ to all these sins. Then as the Psalmist asked, "Drop them in the sea of forgetfulness, never to be dredged up ever again. Forgive me, O Lord I pray. Create in me a new heart. Put a right spirit in me. Lead me in the way everlasting." Oh, how grateful I am for your mercy!

July 1

"You have set our iniquities before You, our secret sins in the light of your countenance. For all our days have passed away in your wrath; we finish our years like a sigh." P. 90:8-9

How would you feel, if I went out and found a nitpicker to look over your life? Can't you imagine all the flaws, errors, and mistakes they could find? Just writing or thinking about that makes me squirm. How would I ever explain away or make excuses for some of them?

God says one of these days I will lift every sin of your life, and will set them out on an eight foot banquet table, where all can see them. This includes your most embarrassing ones.

After that, God will deliberately look for all your secret sins you did in the dark. Similarly, the gossip that you whispered will be amplified through a bull horn by someone sitting on the ridge of a house. That will make you want to shrivel up and crawl under a rug in embarrassment. The Psalmist thought after that he might live in a stupor under the awesome wrath of Almighty God for the rest of his days. If God would continue this day in and out, life for us would end like a sigh of relief.

Praise the Lord, life doesn't have to be lived in dread or in fear. When we sincerely confess and believe on the Lord Jesus, every secret and/or ugly sin is eradicated. In other words, our sins are completely erased from God's hard drive which has no recycle bin. God can not retrieve them even if he wanted. They are forgotten never to be remembered against us ever again. What a liberating joy will flood our lives knowing they are gone forever! No need to ever worry about them again!

Let's live out today knowing God has blotted out every sin. You and I are children of a loving and forgiving God.

July 2

"So teach us to number our days that we may gain a heart of wisdom." Ps. 90:12

Things that are given to us for free, we consider of little value. We look at cars, houses and money as important because we must work to earn these. I read a true statement, "Things That Count Cannot be Counted." What if we lose our family because we spend 10-16 hours a day striving to gain things? Often the love of our spouse is lost while trying to achieve success, money and/or status. In the end, we most often find that the love of our children was ultimately more valuable. So teach us to number our days.

Consider the relative importance of friendship. How many times have we been straining to capture a promotion or sales award and snubbed our friends? Strange, we experienced no exhilaration after reaching that goal. We were just lonely and despondent. Our friends were gone, and we stood alone because we were deceived into chasing glory or honor at the expense of the invisible love of our friend. So teach us to number our days.

Some abuse their body by ingesting or breathing harmful things. Others of us have schedules that stretch our bodies to their maximum. After we experienced ulcers, heart attack, stroke, cataracts or back trouble, we think about the preciousness of the free gifts of sight, hearing, tasting, and feeling. The abilities to drive, walk, talk, or sit in comfort is a tremendous blessing. Teach us to number our days.

Lastly, let us contemplate the gift of salvation so full and so free. May we not overlook this blessing that is so important to our entrance into our eternal home. Lord, give us wisdom to accept the gift of heart purity, our passport to heaven with all its riches. Lord, PLEASE teach us to number our days.

July 3

"I will say of the Lord, 'He is my refuge and my fortress; my God, in Him I will trust.' Surely He shall deliver you from the snare of the fowler and from the perilous pestilence. He shall cover you with his feathers, and under his wings you shall take refuge; his truth shall be your shield and buckler. You shall not be afraid of terror by night, nor of the arrow that flies by day, nor of the pestilence that walks in darkness, nor of the destruction that lays waste at noonday." Ps. 91:2-6

Jehovah is a God of promise. God will be our refuge when the temptations, trials, and burdens of life fall upon us. We can rest serenely as a baby in the safety of God's arms. Picture that!

God will be our fortress when criticism comes like hail, accusations like arrows, and lawsuits like bullets. Like the forts on the American plains, the logs can absorb the lead that would poison our bodies and be deadly to our lives.

Our Deliverer will make the schemes of our enemies backfire and cause their plans to harm them. When a plague of physical illness comes our way, God can divert it from us.

God is our shield of bullet-proof Plexiglas when our co-workers say untrue things about our work, our attitude, or our behavior. Isn't that promise a comfort to us?

With God as our bodyguard, why should we

worry and fret because of evildoers? God is the champion protector. He has never been defeated. Even on the cross God, the Son, was victor in that his precious blood is still efficacious to cleanse all sin from our lives.

Let us sing and rejoice on our way today because God is our refuge, fortress, deliver, shield, and defender. Don't worry! Be happy in Jesus.

July 4

"For He shall give His angels charge over you, to keep you in all your ways." Ps. 91:11

Guardian angels are all around us! Today's scripture confirms that common belief.

Psalm 34:7 states that angels will encamp around Christians and will deliver them out of trouble. God did that for Elijah when he and his servant were surrounded by a hostile army.

Psalm 35:6 says that angels will pursue our enemies. They will chase them down.

The Psalmist urges all angels to bless the Lord. Every angel is created to praise the Lord (Psalm 148:2). In the book of Revelation, it tells of the many angels singing around the throne.

They are doing the bidding of God, the Father. So we can't ask the Holy Spirit to send his angels to protect us nor can we make angels obey us. They are messengers of the Lord exclusively. Angel Gabriel came to Mary and later to Joseph to tell of the 'immaculate conception.' Angel Michael fought demons in the process of delivering a message from God to Daniel.

In today's scripture, He gives the angels permission to watch over you. God will rescue each of us, lift us up, and set us on the solid rock with

His righteous right arm. God promises to keep us in all our ways.

Aren't you glad God created angels before He created Adam and Eve? They are here to minister to us at the bidding of God, the Father. Rest in the security that an angel walks and rides with you wherever you are. When you sleep the angel keeps watch, so rest in peace.

Thanks, God, for sending angels to help us.

July 5

"For He shall give his angels charge over you, to keep you in all your ways. In their hands they shall bear you up, lest you dash your foot against a stone." Ps 91:11-12

Angels take care of me? What a mind boggling reality! There is supernatural help anytime and all the time to divert temptation, get us out of trouble, or just be a close friend. Would you live any differently, if you would actually incorporate this fact into your life?

Let us note who has control of the angels. We, humans can not call on an angel. Neither can we pray to an angel. It is impossible to pray for Uncle Joe, who has passed on, to come help us. At his death, he did not become an angel. Angels were created by God at the beginning of time. They saw Eve, Noah, Moses, Joshua, David, and Augustine and are able to see what you do. Angels only do the bidding of God, whether to guard Daniel in the lion's den, release Peter from the inner prison, or watch over little Moses as he floated down the Nile River.

Satan has angels who, like him, can disguise themselves as angels of light or good. Sometimes they treat you well but always with the intent to hurt you. They can make the roulette wheel win for you.

Good luck? His goal is get you hooked on gambling and put you in poverty.

Our God always sends angels for our good and his glory. The Almighty wants to send angels to keep you on the straight and narrow path that leads to everlasting life. Angels, when sent by God, help you overcome trials, temptations, and sickness.

Angels at one time wanted to help Jesus. It was in the garden but God did not order them to. But every time God orders, angels hurry to help his children.

July 6

"'Because he has set his love upon Me, therefore I will deliver him; I will set him on high, because he has known my name. He shall call upon Me, and I will answer him; I will be with him in trouble; I will deliver him and honor him. With long life I will satisfy him, and show him my salvation.'" Ps. 91:14-16

In this case, God said those who set their love on the Lord as highest priority will have many blessings come upon them. We most often move toward our most dominant thought. If our greatest desire is to love God, we will migrate in that direction. Loving God becomes a joy.

With a steadfast love for Christ, God will come to our assistance when the enemy of our lives comes after us.

When we set God in first place in our lives, the Lord promises to put us in a secure place, safe from the temptations of Satan.

When Christians call on God, we will be heard. Not only will He hear but will answer. Just a Sunday ago, God heard and answered a prayer for me. If He did it for me, He'll do it for you.

Bad things do happen to good people. In our scripture God says when you find yourself in trouble, "I will be with him in trouble." Oh, how comforting!

If our love for God stays number one, God will honor us. How stupendous to be honored by the Creator of the Universe!

Finally, the greatest benefit is our salvation from sin. Being free from sin entitles us to enter through heaven's portals. There we will live in a place prepared specifically for us. God has been building on it before He formed our earth. Oh, Glory, Hallelujah!

July 7

"He shall call upon Me, and I will answer him; I will be with him in trouble; I will deliver him and honor him." Ps 91:15

Every Christian, each Child of God has the assurance that when you pray to God you will be heard! Please take time and read today's scripture again. Check it out for yourself. Isn't it wonderful to know that every night, each morning, or in time of trouble, God takes time out to listen to you? Had you forgotten that fact? Or did you ever read or realize the above promise? How many nights after praying have you fallen into bed and felt like, "Why pray? God isn't listening!" HE IS! Maybe you need to learn from the invalid man, who had an empty chair by his bed. One day the daughter came in and found him dead but his hand was lying on the chair. The daughter knew all was well. For her dad always prayed as if God was sitting in that chair. Her dad had his hand resting on the leg of God, when he slipped away from the bonds of earth.

Job (14:1) knew that our days are few and full of trouble. God disclosed that fact to him. Since

God knows about your constant annoyances called trouble, He promised to be with you. When trouble hits you like as big Mack truck, God pledges to be near you. With God near by, you will have supernatural assistance to overcome or extricate yourself from any trouble that may slam into your life. That is God's solemn oath.

When deliverance is complete and peace returns, God will exalt you. That's right! Almighty God will honor you. I pray that the magnificence of our scripture is soaking into the depth of your being. You are blessed, child of God!

July 8

"It is good to give thanks to the Lord, and to sing praises unto your name, O Most High; to declare your loving-kindness in the morning, and your faithfulness every night, on an instrument of ten strings, on the lute, and on the harp, with harmonious sound." Ps 92:1-3

The Psalmist found it advantageous to start and end each day with God. In the morning, he started out with thanksgiving. Whether it was for restful sleep, comfortable home, or ability to wake up, he was thanking his heavenly Father. Isn't that much better than griping, dreading, and complaining? Thanking God places us in positive frame of mind to face our day whatever it may bring. The Psalmist also recited the attributes of God. The predominant string he plucked strummed was the one of God's loving-kindness. If we would daily realize how big God's heart is and that He is in control, our days would go by so much better.

As his day began to wind down, the Psalmist truly enjoyed getting out his guitar, I mean ten stringed lyre, his flute, I mean lute, or his harp of many strings. He didn't do this in the morning because of the phlegm in his throat. After talking all day, his vocal cords were ready to sing. A Psalmist, like King David, enjoyed singing scriptural songs.

What a joy and pleasure to get the family around and let them all harmonize! Even the harp seemed to praise God with the melodious strings vibrating a praise message to the Lord. O how it calmed the soul and soothed the heart after a rough day!

The way to have consecutive good days is to thank God every morning and sing praise to Him every night.

July 9

"It is good to give thanks to the Lord, and to sing praises to your name, O Most High; to declare your loving kindness in the morning, and your faithfulness every night, on an instrument of ten strings, on the lute, and on the harp, with harmonious sound. For You, Lord, have made me glad through your work; I will triumph in the works of your hands." Ps. 92:1-4

Why did the Psalmist say it is a good thing to give thanks to the Lord? Can he give one good reason to sing praises to God? Why in the world would he go to the closet and pull out an out-of-tune lute, a ten string instrument and a big harp? Would you go to that much trouble to give praises and thanks to God?

The latter half of our scripture discloses the Psalmist reasons for urging each of us to praise God. First, God greets all of us every morning with a sunrise, a rooster, or an alarm clock. The first act of God is to dump his loving-kindness into our heart. This great virtue seeps out to others in the course of our daily lives. This transferred loving kindness gets on others and sticks like honey.

The next reason for the Psalmist was the faithfulness of God throughout every trial and temptation we endure. Sometimes we lose tract of God's imminent presence with us in the midst of our hectic day.

When the evening sun sits, the Psalmist's chest expands in admiration at the works of nature. How dramatically and spectacularly God created the sky to say good-bye to each day. If only the choir from the temple or church were here to sing in perfect harmony to say good-bye to the day as it passes.

How insignificant our effort! How magnificent is our God!

July 10

"But my horn You have exalted like a wild ox; I have been anointed with fresh oil." Ps. 92:10

My horn You have exalted. In western terms the Psalmist is saying, "My business acumen, political clout, and social prestige you have increased." The area of power I had has been enlarged and my influence is more powerful. The wild ox has power, strength, and stamina that can not be measured. In like manner, God has increased my authority over others.

Along with this increase in power, God had anointed the Psalmist with blessing. It is so wonderful to know you have been touched by God! Some have received physical, marital, and/or emotional healing. Others from that powerful touch have been spiritually revived.

When this happens to us, we speak of being refreshed. This is much better than the second day of vacation. It is more like being in the third quarter of a ball game when all of a sudden a hero of ours walks up to the bench and states, "You're doing great! I know you'll win." Your fatigue vanishes in an instant. We run onto the court or field like it was the beginning of the game. "That's refreshed!"

So when the Almighty touches us, we are exalted, energized, and refreshed to step out into the world and witness for Christ Jesus, our Savior.

July 11

"If I say, 'My foot slips,' your mercy, O Lord, will hold me up. In the multitude of my anxieties within me, your comforts delight my soul."   Ps. 94:18-19

How often in the last month have we knowingly sinned? Or has there been a temptation so strong that we yielded? Most of the time we realized our determination to resist was unequal to the temptation. This is when the Psalmist called on God for mercy. You and I know in many cases it is only the mercy of God that can prevent us from sinning. Or it is God's mercy that will lift our feet from the mucky miry clay of sin. Stepping into sin for us is similar to a fly stepping on flypaper. We are stuck forever without outside help.

Even in the Psalmist's day, life could be hectic. He declared it in these words 'multitude of anxieties'. That's a bunch of worries! Most of us go through times like these.

The Psalmist discovered that as God revealed himself, the more he learned about: the mercy of God, comfort, assurance, loving-kindness, recollection of pertinent verses of scriptures, patience. God counteracts our bungling with his ever abiding presence. God controls our mortal lives but also warms the corners of our eternal soul. This helps us carry on from day to day.

The Psalmist re-affirms, there is always help in the Lord, if we but call on Him. Oh, Lord! Today we cry out as the Psalmist to be held up. Lift us up and beyond what we can do on our own. Amen

July 12

"Oh come, let us sing to the Lord! Let us shout joyfully to the Rock of our salvation. Let us come before his presence with thanksgiving; let us shout joyfully to Him with psalms. For the Lord is the great God, and the great King above all gods."

Ps 95:1-3

Throughout the Bible it states that sin will always bring punishment and definitely never evoke joyful shouts of praise. When we participate in homosexuality which is an abomination to God, 'watch out' for you may scream in anguish. When people commit adultery, they are breaking one of God's Ten Commandments. Surely these people will only scream in pain from God's wrath. When we put things, pleasures, or people before our love for God, surely we will receive God's disciplinary actions.

God really is pushing us toward a feast of thanksgiving. Some shout to encourage their pony to get out front. Many parents shout encouragement to their children at the athlete event. Others shout and root their pro team on to victory in the living room, where the team can't even hear the shouts. Then amid the shouts of praise and thanksgiving there are words of encouragement. St. Paul encouraged his students Timothy, Titus, and Aquilla and Priscilla in their Christian life. Barnabus was known as the encourager for all who called themselves a Christian at Antioch.

Some of us love to shout "Hallelujah" when Handel's Chorus is sung. Any time "alleluia" comes in a song; we sing it as loud as we can. Some people in church shout "amen" right in the middle of the sermon. They're afraid if they don't let it out, they might explode. That is an encouragement to the preacher. If we would dare shout when God is filling up our emotional cup, God would be much encouraged and well-pleased with us. The advice of being quiet in church is not what this Psalmist is advocating.

July 13

"For He is our God, and we are the people of his pasture, and the sheep of his hand. Today, if you will hear his voice: 'Do not harden your hearts, as in the rebellion, as in the day of trial in the wilderness.'" Ps. 95:7-8

The Psalmist warns us not to go down the path of rebellion with God. When we get spiritually hardened, it is difficult to hear the Holy Spirit urging us to do right. An example is the children of Israel while they were wandering in the wilderness. They rebelled and thousands died because of the Lord's anger.

It would be to our advantage to pay attention to God's admonitions. If we are in church and are upset at someone, we are to leave the service and go make up with the one who has something against us. (Matt. 5:24). Only then can the Word of God abide securely in our heart. With the Divine dwelling inside, we can be thankful (Colossians 3:15). Pursue what is good for everyone (I Thessalonians 5:15). I wonder, do we always vote for what is good for all the church in board meetings? St. Paul recommends that all Christians be examples of keeping our word, upright in our conduct, show a spirit of love, obey the Holy Spirit, have great faith in God, and live a life of purity (I Timothy 4:12). Our Christian witness should be steadfast, immovable, and always abounding in good works (I Corinthians 15:58).

Remember through all the hustle and bustle of life, that we are the sheep of his pasture. We can lean back and rely on God to provide our needs. The most satisfying is when the Great Shepherd tousles our hair as we would a dog which sidles up to us. At times like that, it almost seems like power flows from our great Shepherd into our being. What a positive charge to our low spiritual batteries. Praise our great God!

July 14

"For forty years I was grieved with that generation, and said, 'It is a people who go astray in their hearts, and they do not know my ways.'" Ps 95:10

Over a long period of time, God has been watching his people. He has been looking over America for the last two hundred years. I have a suspicion that He has been seeing the same thing as occurred in Israel's years in the wilderness. Theirs and our devotion has been diverted to things of this world. We have given more love to possessions, acquisition of wealth, or another person than we have given to God. Oh, how God longs to be first in our lives. We have let projects and hobbies consume our time to the exclusion of daily devotions or regular attendance at worship services. Some have permitted addictive habits, or vengeful thoughts control us psychologically or mentally. Christ can set us free.

The action that hurts God most is indifference to Him. The Israelites and we Americans have left the Bible unopened too long. We have forgotten the commands of God, therefore, we have not obeyed them. One of the hardest commands is to love our neighbor as ourselves. After the Lord's

Prayer, Jesus urges us to always forgive. Never ever should we hold any resentment. None of his commands seem easy, do they? God wants us to return good for any evil that people do to us. St. Paul asks us to not think more highly of ourselves than we ought. Do not grumble nor complain. Those two actions made the life of the Israelites more difficult in the wilderness. We are to love the Lord our God with all our heart, mind, and soul.

If we keep our hearts soft and sensitive to the will of God and obey his commands, He will bless and protect our nation. Let's do our part at least for today. God is always available to assist us in keeping his commands.

July 15

"Say among the nations, 'The Lord reigns; the world also is firmly established, it shall not be moved; He shall judge the peoples righteously.'" Ps 96:10

Travelers fly to China, Europe, Australia, and around the globe. The Psalmist says it is imperative to tell the world that the God of Israel reigns. That is not the preacher's job but our responsibility. This command falls on our shoulders. How are we to tell everyone that our God is in control? Most of us are so timid that we don't even volunteer to mention what church we attend. Satan has us afraid of those we talk to. They may ask us a religious question that we can't answer. We're so intimidated we can't or we fail to yell to the world that our Lord is the one to worship and praise.

Our God is the one who raises kings, rulers, and presidents to office, as well as the One who deposes them. He is the one who is in control. Nothing happens that He has not permitted. God set the world up in Genesis and continues to reign today. Nothing nor nobody can change that.

God shall judge all nations. Those who have never heard about Jesus will have few commands to follow. We, who have heard the gospel of salvation from our youth, will be judged more severely. We are required to walk in all the light we have. Others will not be judged by what we know.

God's judgment is righteous. There will not be a single case of miscarried judgment. God does not have a room of cold case files. God knows so there is no need for a DNA match from the scene of disobedience. This is difficult to imagine. We are dealing with Almighty God, not fallible humans with incomplete knowledge.

The Psalmist was positive the God of Israel was the Creator of the universe. God established all the laws of nature and no human is going to change that. At the end of time Almighty God is going to correctly judge the people of every nation on earth.

July 16

"You who love the Lord, hate evil! He preserves the souls of his saints; He delivers them out of the hand of the wicked. Light is sown for the righteous, and gladness for the upright in heart. Rejoice in the Lord, you righteous, and give thanks at the remembrance of his holy name." Ps. 97:10-12

There is a prerequisite to meet before receiving all the blessings described in these verses. God is calling the Christians to love all things less than their degree of love for Him. If we don't meet this first requirement, we probably won't be able to handle the next obligation. That hurdle is to hate evil. It is so easy to accommodate a little sin. Similarly, we can tolerate a little cancer but in time that small amount of cancer will kill us. A little sin will eventually send us to a devil's hell.

Since we qualify as true children of God, the Father promises to preserve our soul. Daily God will deliver us from the schemes of the wicked. The light of the Word will shine on our daily path and prevent us from falling into Satan's traps. God will beam gladness from heaven straight into our heart. Our blessings will never be sent to another person. His global positioning system never fails to be anything but 100% accurate.

With all these blessings, we ought to be bubbling over with joy. Rejoicing should boil over from our lives. Each time we think of God's generosity, praise should flow out of our life, like water after a rain in a water soaked field. If our life stays saturated with blessings, all additional blessing should splash on those around us.

Today, I vow that I will love God and hate evil so I might be eligible for all these blessings.

July 17

"You who love the Lord, hate evil! He preserves the souls of His saints; He delivers them out of the hand of the wicked. Light is sown for the righteous, and gladness for the upright in heart. Rejoice in the Lord, you righteous, and give thanks at the remembrance of His holy name." Ps. 97:10-12

Can a Christian hate? The Psalmist thinks it should come natural for God's children to hate – evil, that is. It should sicken our stomach, when we see: shows that kill adults or embryos, programs that glorify adultery, series of films that condone lying, videos that lift up greed, and talk- shows that promote harming our bodies. So much of the sin in this generation seems to stem from self-gratification instead of glorifying God.

God has special promises for his beloved saints. Almighty God will save our souls from a Devil's hell. When this happens, we change our destiny frm punishment to living throughout eternity in heaven. O what a time that will be!

Also we will be rescued out of the wicked hand of Satan. Only God can perform such a feat and believe it or not, He will do it for little old you and me.

As Christians, we can walk in the light of God's Word and don't have to stumble through life like our non-believer counterparts. Our path leads up to heaven, while the sinners' path leads to a very warm reception.

Gladness and singing can be and should be the obvious sign of a Christian. When God pours blessings into our lives, we should unashamedly rejoice in the Lord. How often do people see us with a tune in our heart and a song on our lips?

Christians are also always thankful. Our witness is bright and clear, when we are thankful for all God has done for us. Praising and thanking God should be the two strings our Christian guitar plays. Thanks, Lord, for our scripture today.

July 18

"The Lord has made known his salvation; his righteousness He has revealed in the sight of the nations. He has remembered his mercy and his faithfulness to the house of Israel; all the ends of the earth have seen the salvation of our God." Ps. 98:2-3

I challenge you to revisit the time Christ became your Savior? How did you feel when the Holy Spirit convicted you of your sin and/or the style of life you were living? Was the burden heavy on your heart? Did that load of past sin put the fear of God in you, so you were afraid to wait until tomorrow? Because if you had a fatal car wreck or a massive heart attack, you were positive you wouldn't make it into heaven.

How wonderful did it feel when God rolled that burden off your back? Was there a joyous feeling that swept all over you? Did it feel like you were walking on air? Or did the sky seem brighter and the clouds more heavenly? The guiltiness vanished and the fear disappeared. Were you filled with a desire to tell the whole world about what happened in your life? Or was it an insatiable appetite for the Word of God?

Have you been around a group of born again Christians for any length of time? Sometimes the feeling of love and serenity is so powerful; you are not sure how to respond. You may laugh, cry, or just absorb that holy living presence.

Jesus said that whosoever comes to him, He will never reject. The entire world can see and experience this salvation of the Lord. I urge you to accept his salvation by confessing, believing, and living in the presence of God. Or can I praise the Lord you have this precious salvation?

July 19

"The King's strength also loves justice; You have established equity; You have executed justice and righteousness in Jacob. Exalt the Lord our God, and worship at his footstool – He is holy." Ps 99:4-5

The Psalmist is urging us to exalt the Lord, our God. To exalt God, we need to lift God from indifference or the common place to an exalted position of honor in our life. In this esteemed place of honor, we should neither defy the commands of God, take God's name in vain, nor make derogatory remarks about God. The most appropriate thing to do is to adore Him. In other words, we should love God with all our heart, mind, and soul. Don't let any earthly allegiance knock Him out of first place in our priorities.

We should praise God with words. Another way to praise God is to show our love for Him by the Christ-like life we live. A genuine Christian life is truly effective. We think about praise only as verbal praise most of the time. There is another out-of-the-ordinary way is to testify in church about what God has done in our life. That is to praise God is through shouting. My two aunts were able to praise God in this manner while my grandfather shed tears of joy.

The most common way is through congregational singing. We can elevate his name through worship. In a church service during the Prayer of Confession or the Lord's Prayer, we confess our faults and sins. In this humble attitude, we trust God to forgive and cleanse us. Then in the atmosphere of holiness we can easily exalt our Lord through praise.

July 20

"The King's strength also loves justice; You have established equity; You have executed justice and righteousness in Jacob." Ps. 99:4

Oh, how often we want justice to come to all the evil people of the world! Many of us at one time or other have received the wrong end of the club of justice. We did what was right but received what we perceived as punishment. When will the perpetrators of evil receive what is rightfully theirs? It is truly a comfort that God, who rules the world, will finally see to it that fairness will be dealt to all. How could each of us endure life without the certainty that right will finally prevail? We truly wonder when we are in the depth of self-pity that God is fair.

King David loved to mete out justice. Since he was rich, he could not be bribed into administering punishment to the innocent. The most important trait of King David was a driving desire to live according to the commandments of the Scriptures. One man literally pelted him with rocks when his son, Adonijah drove him out of the palace. King David would not let the soldiers hurt him. The King thought it might be God using that man to correct something in his life. I can't imagine the FBI letting anyone hit our president with a rock.

King David wanted to live a such righteous life that God would be proud of. Not only was he wanting to be like the coming Christ, but wanted his people see God through how he made decisions and judgments. Let us take the same vow to live like Jesus and attempt to treat others like Jesus did – with justice, and with completely righteous motives.

July 21

"I will sing of mercy and justice; to You, O Lord, I will sing praises. I will behave wisely in a perfect way. ..." Ps 101:1-2a

This may not have been New Year's Eve when the Psalmist wrote this verse. At this precise moment the Psalmist decided to do better. Let's see what he resolved to do:

I will sing of the times You extended your mercies to me, O Lord.

I will declare to everyone of how You mete out justice that is fair to all involved.

I will behave wisely before everyone I meet.

At home in front of my family, I will walk with a

heart of devotion to You. I won't dump my troubles on them but will treat them as You would.

I will set nothing evil before my eyes. I will shun the very appearance of evil.

I will not participate in any evil or wicked scheme. That kind of dirt will not be on my hands.

In the remainder of the chapter, God replies and states emphatically that He will destroy those who secretly slander their neighbor. It is hard for God to stomach those who have a haughty look and possess a proud heart. He will banish those who lie whether a lot or a little. None of the evil doers will enter the city of heaven.

The eyes of the Lord will carefully follow the faithful of the land. Someday they will live with God in the sweet by and by. The saved will serve the Lord and live in this world but will not be like the world.

July 22

"I am like a pelican of the wilderness; I am like an owl of the desert. I lie awake, and am like a sparrow alone on the housetop." Ps. 102:6-7

The pelican is not created as aerodynamically correct as an eagle. Yet the pelican can fly two feet above the water for miles. Their pouch or craw holds the fish yet they can strain the sea water out and retain the life supporting food. They may fly in pairs but seldom associate in flocks. So they are solitary birds. In our crowded world, there are multitudes of people but most of us feel oddly unique like the lonely pelican. There are families who cause their members to feel lonely even in their own homes.

There are times we feel like an owl. The owl seems to twist its head 360 degrees in search of food and or keeping vigilance for an enemy. Some search hour upon hour for pleasure, a good time, or some gratification. Others are climbing the social ladder and keep their unblinking eyes on those in the office aiming to bring them down. Still others live in crime infected areas and must be ever on guard for thieves, crooks, and murders in order to prolong their life.

The Psalmist says that sometimes he feels so little. His comparison is to a lonely, defenseless, vulnerable sparrow sitting all alone on the gable of the house. God is in heaven far away. All the other snow birds are flying around socializing but here it sits all alone on the roof of a house. He neither experiences the boundless freedom of being in the trackless limitless sky nor down on the ground where the food and animals are.

Whether we feel odd, like the pelican, wary and afraid like the owl or lonely and defenseless as a sparrow, the God who never broke a promise, said he would never ever leave neither us nor the birds alone. Hallelujah!

July 23

"Bless the Lord, O my soul; and all that is within me, bless his holy name! Bless the Lord, O my soul, and forget not all his benefits: "   Ps. 103:1, 2

Have you ever made a vow or resolution to yourself? Was it to lose a certain number of pounds? Was it to exercise **every** day? Was it to keep a positive attitude at work? Was it to keep forgiving and loving toward a family member? Maybe the vow was to practice the presence of the Lord every minute of each day.

You were and are in good company. The Psalmist of old declared his weak self-discipline too. He commands his soul to "Bless the Lord." He goes even farther and urges his entire being to proclaim praises to Almighty God.

The Psalmist gave order to his mind to both now and continually praise the name of God. A name during his era of time held the power and authority. YWH, Yahweh was so sacred that the Jewish people did not dare try to pronounce God's name. So the Psalmist thought it was an ultimate honor to raise such a holy name.

The Psalmist thought that repetition would be a good way to program his subconscious to remember the vow he made to bless the Lord. Every time he noticed a blessing or benefit from God, he was reminded to praise the Lord from the bottom of his soul. Our scripture did not tell us how successful he was in his continual praise to God.

How would you like to join me in following the example of the Psalmist? Let's challenge our mind to remind us often to praise God. Oh, come on, be a good sport and try it for at least twenty four hours and see if God changes us or anything in our life.

July 24

"He will not always strive with us, nor will He keep his anger forever. He has not dealt with us according to our sins, not punished us according to our iniquities. For as the heavens are high above the earth, so great is His mercy toward those who fear Him; as far as the east is from the west, so far has He removed our transgressions from us." Ps. 103:9-12

Could God accuse us of continually and intentionally breaking his commands? The Psalmist knew many who were rebellious and stubborn about obeying all that God wanted them to do. Here he warns them to be careful because God **does** have a limit. After that limit, Sodom and

Gomorrah, for instance, was dealt severe punishment.

The last half of our scripture describes the inexhaustible mercy of our loving God. First of all, God has not dealt with us according to all our lies, times we stole, people we cheated, and not made restitution. How about the time we intentionally did what we knew for sure was a sin? Like you, I'm glad God is not sending me to the Lake of Fire for stealing those green apples or those watermelons, especially since I confessed them.

You and I might forgive someone three times but would we forgive others as many times as God has forgiven us? We have to stop and think about that one, don't we? If that stretches our mercy, the Psalmist emphatically proclaims that in comparing our mercy to God's, his is the distance from earth to heaven more merciful than we are. Can you even imagine a forgiving spirit that enormous? Oh, how wonderful to be serving a God who is not mad or vindictive but showers us constantly with love and mercy. Are you glad you are a child of the God of Israel?

July 25

"As a father pities his children, so the Lord pities those who fear Him. For He knows our frame; He remembers that we are dust." Ps. 103:13-14

The Psalmist compares the Lord to a father. He is our heavenly Father. Many virtues are needed to be a father.

Our Lord is sympathetic to the needs of his child. Sympathy boils to the top when one of his children tries hard but is incapable of achieving the task.

God extends help to his children starting with two fingers for the baby to hold on to while they learn to walk. This mercy continues through marriage or stages of setting up house.

The Father is patient as we young Christians try to be like Jesus. The Heavenly Father's long-suffering nature endures to our last breath.

The Lord has delegated the Holy Spirit to guide us. He lives within us and guides our attitudes, our financial strategies, and our social conduct.

As our dad sets up and enforces boundaries for us as an adolescent, so our Lord chastises us when we stray and sin. This discipline comes when it is justified or physical punishment when it is due. Our Heavenly Father is more than glad to reward us, when it is appropriate.

Our Heavenly Father does not regard love as weak. Each day in many ways He lavishes love upon us. There is never a time that we should doubt his love for us. Many earthly fathers are buddies, friends, and yet a father is the authority figure in their children's life.

God is the great provider. He provides for your father to make a living and provides for all our needs. On top of that, God cares for all the animals of the world.

What a great dad we have! What a wonderful Father our Lord is!

July 26

"As for man, his days are like grass; as a flower of the field, so he flourishes. .... But the mercy of the Lord is from everlasting to everlasting on those who fear Him, and his righteousness to children's children, to such as keep his covenant, and to those who remember his commandments to do them." Ps. 103:15, 17-18

Would you like to leave a sizeable inheritance to each of your children? I mean three million in stocks and half a million in liquid assets? Oh, wouldn't that be nice!

You might say, "I don't have a ghost of a chance of leaving that much to my kids!" The Psalmist gives us the recipe of how to leave an even greater inheritance than three and a half million dollars. Are you ready?

First, we parents need to fear God. In other words, we need to confess our sin, as the Holy Spirit brings things to our mind. God will then forgive us of all unrighteousness. After we have given God all our sins, we give our body, mind, and soul to Him. Through this process we become a blessed child of God instead of being a child of Satan. While going through this transforming experience, we become thirsty for righteousness. Personally, I couldn't get enough of reading the Bible. That lasted for several months. The more we learn from his Love Letter the more we want to please God by obeying everything we read in the Bible. Then God's mercy and righteousness will follow every action of our life.

After becoming a Christian, blessings begin to flood our life. The Psalmist promises an inheritance of God's blessings to our children which exceed three and a half million dollars. The wonderful part is this inheritance extends to all your grandchildren. Isn't that better than giving them gold, silver and money which can cause the children to squander or create bitterness and strife? This inheritance is so much more enduring. The most wonderful part is you'll enjoy your children and grandchildren's presence throughout eternity.

July 27

"Bless the Lord, you his angels, who excel in strength, who do his word, heeding the voice of his word. Bless the Lord, all you his hosts, you ministers of his, who do his pleasure." Ps. 103:20-21

Visualize yourself among the angels who are praising God! At first glance, we see row upon row of angels and archangels standing around in the holy presence of the Heavenly Father. Next, we notice that some have their arms raised in adoration while others are on their knees with faces to the ground in humility and the remainder is singing celestial music that harmonizes with the joy that is within us. Strange, how we feel in one accord with all who are worshiping God. Several of you have experienced that feeling at one time or another in a worship service.

Upon further observation, we see strong well-built angels who have sufficient strength to defeat all the imps of Satan. Their rich baritone voices can clearly be heard among the other singers. Some angels leave to do the will of God on earth. Oh, how we wished we might instantly obey God when the Holy Spirit urges us, like his angels do. Other angels keep arriving from fulfilling God's promises to his saints.

All these angels are blessing their God and Creator. Likewise, God wants all his saints to praise him as sincerely as the host of angels we visualized. It is a real pleasure to God, when we bless and praise Him continually. The Lord actually inhabits the praises of his people. If we consistently praised God, God would be near us and within us. Wow, what a magnificent thought and that it could be an actual reality!

July 28

"He sends the springs into the valleys; they flow among the hills. They give drink to every beast of

the field; the wild donkeys quench their thirst."
Ps 104: 10-11

Do you have a busy life? Are you so busy you have to have a Day-Timer or palm pilot to remind you of all your engagements? If you think your life is a rat-race, let's look at God's daily schedule.

He has to get the sun up at the precise time each morning.

He has to keep you breathing, as well as, everyone on earth.

When someone dies, God takes care of all the grieving family members.

God listens to every prayer as the earth rotates. He then must decide whether to say no, yes, or postpone the answer. I've never known his answers to be late.

Oh, by the way, God keeps track of every hair in every head around the world. He can give you an exact count at any time.

God translates every language of each prayer and completely understands.

God keeps the bacteria and viruses in balance.

He also keeps the animal population in balance.

God feels our pain, as well as, all others and sympathizes with us. Sometimes he heals us.

He performs miracles every hour. He creates from two cells babies who not only look like their parent but act like them, too.

An even larger miracle is, if we confess our sin and trust God, He can take the blood of Jesus and cleanse our soul completely. No human or earthly power can do that!

Let us thank God for being our Father and Father for everyone on this earth.

July 29

"He waters the hills from his upper chambers; the earth is satisfied with the fruit of your works." Ps. 104:13

People of the Old Testament always thought of God as living up there. He took care of the earth from up there. Remember this is before his only Son came to earth to give us a better idea of who God really is. So the Psalmist states that God opened his upper flood gates and let the water fall as drops upon the earth to help the vegetation to grow. When the waters failed to come at the appointed times, it was a sign of his displeasure with the actions of humankind.

The earth flourishes and brings forth abundant crops most of the time. That is when the farmers, fruit growers, and cattlemen make a profit. We, like the earth, are satisfied with God's control of the weather.

Another area in which God pours out his blessings is on the fruit of our labors. If we are lazy and fail to plow and plant, we reap a measly harvest. But those who diligently work, invest thought, time, and effort, God blesses with salary increases and sometimes satisfaction of a job well done. Many mothers receive a great pleasure in watching their children take on many socially accepted personal skills. Parents really enjoy seeing their children marry and raise wonderful families, especially when in their growing up years doubts frequently arose as to that possibility.

Though all of life, we, like the Psalmist, can say, "God blesses and we are satisfied with the fruit of Your works".

July 30

"These all wait for You, that You may give them their food in due season. What You give them they gather in; You open your hand, they are filled with good. You hide your face, they are troubled; You take away their breath, they die and return to dust. You send forth your Spirit, they are created; and You renew the face of the earth." Ps. 104:27-30

How truly independent are we? How dependent on God are we? I can do my work at the job, but what if God erased your memory? I can feed myself but what if your nerves failed to function? I am a good business man but what if God gave you only part of the plan? So we can quickly see that God provides for us to make or earn our food.

When a pay raise, blessing, or windfall comes our way, we often call it a coincidence. We need to give the praise to Almighty God. When He opens His hand, we take and enjoy each precious blessing.

It doesn't take much trouble to occur in our lives before we begin wondering if God is upset with us. It is even worse, if God removes his protecting hand from us. A man came to work yesterday and told me that the night before last he was at a funeral home talking and joking with a friend. By the next morning his friend was being worked on at that same funeral home. That is how quick God can remove his protecting hand.

There are times when the world seems to be caving in on us, and then God breathes his spirit into our chaotic situation. O what a relief it is, when God lifts the burden! The winter period of our life changes into a budding, blossoming, and blooming time. Oh, how gracious our Lord is!

Some senior citizens have seen these periods appear and reappear throughout their long tenure on earth. Praise be to the Lord for his faithfulness to all generations.

July 31

"You hide your face, they are troubled; You take away their breath, they die and return to their dust. You send your Spirit, they are created; and You renew the face of the earth." Ps. 104: 29-30.

Many of you can remember the day Mount Helena erupted. The Psalmist may have heard about Mt. Vesuvius. It filled the sky so it was dark at mid-day. The vegetation was burned, scarred, or crushed. It was useless ecologically. After a few rains and spring rolled around new sprouts shot though the fly ash.

The Psalmist used a similar situation. When God turns his back and doesn't listen to our prayers, we get disheartened. Working on our own, we soon get discouraged. During our down time, we look for and truly enjoy the smile of God.

At anytime God could stop our breath. When God moves, we are helpless. Our spirit departs and our body dies and begins to decay. In time that corpse turns to dust.

When God gives us attention, we light up like a kid at a surprise birthday party. When God sends blessings our way, our life blooms as the American Beauty Hybrid Tea Rose. It is similar to living an entirely new life walking in the sunshine of God's love.

August 1

"You send forth your Spirit, they are created; and You renew the face of the earth." Ps. 104:30

The story of mankind begins with the earth being without form and shrouded with darkness. The waves lapped on the shores in the jet black of night. The Spirit of God hovered over the earth changing the atmosphere from the gloom of evil to brightness of day.

During creation as the words were spoken, things were created out of nothing. Animals and vegetation were brought into existence. All things were created. Nothing was made; all was created as the Psalmist states.

Mankind is foolish and careless with the use of the earth on which Adam and Eve were created. We pollute our streams and rivers. God sends the water over rocks and re-purifies and aerates the water. If that does not do it, God has it evaporate, condense, and send it back as pure rain water.

When man carelessly starts a forest fire or God sends lightning, it scorches the earth. It looks desolate, but the next spring flowers start to grow. The following year seedling trees poke their little green head up to renew the land.

When we seemingly ruin our lives with alcohol, drugs, or pornography, God can cleanse it from all sin and all unrighteousness. After that process, God recreates within all of us a new soul, one that is soft and submissive to the will of God. Hundreds in prison of Columbia, South America have had their souls recreated and are living a righteous life.

God renews nature even when we abuse it. God renews our spirit even after we have rebelled and disobeyed God's commandments. If you haven't already, let God renew your soul today.

August 2

"Oh, give thanks to the Lord! Call upon his name; make known his deeds among the peoples!" Ps 105:1

Mr. William Carie was happy with his life as a cobbler in England. He was making a contribution to society by manufacturing and repairing shoes.

As he read the Bible, the Lord high-lighted several scriptures about sharing the gospel aboard. Today's scripture may have been one of them. Against the prevailing thought of his day, he gave up his business and sailed to India. There he preached until he got sick and had to return home. He went unto the uttermost parts of the world.

David Livingstone left his home and family and headed into the heated jungles of Africa. He was sure that without Christ they would not make it to heaven. The command of "Go ye therefore and make disciples of ALL NATIONS..." was uppermost in his heart.

The Psalmist recalled the days when King David reigned over all the neighboring states. The King was neither timid nor afraid to make known all the mighty deeds of the God of Israel. For such a powerful king, he was humble before the Lord. He knew that all good and perfect gifts come from God. This he proclaimed among all peoples of his kingdom.

We may not be great. We may not be powerful. We may not even be wealthy. But we can make known all the good things God has done in our life. That is not hard to do. It only takes a little courage. The benefits are multiplied, when it returns to us.

This week let's make up our mind in one way or the other to tell someone about how great God is. Pray that if God gives us the opportunity, we'll have the bravery to speak up. If we can do that, we are a missionary to the people we live with.

August 3

"Glory in his holy name; let the hearts of those rejoice who seek the Lord! Seek the Lord and his strength; seek his face evermore!" Ps. 105:3-4

We are to glory in the name of the Lord. To do that, one should stand in awe of the majesty of the Creator of the Universe. Some earthly people might be in awe of: Queen of England, Billy Graham, Joel Osteen, Robert H. Schuller, Barack Obama, or U. S. Supreme Justice. Their prominence and their fame cause us to be humble in the room with them.

Our hearts rejoice in their achievement. Let this same feeling of joy spill over when we are in the presence of the Lord. We can rejoice because he loves us, cares for us, and dwells in us. Be happy! This happiness is enduring, not temporary or momentary. Be happy through and through.

For those who have never experienced this feeling of joy, the Psalmist directs us to seek the Lord. The scripture seems to say that God is most easily found through humility and contrition. Those, who seek the Lord with all their heart, will find Him (Deut. 4:29). If at first you don't succeed in finding God, keep trying for God is ever present. If we seek, we shall find (Matt. 7:8).

The initial question might be, "Where are you looking for God?" If we following the desires of our natural inclinations, that will lead to evil. If we are reading lewd books or watching filthy television, God will not be found there.

We must turn our eyes upon Jesus. His name is glorified through the hymns of faith. His love letter, our Bible tells of his will for our lives, explains the extent of his love, and forecasts our eternal destination. The Psalmist concludes by urging us to seek His face evermore.

August 4

"He sent a man before them – Joseph – who was sold as a slave. They hurt his feet with fetters. He was laid in irons. Until the time that his word came to pass, the word of the Lord tested him." Ps 105:17-19

The Psalmist today is using hindsight. He is looking back many generations to one of his forefathers. Joseph's life was lead by God. Like us, he could not imagine why he was sold into slavery by his own brothers. His oldest brother, Reuben tried to help him escape before the traders came along. The traders bought and took Joseph to Egypt and sold him to the general of Pharaoh. Why did God permit him to be a slave, when he could have stayed in the family and been treated like a prince by his father? Through the affliction, Joseph learned to trust God and be faithful. The general's wife got him put in prison. There they put his neck and feet in stocks. How could a guy, who trusted God and did right, end up like that?

Even with cases like this, the Psalmist came to the conclusion that God guides his children, you and me. While things are adverse rather than pleasant, God is working that to our benefit. Different facets of our character are being strengthened. After the crisis, we, like Joseph, are better prepared to handle the reins of leadership. Maturity produces in us a more steadfast personality and much less likely to fall to evil temptations.

The Psalmist noted, when God thinks we are done, He will take us out of the oven of affliction and/or trials. God can then effectively use us, if we make ourselves available, as Joseph did.

August 5

"That they might observe his statutes and keep his laws. Praise the Lord!" Ps. 105:45

How many different instances in your life can you recall, when God really blessed you? I mean the times you would call it a miracle. No one but God could have saved you! Did you fall a long distance and yet have no back injuries today? Was it a head-on collision where four were injured and two killed? You were one of the slightly injured. Was it the time your child had a dangerously high temperature but the fever broke with no damage to their brain? These came to you that you might have more reasons to follow the commands of God and obey the prompting of the Holy Spirit.

The Lord blessed the Israelites. First, God brought them out of 400 years of slavery. Next God made the mud hard on the bottom of the Red Sea and the million plus walked through the dust to the other side. Following that God lead them with a cloud that air-conditioned the desert heat in the daytime and a pillar of fire to make it comfortable sleeping each night. Next, they wanted some meat to eat so he sent quail whose breast is eighty percent of its body. To go with that God sent manna every morning so they could have sandwiches of bread and meat. After the Israelites complained a lot, God caused a spring to pour forth enough water to quench the thirst of the approximately one point six million Hebrews.

After they reached Canaan, God blessed the work of their hands as they planted olive trees, grape vines, and wheat in their new land. God performed all of this for them so they might learn and obey all the commandments of God.

God has blessed us abundantly. The least we can do is praise God with our voices and our actions.

August 6

"Praise the Lord! Oh, give thanks to the Lord, for He is good! For His mercy endures forever. Who can utter the mighty acts of the Lord? Who can declare all his praise? Blessed are those who keep justice, and he who does righteousness at all times!" Ps. 106:1-3

Can our actions be judged good or bad according to the situation in which they occurred? Can all our actions be relative according to the people present and what impression it makes on believers, as well as, non-believers? Would a white lie or stretching the truth be a punishable offense, if the whole truth would emotionally damage the person we are talking to? Is it alright with God, if we withhold some of the facts to keep ourselves from taking the blame or punishment?

Will God hold us guiltless, if we keep our promises, obey his commandments, and maintain our temper 97% of the time? That is almost always! Would God be upset, if we told the truth all the time except to one intimidating person or the person we dislike? How similar to offer you 97% pure mountain spring water and 3 % ditch water?

Our scripture today states that God's blessings will fall on those who don't compromise, give favors, or pronounce unfair judicial discussions advantageous to the rich. God promises more than happiness. Blessings are the divine fulfillment to those who consistently, without fail, live a Christ-like life.

The Psalmist gives us a start on living a Christ-like life all the time. This may be too simple for us. Praise the Lord always. Never fail to give God thanks for every blessing, small or great. Such living keeps the presence and power of God's spirit near us. Take a minute and remember and the enjoy the times God has blessed us in our life? The Psalmist tells us that we will never run out of things to praise God for.

August 7

"We have sinned with our fathers, we have committed iniquity, we have done wickedly. Our fathers in Egypt did not understand your wonders; they did not remember the multitude of your mercies, but rebelled by the sea – the Red Sea." Ps. 106:6-8

Is there anyone who can say, 'We have not sinned along with our forefathers'? Have we held ill-will against someone (Deut. 15:9)? Do we put something we own ahead of our love for God (I Kings 12:28-30)? Have we sinned by not following God's orders as printed in the Bible (II Kings 21:11-13)? Do curses and lies pass through our lips (Ps 59:12)? Have we broken a promise to someone or God (Ecclesiastes 5:4-7)? Did our eyes see things that caused us to sin (Matthew 5:27-30)? Did we ever rebel against God and do evil even though we were well aware it was a sin (Job 34:37)? Have we intentionally done something that we were positive a friend considered a sin? That is a sin on our part (I Corinthians 8:9-13). All sins lead to spiritual death (James 1:13-15).

Since Jesus came, there is a cure or remedy to the sin each of us may have committed (Heb. 10:12-14). Jesus willingly gave His sinless life so we might be cleansed as white as snow (Heb. 9:26). His precious blood washes our souls clean (I John 4:7). If we confess our sin, He will faithfully and willingly forgives us of every sin we ever committed (I John 1:9). Christ has the authority to cancel sin (Matt. 9:6). After our spiritual cleansing, we will be blessed as Christians because we will be constantly dispensing love and kindness as Jesus did (Proverbs 14:21).

Let us not sin, do wickedly, nor commit evil deeds as our forefathers did. Instead, let us humbly come before our Heavenly Father asking for his mercy, his forgiveness, and his blessings on our lives. Today, let us live as Jesus would like.

August 8

"When they envied Moses in the camp and Aaron the saint of the Lord, the earth opened up and swallowed Dathan, and covered the faction of Abiram." Ps 106:16-17

Do you recall what it took to bring down the wrath of Mom and Dad on your head? Did it really light your Dad's fuse to dent this car and not tell him but wait for him to find it? Then the explosion came! What was the hot button for mom? Was it to sass or defy an order that she gave you to do? Her voice would go up three notes, the voice volume tripled and the veins would pop out on her neck so her face got nearly as red as a beet.

As the Psalmist peered back into history, he was somewhat amazed at what actions made God red in the face. He takes us back to the wilderness walk in the history of the children of Israel. They had a few people who were jealous of Moses and Aaron. As the people got on board with them, these leaders became more envious of Moses being the leader of the million plus Israelites. Others were jealous of the authority of Aaron. This stirred the wrath of Almighty God to the boiling point.

Moses had those particular families assemble out in the field away from the other Israelites. All at once God cracked the earth open like a nut. Momentarily, they were suspended in space. Then the men, their wives, their children and their possessions including their cattle fell down into the crack. Moments later it came back together like a clam. God's blood pressure dropped back to normal. Now you and I know what it takes to keep God on an even keel. Don't be envious or jealous of the leader whom God has appointed over you.

August 9

"They forgot God their Savior, who had done great things in Egypt, wondrous works in the land of Ham, awesome things by the Red Sea. Therefore He said that He would destroy them, had not Moses his chosen one stood before Him in the breach, to turn away his wrath, lest He destroy them."   Ps. 106:21-3

When was the last time you came face to face with fear? Did it seem as large as Goliath?

The children of Israel came to the border of Canaan and were afraid of the Amelikites. It only took about ten days from the Red Sea to Canaan. The whole nation believed the report of the ten negative scouts, even though Caleb and Joshua gave a glowing report. God got angry and said "No one over twenty years old now shall step foot on the land blessed with milk and honey". Moses told them what God said yet they disobeyed God and said, "We will now go into Canaan because God said we never would". Like a child the children of Israel want to march into Canaan. Moses, the priests, and the Ark of the Covenant stayed in camp. A group of Israelites took off to go into the land from the south. The two kings routed the Israelites and chased them back to Hormah. So Moses took the people back toward the Red Sea and wandered a year for every day the scouts took to spy out the land.

God may not punish each of us that severely when we face fear and turn around. Caleb knew God was going to help them capture their giants of fear. He will do the same for you and me. When the Holy Spirit urges us to witness, to tell others about Him, or go where we have never gone before, He will accompany us. When God sends us forth, who of any consequence can be against us? We are more than conqueror through Him who loved us and gave his life for us.

August 10

"But complained in their tents, and did not heed the voice of the Lord. Therefore He raised his hand in on oath against them, to overthrow them in the wilderness," Ps. 106:25-26

In the United Methodist Church, they have district superintendents. Each one has oversight of approximately 100 charges. Some charges are one church. Some are as many as six churches. At the annual conference in June, one district superintendent passed out buttons that had, "Thou Shalt Not Whine" on them.

God gets just as frustrated, irritated, or disgusted with whiners, gripers, and complainers. The Israelites were complaining in their tents that all they had was bread (manna) to eat. Finally, God got his belly full of this complaining. He told Moses He would sent so much meat on the wing that they will gorge themselves until it comes out of their nose (Numbers 11:19-20).

God is just as displeased when we do not follow his ten commandments. All the blessings God promises are conditional. If we listen and obey, God will dispense blessings our way. Often God can not bless because we are not fulfilling our part. Our indifference arouses the anger of God.

"Enough is Enough" has been used lately by protesting groups. God gets to that point at times. In this case, he said to the children of Israel I will raise my hand and take an oath to overthrow you in your complaining and indifference to my love for you.

Today, when we catch ourselves complaining, remember that makes God upset. Let us stop, no matter how we can rationalize the reasonableness of the complaining. Each time we succeed in stopping, God may smile on us.

August 11

"They did not destroy the peoples, concerning whom the Lord had commanded them, but they mingled with the Gentiles and learned their works; they served their idols, which became a snare to them." Ps. 106: 34-6

Are we following the ways of the world? Is it okay because everyone is doing it? It is alright to break the law as long as you don't get caught, right? Is it permissible in God's eyes to trade spouses? Are you sure an alternate life style is sanctioned by God since thirty percent of the world is doing it? The religions of Canaan infiltrated Israel urging the people to present their babies as a sacrifice to Moleck. We, in like manner, have let the world under Satan's control guide our children. Many are ingesting or inhaling harmful chemicals to damage the house that God built for us to live in. It's okay to cheat in business because it is a 'dog eat dog' world, right? All contractors use second grade material and charge for prime products. The speed signs are like the ten suggestions that God gave Moses on Mount Sinai.

I am afraid that all the above are not true! All who sin will die, both physically and spiritually. God wants his children to be peculiar person, which means be different than society. God hears those who have a pure heart and clean hands.

Children of God use accurate scales. Those who lie are children of the Evil One. It is as simple as that. Blessed are the pure in heart for they shall see God. Born again Christians walk in the light as He is in the Light and have fellowship with the Lord. Jesus sacrificed his life on the cross because of the hardness of the hearts of humans. God's original plan was for us to live like his son, Jesus.

Let us not rationalize our behavior but follow the true Word of God as the Holy Spirit reveals it unto us. Could we start now – this very moment?

August 12

"Nevertheless He regarded their affliction, when He heard their cry; and for their sake He remembered his covenant, and relented according to the multitude of his mercies." Ps. 106:44-45

Have you ever called on God when sickness, disease, and pain were pelting you like a sleet storm? Hey, God! Hey, down here! Look at my condition! Can't you see how bad I'm hurting? Come wipe my brow and heal me!

The Psalmist says we don't have to get God's attention. He loves us so much that He is ever aware of our needs. He pities us when we are in distress and hears any call of distress we might make. We don't have to pray like God is half deaf. He is as attentive to our need, as a new mother is for the cry of her first baby in the bassinet.

God remembers the contract He made to never leave us nor forsake us. Isaiah mentioned that God answers our prayers before we finished praying (Isaiah 65:24). God has adopted born again Christians into his family. He will never abandon his own!

God possesses an limitless amount of love. Can you imagine that if you were the only one to sin in the world, Jesus would die just for your forgiveness? Wow! Because of this extraordinary love, He searches for those who are hurting. His compassion is perched out on his sleeve, so to speak. It only takes a little hurt for God to reach out his big burly arms to hug us and chase the fear away and relieve the pain.

So today if you are in pain, God is aware of it. He feels for you and if it is His will, He will kiss it away. Rely on God because He will do what is best for you.

August 13

"Oh, give thanks to the Lord, for He is good! For his mercy endures forever. Let the redeemed of the Lord say so, whom He has redeemed from the hand of the enemy." Ps. 107:1-2

"Let the redeemed of the Lord" speak up. Who are those considered "redeemed"? In the Old Testament, it was the persons who had presented an animal sacrifice as atonement for any and all their iniquities and transgressions. The redeemed or saved in Jesus' day are those who believe that Jesus was the Son of Almighty God. Since Jesus' death and resurrection, the Christian is one who has confessed their sin and permitted God to cleanse them of all unrighteousness. At that point a personal relationship develops and grows stronger between the saved and the Savior. Similar to a parent and a child, the two continually seek for ways to please the other.

The parent is always proud to proclaim to the world, "That's my son or my daughter". Just as some children are rebellious and publicly disown their ancestors, so the Psalmist noticed that some children of God fail to speak up for their Savior. So he asks each of us Christians to speak up at the store, the office, and out on the job. Could it be possible that if we are ashamed of Jesus here on earth, He will be ashamed to claim us as his child before all the angels in heaven? Hey, I don't want to take a chance on being embarrassed up there and be sentenced to down there. How about you?

So let's take the admonition of the Psalmist and publicly speak up and claim Jesus as our Lord, Savior, and King.

August 14

"Let the redeemed of the Lord say so, whom He has redeemed from the hand of the enemy," Ps. 107:2

The Prophet Hosea married a woman. She was unfaithful in the relationship. To redeem Gomer, Hosea had to give fifteen pieces of silver, five bushels of grain and some wine. She was rightfully his again. Hosea had redeemed her.

God gave us life with the intentions that we would honor Him with our life. We began by being selfish, then overly ambitious and finally greedy. We forgot completely about God. Then the Heavenly Father sent His only Son, Jesus to earth. His death on the cross was the price He paid to redeem us.

Gomer should have been happy to have good food, a roof over her head, and someone who loved her. She wasn't even grateful. After Christ redeems us from sin, we should be thankful. But how many times do we gripe about having to go to church, being strapped down to all the rules in the Bible, and want excitement instead of the peace Jesus places in our heart?

The Psalmist gives us a prod in the posterior to perk us up for God. He asks us to remember that

God lifted our feet from the stinking miry clay of sin. We should be thankful before our friends. He has set us on a path that leads to eternal glory. When we are in church and the joy of God comes upon us, let us sing loud or possibly shout. When we recall how Jesus is already building a mansion for us over there, songs of praises, Christ-like actions, and words of testimony should boil out of our lives, like lava from on active volcano. May our spiritual light shine so people will know we are Christians this week.

August 15

"Let the redeemed of the Lord say so, whom He has redeemed from the hand of the enemy,"
Ps. 107:2

Has the Lord redeemed you from a life of sin? Has there been a time in your life, when you felt burdened by the wrong you had done? At that point, you told God you were sorry for all those actions and promised to change your way of living. You believed that Jesus was truly the Son of God. At that moment, you felt your burden lifted. You fell in love with Jesus Christ. You loved Him more than anyone you had ever met in all your days. It was your main desire to do things that made Him happy.

If this experience has come into your life, then speak out. Tell others that Christ has saved you from sin. Relate how joy has replaced guilty feelings. List the blessings you now receive daily. Recount the happy days since you were adopted as a child of God. Could you speak up and tell others that God promised you could spend all eternity in heaven? Could you describe how God snatched you from the slippery slope heading to a hot destination? Happily convey to them how eager

God is to do the same for them. Wouldn't an endless fiesta be better than eternal heat and endless torture? Articulate how blessings now flows out of your mouth as easily as curse words used to. It is almost an unconscious action because you love God so much!

I would feel guilty, if I kept how God has saved me from sin a secret from the world. How about you?

August 16

"Those who sat in darkness and in the shadow of death, bound in affliction and irons – because they rebelled against the words of God, and despised the counsel of the Most High, therefore He brought down their heart with labor; they fell down, and there was none to help. Then they cried out to the Lord in their trouble, and He saved them out of their distresses. He brought them out of darkness and the shadow of death, and broke their chains in pieces. Oh, that men would give thanks to the Lord for his goodness, and for his wonderful works to the children of men! For He has broken the gates of bronze, and cut the bars of iron in two." Ps. 107:10-16

Have you enjoyed the heat of the warm sunshine on your back on a cool March day? Then all of a sudden you walked into the shadow of a building. Wow, what a difference! The Psalmist compares this to living in the radiance of God's presence and entering the shadow of our mortal finality.

Sin binds us with bronze hand cuffs and our legs with iron shackles. God in Christ frees us to serve in love, not in slavery and drudgery. With Satan there is no one to help us when we fall and fail. Satan can control of our senses. With Christ is instantly available. We can always be victorious! God never leaves us to walk the road of life alone. Like the apostles on the road to Emmaeus, he accompanies us and makes our hearts rise up within us.

O how the Psalmist yearns for each and everyone to give thanks to God. Thank Him for delivering us from the bonds of sin, changing our destination from hell to heaven, and splashing wave upon wave of blessings onto our lives.
God is good – All the time
All the time – God is good.

August 17
"Then they cry out to the Lord in their trouble, and He brings them out of their distresses. He calms the storm, so that its waves are still. Then they are glad because they are quiet; so He guides them to their desired haven. Oh, that men would give thanks to the Lord for his goodness, and for his wonderful works to the children of men! Let them exalt Him also in the assembly of the people, and praise Him in the company of the elders." Ps. 107: 28-32

A beloved pastor friend of mine last Sunday opened the morning worship with a time of testimonies. He bemoans the fact that only one person had been blessed enough to stand before his peers and tell what God had done for him. Were the others not blessed or were they afraid to stand up for Jesus?

Many of us have cried out to God in our distress. Our merciful God miraculously brought us through, yet we failed to tell others. Some families have gone through marital and childhood storms that only Almighty God could calm, why don't we testify to that? Oh, how glad we were when peace and quiet finally prevailed! Oh, what a relief it was! Have we taken time to thank God? How long has it been since we have testified even to friend about the wondrous things that God has performed in your life?

Take the challenge with me to search for any opportunity to tell someone how God has blessed us. Since we haven't done this before, we may have to observe for a day or two. Oh, maybe God will provide that chance the very next person you encounter. We may have to be brave and speak up in Sunday School class, just to give God glory and honor for His love and blessings.

August 18

"O God, my heart is steadfast; I will sing and give praise, even with my glory."   Ps 108:1

Do you trust your friend? Would you trust them to drive your new car? One more question, would you trust them with your wallet, checkbook, or credit card? If you can say 'yes' to all the above, you have confidence in your best friend.

The Psalmist went one step farther. He trusted his heart, life, and future to God. That is 100% confidence! He had no doubt that God could watch out for his welfare. So his heart was steadfast with no idea of changing.

In other words, he had no worries. He didn't fret about what might or might not happen each day. Being worry-free, he had time and the inclination to hum, whistle, or sing hymns and gospel songs. Many search for songs that have praise words in them like: Alleluia, Glory, Hallelujah, and Amen. How good it feels to praise the God who created us, guides us, and protects us.

Wake up my soul and attribute all glory to God. Don't wallow in self-pity, depression, or low self-esteem. Stand up, soul, look to God whose smile feels like warm sunshine. Any glory we get from our achievements, performances, or compliments, let us direct that glory to our Savior and Lord. When persecutions come or people make fun of us, we definitely look to God. When times were good, the Psalmist had an earnest desire to divert all glory and words of praise from himself to God.

August 19

"Do not keep silent, O God of my praise! For the mouth of the wicked and the mouth of the deceitful have opened against me; they have spoken against me with a lying tongue. They have also surrounded me with words of hatred, and fought against me without a cause. In return for my love they are my accusers, but I give myself to prayer. Thus they have rewarded me evil for good, and hatred for love. Set a wicked man over him, and let an accuser stand at his right hand."   Ps. 109:1-6

Have you ever been in a long term situation that ground you down? Trials were creating a stress level of ten. The problem never seemed to take a rest. Finally, you began pleading with God to listen to you and relieve you of all this internal pressure and external conflict. God didn't immediately answer nor did He intervene after thirty prayers. You were desperate for help. Problems continued to mount and constantly upset you. In complete exhaustion you flop across the bed in prostrate form and mentally yell, "God, do not keep silent! Oh, Lord, change THEM or if You have to, change me."

Most of the time, we tell God that the trouble is coming from people we love or have been more than generous to. We haven't in all our life given them the slightest reason to do what they are doing to us. They are returning the good we did for them with evil. We have loved them through thick and thin, and then they act like they hate us.

Prayer: Lord, only You can right this crisis of mine. If it please You, give them ulcers or trip them up in the scheme they set for me. I also give You permission to change me to help release the stress that is in my life. Please, Lord, take out your ear plugs and don't delay. I need your assistance now! Thanks, Lord. Amen.

August 20

"Let them curse, but You bless; when they arise, let them be ashamed, but let your servant rejoice. Let my accusers be clothed with shame, and let them cover themselves with their own disgrace as with a mantle. I will greatly praise the Lord with my mouth; yes, I will praise Him among the multitude. For He shall stand at the right hand of the poor, to save him from those who condemn him."   Ps 109:28-31

If we feel the world has singled us out to pick on us, listen to the Psalmist litany of woes. The evil people tried to demean and belittle him. They told lies about him. Many of them are experts at pushing the Psalmist hot button and their spiteful tongues really hurt. They seem to get a pleasure out of picking on an innocent person. These cruel people continue to try to destroy while the Psalmist attempts to love them and pray for them. They return evil for the good. The Psalmist does good for them in return for their hatred. He attempts to love them, but these gossips keep hounding him.

The Psalmist's Prayer to God.
God, let them curse me -- You bless me!
When they attack me -- Let them be disgraced!
My life shows love for You – make their humiliation obvious to all.

It is my firm decision:
Lord, help me to continue rejoicing.
I will give repeated thanks to you, O Lord.
I promise to keep praising You before everyone.
In conclusion:
Save me because of your unfailing love.
Save me for I am condemned by others.
Amen

August 21

"Let them curse, but You bless; when they arise, let them be ashamed, but let your servant rejoice. Let my accusers be clothed with shame, and let them cover themselves with their own disgrace as with a mantle. I will greatly praise the Lord with my mouth; yes, I will praise Him among the multitude. For He shall stand at the right hand of the poor, to save him from those who condemn him." Ps. 109: 28-31

Don't you enjoy this metaphor the Psalmist uses? "Let my accusers be clothed with shame, and let them cover themselves with their own disgrace as with a mantle." So often we don't want bad things or a terrible tragedy to happen to our enemies but we sure would like for the world to see them for what they truly are. Especially let it happen to the person who lets us do all the work and then takes all the praise for it in front of the boss.

The Psalmist said we should have an "attitude adjustment". Nothing changes attitude, like praising God or a session of thanksgiving. Let us make a mental decision and say, "I will greatly praise the Lord with my mouth." That's more than just thinking happy thoughts. It takes courage in hard time to verbally praise God.

You and I both know the character of God. He is loving and kind whether we are nice or mean.

He is always forgiving and full of mercy especially when we are down. He sends peace when we lest expect it. He pours joy into our heart when Satan would have us sulk or live with depression. God is so good to each of us that we should be ashamed of our attitude most of the time. He is faithful even when we intentionally disobey Him instead of doing what we know is right. He is preparing a place in heaven for all his children. Hopefully, we have permitted Him to cleanse any evil from our heart so we now enjoy a vital relationship with Jesus Christ now and later in heaven.

August 22

"Your people shall be volunteers in the day of your power; in the beauties of holiness, from the womb of the morning, You have the dew of your youth." Ps 110:3

Just as God hears our calls for mercy, the Psalmist feels like we should hear the cry of the sick and hurting. We should extend mercy, not judgment nor condemnation, no matter how well deserved we think it is.

God's compassion is like grandmother's home-made biscuits, new every morning (Lamentations 3:22-23). His tenderhearted concern never runs dry. I marvel especially at the nurses on oncology wards. Their love goes out every day with the full knowledge that their patient may die before they return. The passing of their patient profoundly affects their emotions, similar to the affect as one of their family. Still they routinely lavish love and dispense compassion on their patients. What a great human example of compassion!

When we are tired, compassion is difficult to locate within and share outwardly. God promises to provide strength as we have need. Therefore, if we search within, we will find compassion for the poor and the hurting. The strength that comes from above can assist us in loving enemies, as well as friends.

This kindness and love emanates from God's heart of love. Our love first dwelled in God, who loved us first. The compassion that flows from us should be humbly distributed. Our attitude will not be arrogant but gentle and merciful. Our compassion will show through our good deeds.

Compassion forms in an atmosphere of holiness. Holiness is a lifestyle that duplicates or attempts to reproduce the sinless life of Jesus. Holiness is everyday, not a holy moment in our lives. To live this holy life, we must shun every evil and pursue every noble and worthwhile action. As we continue with this mind set, the way of holiness becomes somewhat easier. What a joy comes from being Christ-like!

August 23

"...In the beauties of holiness, from the womb of the morning, you have the dew of your youth." Ps 110:3b

The beauty of holiness is an intriguing phrase! What would the beauties of a pure Christian life be? Holiness is being holy before God. Not only is it a state of being but a way of life. One of the prophets called it a highway of holiness (Is. 35:8).

The beauties of holiness can be seen in saints of the Lord. Do you presently know a saint? Or do you recall an aunt or grandparent who truly lived a holy life? There was a serene joy in all they did. It was similar to happiness but continued despite pain, or adverse conditions. Kindness and consideration surrounded them like a magnetic field. They somehow made you feel important.

That part I can't explain.

This outstanding saint you remembered matured from a new-born Christian like you and me. Each day they searched God's Word to discover truths they could incorporate into their lifestyle. Each improvement made them more like Jesus. When the Holy Spirit would high light a trait in their personality that might hurt the cause of Christ, they would eliminate that from their life. The longer they walked with God the more they looked and acted like Jesus. The slightest indiscretion seemed to wound them. Corrections, apologies, or confessions were quickly done. They didn't want to hurt God. In fact, they did all they could to please their Savior.

Maybe they sang a song like, *Let the Beauty of Jesus Be Seen in Me.*

August 24

"Praise the Lord! I will praise the Lord with my whole heart, in the assembly of the upright and in the congregation." Ps. 111:1

How do we love and praise God with all our heart? Haven't we swung at a ball with all our might trying for a home run and missed? In basic training I tried with all my might to do one more chin-up for Drill Sergeant Douglas and failed. Haven't we loved our new born baby with all that was in us? The strange thing was I still had more love to give to my second child. I was almost positive I loved the eldest with all my love.

There are times in our lives when we try hard but there is always an ounce or two more of energy or dedication we didn't put out. One example is studying for a test. We could have concentrated a little more on our class notes. During a test our mind wandered instead of staying focused, so we lost 100% effort there.

The Psalmist wants us to praise God with all our heart. God wants us to love Him with all our mind, soul, and strength. We will find God, if we search for Him with all our heart.

St. James says if a person vacillates, how does he ever expect to get anything from God (James 1:6)? We must ask God and have no doubt. For he who asks, receives. He who seeks will find. The one who knocks, to him the door of opportunity will be opened (Matt. 7:7-8).

Soldiers of all wars who gave their lives loved their country with every ounce of devotion. Jesus loved each of us enough to lay down his life for us. Maybe if we focus all the love within us, we can praise God with all our heart. I invite you today to take the challenge that the Psalmist lays before us. Praise God with your WHOLE heart!

August 25

"The works of the Lord are great, studied by all who have pleasure in them."   Ps. 111:2

Who but God can create a sun that burns at thousands of degrees but hasn't burned up in 4,000 years?

Who but God can recycle water by the ton and hold it suspended in space?

Who but God can keep ice balls the sizes of golf balls to baseballs in that same space?

Who but God can create seeds that can be stored a thousand years in a pyramid but grow when planted?

Who but God can create a creature that weighs many tons and can submerge one mile deep yet live on animals as smaller than a radish seed?

Who but God can create humans capable of getting mad enough to kill another person yet compassionate enough to run into burning building to save a child?

Who but God can love a group of human beings so much He provided a pillar fire to warm chilly desert night air and give them a cloud to air condition the hot dry desert heat? Their original sandals were still in good shape after walking the desert for 40 years. He provided enough quail to feed one and a half million people daily.

Who but God could grow a seventy foot oak tree from something as little as an acorn?

Who but God can cause a boy or girl to fall in love so much that the rest of the world doesn't matter to them?

Who but God would send His only Son to take care of the sins of someone as insignificant as you and me?

August 26

"The works of his hands are verity and justice; all his percepts are sure. They stand fast forever and ever, and are done in truth and uprightness. He has sent redemption to his people; He has commanded his covenant forever: holy and awesome is his name. The fear of the Lord is the beginning of wisdom; a good understanding have all those who do his commandments. His praise endures forever." Ps. 111:7-10

God truly is "awesome!" Whatever He did or does is **always** right. Never is there a mistake nor has He ever said, "Oops." Every rule or principle that God inspired or Jesus said is as sure as the Plymouth Rock. You can stand on it with complete confidence.

God set down a plan for the redemption of

every person who has sinned. If we don't avail ourselves of the plan of salvation, we will be far away from God forever. What generosity to provide such a valuable sacrifice! Jesus was both holy and awesome. Who but Christ can cleanse us from all sin!

Magnificent is this Lord of ours! The Psalmist flatly states that when we hold him in awe, we begin to obtain wisdom. Our sage thinks books and learning are of lesser value or second rate as compared to observing God and how He works. God is first rate, when it comes to getting understanding. If we use the scriptures while walking through the school of hard knocks, we will gain understanding. For everyone who works this plan, God promises that they will achieve wisdom and understanding.

God's praise endures through all time. God so enjoys it, when each of us praises his name! If we refuse to praise God, He will cause the waterfalls, babbling brooks, majestic mountains or the dainty daisy to praise God in our place (Luke 19:40). The Psalmist is quite sure his praise will endure forever.

August 27

"The fear of the Lord is the beginning of wisdom; a good understanding to all those who do his commandments. His praise endures forever." Ps. 111:10

A friend of mine refrained from giving his heart to the Lord for over sixty years because he couldn't understand why we were to fear God. He spent his latter years in a nursing home in a distant state so I don't know if he ever surrendered his life to Christ. Here the Psalmist states that the fear of the Lord is the genesis of wisdom in our lives. God will generously give us wisdom, if we will but ask for it.

Understanding comes from keeping God's commandments. We are never to let anything on the earth become more important than God. We are to be content with God as an invisible God. As we speak, let's be careful to reverence God's name. If we must take our shift at work on Sunday, we are to rest another day in which we remember God. The rest of us should not fill each Sunday with business to the point of missing worship services. If we still have your parents, honor them to the best of your ability. Recount the good qualities of your parents/grandparents to your children and grandchildren. We are not to take the life of any person God has created. When a married person's mind goes to thinking lustfully about another person, we must stop those thoughts to keep from committing adultery. Children of God do not steal even a penny or any time from the company they work for. Integrity is your calling card. Neither will a Christian lie for any reason. Lastly, we must not want what others have whether antique or brand new.

As we begin receiving this new wisdom and new found understanding, let us continue to praise God. All praise belongs to the one who created us, saved us, and is building a mansion for us.

August 28

"Praise the Lord! Blessed is the man who fears the Lord, who delights greatly in His commandments." Ps. 112:1

What is our greatest delight during the day? Is it quitting time or school recess time? Could our greatest delight be coming home after work to our children? Could our most treasured moment of the day be the time we spend in Bible reading and conversation with God?

Hopefully, as Christians we thoroughly enjoy doing good things for others. Especially do we get a pleasure from helping others who really need assistance. Another area that gives rich rewards is being generous. Some can give money while others lend their talents and skills. Others of us can only afford smiles and our cheerful spirit, but we are generous with them.

God wants us to be liberal with our mercy. In other words, we can be lavish in showing compassion to those near us who are hurting, depressed, and lonesome. Sometimes it may actually cost us financially, but we enjoy showing our concern for the hurting.

Blessed is the person who delights in living a righteous life. Oh! How God enjoys pouring out blessings on those who are determined to love Him and obey any and every suggestion they find as they daily search their Bible. Another suggestion is to lend freely. We mentally know we can't out give God. The more seeds of generosity we sow, the greater our harvest. If we enjoy serving Jesus, God, the Father guarantees to open his door to happiness, joy, and serenity.

August 29

"Praise the Lord! Blessed is the man who fears the Lord, ...Unto the upright there arises light in the darkness;" Ps 112:1a, 4a

The Psalmist was contemplating one day. Instead of dwelling on the negative, evil, and bad, he got to pondering the life of the righteous.

Happy are the persons who consistently hold a respectful awe of God.

Persons who seem most happy are the ones who take a special delight in following God's will.

They get a distinctive pleasure from following Jesus.

God apparently not only blesses the Christian but also pours good fortune upon their children and grandchildren. Their whole generation is under the beneficent gaze of Almighty God.

The godly appear to have a divinely given ability or acumen, when it comes to finances. They always come out on the good end of the deal.

Outstanding community leaders never mention the good deeds they have done in the church, accomplished in the community, or how they secretly helped the poor.

It is a well-known fact that Christian businessmen deal fairly. It is acknowledged by all that Christians are generous when a need is noted.

It is strange how these upright people are never frightened at bad news. After much thought the Psalmist concluded they trust God completely. Christians have influence and honor everywhere they go.

How pleasant it has been to think about the blessing and influence Christians have!

August 30

"A good man deals graciously and lends; he will guide his affairs with discretion. Surely he will never be shaken; the righteous will be in everlasting remembrance." Ps. 112:5, 6

A good business man deals graciously and kindly with every customer whether they are pleasant or irate. One chain store has two rules for customer satisfaction. Rule one: The customer is always right. Rule two: When in doubt refer to rule one. Christians are like the business man who is always friendly to others. The business man is friendly so the customer will return. That translates into success or money. The Christian is cordial and courteous because Christ was gracious to them before they thought about giving their heart to God.

A successful business person is never too stingy with his profit for if he does his defeat is assured (Prov. 11:24-26). He lends and invests wisely to get a good return. When one is urged by the Holy Spirit to give money, God will multiply it and bring it back on every wave (Ecc.11:1). A minister friend calls that "need-seed". Only the Holy Spirit knows when we are to 'lend' to the Lord.

A respectable business consults counselors in making wise decisions (Prov. 11:14). Whimsical judgments or snap conclusion are not part of their character. Sound and prudent decisions keep him from being shaken when a partner splits, the stock market turns bear, or adverse economy comes.

A prosperous business is run on Christian principles. All the business principles are written in the Bible. The Creator of the World inspired its writing. So if you are in business or planning on founding one, take a serious look into the Bible. Then surround yourself with wise counselors, like King David and our present president did.

August 31

"...The righteous will be in everlasting remembrance. He will not be afraid of evil tiding; his heart is steadfast, trusting in the Lord. His heart is established; he will not be afraid, until he sees his desire upon his enemies. He has dispersed abroad, he has given to the poor; his righteousness endures forever; his horn will be exalted with honor. The wicked will see it and be grieved; he will gnash his teeth and melt away; the desire of the wicked shall perish." Ps. 112:6b-10

FEAR! Oh how some of us fear! Some of us have fears that even affect our digestive system enough to produce ulcers. Others of us have small fears and these are correctly labeled worries.

The Christian man or woman according to the Psalmist should not be afraid. Their trust in God should be so strong they don't fear phone calls, faxes, voice mail, or beeper calls. Whatever the message might be, God is going to turn it out to their good and God's glory (Rom. 8:28).

The born-again person has a steadfast heart. They have an abiding self-confidence and/or serenity that exudes a healthy well-balanced personality. With God on their side, how can they be otherwise? This Christian is not arrogant but knows whose they are and what they believe.

Those, who put their total trust in God, enjoy life. All who walk in God's ways will have their desires come true (Ps. 37:4). The Psalmist goes one step farther and says the Christian will even see their desires fulfilled upon their enemies. The righteous will gain authority and honor through their integrity. Evil persons will see their desires evaporate; their trouble will be so awesome they will grind their teeth. These servants of Satan will endure torture throughout eternity.

The Christian will be remembered after their demise. What a legacy to leave this world! It far exceeds a plaque or monument with our name engraved on it which no one reads.

September 1

"Praise the Lord! Praise, O servants of the Lord, praise the name of the Lord! Blessed be the name of the Lord from this time forth and forever more! From the rising of the sun to its going down the Lord's name is to be praised." Ps. 113:1-3

Could you pretend you are the American Ambassador to the United Nations in your seat in New York City in that beautiful building? Often you would call the President of the United States while he is in the Oval Office. As you talk together, you get the drift of what his goals are. When the council meets, you speak for the President. When you were ratifying a treaty, your signature is backed by the U. S. President.

We Christians are ambassadors for Christ. When we speak, the authority of God is behind it. According to these three verses our main job is to say good things about the One who formed us, who saved us from sin, and who constantly walks beside us. We are to praise Him always. Let us sing the praises of Jesus every day and everywhere we go. We never speak derogatorily of our Savior.

When we say, "I am a friend of our President" we have status in other people's eyes. The same is true when we state, "I am a Christian". Others look at us differently. Our actions as Christ's ambassador should always make Christ look good.

September 2

"The Lord is high above all nations, his glory above the heavens. Who is like the Lord our God, who dwells on high, who humbles himself to behold the things that are in the heavens and in the earth?" Ps. 113: 4-6

The Psalmist on this day was greatly awed by the immenseness of the God he was serving. God's reign is more than just over the Gentiles or Jews. God holds the venerable position of Lord over **all** nations. God is not only over us but all humanity on our tiny globe. The Psalmist realized that God was master of all the galaxies and universes, as well. We, humans are fortunate that God is humble enough to be concerned about our planet, and the welfare of each individual.

Often people of this world take his name in vain. Many live lives, like they drive their cars at night. They think that since they can't see the state policeman, he can't see us. Therefore, they drive at the speed they want. Some thoughtless people practice evil, as though God doesn't exist since they can't see Him.

Each of us should hold God in high regard. Could it be at times that we value ourselves more highly than we do God? Help us, Lord, to see ourselves as we ought! Help us comprehend how finite and insignificant is our place in the entire universe. This will surely invoke praise to Lord.

You, O Lord, are: august, regal, noble, overwhelming, and impressive. We should be: awe-struck, solemn, reverent, speechless, dumbfounded, astounded, and filled with wonder. After mediating a little, it seems we come to the same conclusion as the Psalmist. God is AWESOME!

September 3

"The sea saw it and fled; Jordan turned back. The mountains skipped like rams, the little hills like lambs. What ails you, O sea that you fled? O Jordan that you turned back? O mountains that you skipped like rams? O little hills, like lambs? Tremble, O earth, at the presence of the Lord, at the presence of the God of Jacob," Ps. 114:3-7

Isaiah was in the temple one Sunday. It was a regular trip to church but this Sunday it became the greatest service of his entire life. That day he stood in the presence of the Lord.

First, he saw that the whole sanctuary was filled with smoke. It created a sense of the awesome presence of Yahweh in the room! The feeling does not bring fear but the air was electric with anticipation! Similar to Moses, Isaiah just knew he was standing on holy ground.

Second, in this majestic presence, Isaiah realized his inadequate preparation and unworthy condition. After being cleansed by the fire of God from off the altar, he stood in the presence of the Creator.

In this anointed condition, the Psalmist spoke of nature. He visualized the feeling of the Red Sea when God's presence came close. Also he imagined the Jordan River backing up during flood time when the children of Israel walked across on dry ground. In his mind, he expressed the joy the hills might have had, when God comes close to them. They would skip and prance like rams and the little hills would act like frisky little lambs. All the earth would tremble and shake before the awesome majesty of Almighty God.

Can you imagine how you might react, if next Sunday as you step into the sanctuary you would enter into the glorious presence of the God of Israel?

September 4

"Not unto us, O Lord, not unto us, but to your name give glory, because of your mercy, because of your truth." Ps. 115:1

Have you worked your way up to foreman or supervisor? Good! Have you made your way up to vice-president? Great! Have you earned your way up to number one in wisdom, as well as, tenure in your department? Wonderful! Did you get the title of 'Mother of the Month or Year'? I am glad for you. The Psalmist was saying all the glory should go to God. None of the praise should go to us, our prowess, our financial acumen, or our pleasing personality.

There are two solid basic reasons to give God the glory. One good reason to praise God might be that his truth keeps us free. With the golden rule in effect in our life, many wrongs will be missed and many blessings garnered. God's truth is like a rock, it does not change. The situation in which an action happens does not change a right to a wrong or vice versa.

The second reason, God's unfailing mercy should call forth our praise. How often in our short life have we had to yell, "Help me, O God"? The Heavenly Father has always extended his long arm of mercy to us. God's mercy flows like a never ending stream fed by an underground spring. His heavenly mercy is never rationed but always generously bestowed on all who call for it.

The next time we brag, let us check and see if in reality the praise rightfully belongs to God. If it belongs to Him instead us, then we can redirect the praise and compliment God, who deserves **all** praise.

September 5

"But our God is in heaven; He does whatever He pleases." Ps 115:3

Some people of this world degrade God by lowering their opinion of God and addressing Him with nicknames or by adding negative modifiers to his name. Because they can't see God personally, they feel they don't have to honor or respect God. Since He is in heaven, they could care less how they treat him. How short sighted!

Sure God is in heaven and does whatever He wishes. God, like a king or president, does things that are good for their subjects or constituents.

Some earthly kings or rulers are insecure in their position and may kill or destroy people that are a threat to them. Our God is not so capricious. Everything He does is for his children's good. Sometimes He permits us to endure some difficult times, so we may grow stronger. During these times, he may skim off the impurities in our character. In Uncle Bud Robinson's day, they would cook sorghum. The farm hands would skim off the froth. He once stated that God kept skimming his life. He was afraid he would be all skimmings. A little humorous, but sometimes we may feel that way.

It is the wish of God that all should be saved and that none should perish nor experience the second death. So God, the Holy Spirit urges each of us to confess our sin and permit God to cleanse our soul from all unrighteousness. Jesus died to offer to everyone on earth eternal life in heaven. No human has to earn a right to heaven. For if there happened to be one handicapped person who was incapable of doing the good deed or earning their passage, God would be unhappy. It is through the grace of the Almighty and your faith in his precious blood that we can all make it to that wonderful land of endless day.

September 6

"O Israel, trust in the Lord; He is their help and their shield. O house of Aaron, trust in the Lord; He is their help and their shield. You, who fear the Lord, trust in the Lord; He is their help and their shield." Ps. 115:9-11

Have you ever marveled at how the men from the Federal Bureau of Investigation guard the President of the United States? They take his calendar and check out each place where he is to stay, his bedroom, and the cafeteria and/or chefs. Once while he is in New York City, one of these men watched from the roof of the apartment building where my son lived. Great pains-taking care is invested in the safety of the person they guard.

The Psalmist never witnessed such a protective team yet he explained an even better security system. First, of all the FBI has to change men every eight hours, while God is always awake. Second, the FBI has to learn the emotional and mental quirks of the guarded, while God knows our every thought. Third, the FBI only puts down someone who looks suspicion or brandishes a weapon, while God knows the meditation of every person whether for evil or for good. God can change their thoughts and intentions. Fourth, the FBI only follows the guarded person while God can lead the President around harm. Fifth, the FBI must stop the enemy before the bullet is fired, while God can send an angel to deflect the bullets even after it leaves the muzzle of the weapon.

The Psalmist assures us that God not only can shield us from all forms of harm but is an ever present help in our time of need. So every one who is a born-again child of God has this ultimate protection, greater than anything the government could arrange. So let us not fear what others might do to us, but rest comfortably and unmolested in the loving protection of Almighty God.

September 7

"You, who fear the Lord, trust in the Lord; He will be their help and their shield." Ps. 115:11

Do you have the right qualifications? If you are a current member of the AAA, they will tow your car, when your car breaks down. If you are a member of the country club, you can use the swimming pool. If you have the right clearance on your swipe card, you can get into the Pentagon. If you are of the right political party, you can sit on the inaugural stage with the brand new president.

May I mention one more qualification? If you hold God in awe and truly trust him, He will help you in trouble and will even shield you from harm. The central question then is do you meet that qualification?

Most of us must meet Christ personally though urgings from the Holy Spirit before we can comprehend the awesomeness of the Almighty. After we have an inkling of the grandeur of God, we will have a high respect for Him. Sometimes this awe is portrayed as fear.

Again when Christ has cleansed our heart, we will instinctively put our hope and dependence in Him. One indicator of our trust is how much or how little we worry? If we trust instead of worry, God promises to help us. There is no time limitation in our scripture. So it must mean that any or every minute of our life, God will be willing to help **us.**

Another advantage the Christian has is that God will shield us from many of the storms of life. When the temptation to do wrong is very severe, God will step in and shield us so it will not be more than we can withstand (I Cor. 10:13).

So let's take advantage of this promise of help by holding God in awe. Don't worry, trust God.

September 8

"I love the Lord, because he has heard my voice and my supplications. Because He has inclined his ear to me, therefore I will call upon him as long as I live." Ps. 116:1-2

I love the Lord because his son, Jesus died in my place on Calvary.

I love the Lord because when I confess my sin, He always forgives me.

I love the Lord because He loved me before I loved him so I might be attracted to God's salvation.

I love the Lord because He is building a mansion for me over there.

I love the Lord because He is leading me in the paths of righteousness for his sake.

I love the Lord because He hears and literally answers my prayers according to his perfect plan.

I love the Lord because He has supported me during the death of one very close to me.

I love the Lord because He supplies my every need while he listens to and some times provides my wants.

I love the Lord because He continuously walks beside me and lives forever in my heart.

I love the Lord because He protects me, when I walk through dangerous places.

I love the Lord because He surrounds me with people to love and people who love me.

I love the Lord because He keeps molding me into a mature Christian.

I love the Lord for His love is unconditionally given.

I love the Lord, because he hears my prayers and answers my requests.

Like the Psalmist, I will call upon the Lord as long as I live!

September 9

"Because He has inclined his ear to me, therefore I will call upon him as long as I live." Ps 116:2

Some fortunate people have in their possession a personal letter from the President of the United States. Those persons hold them in very high esteem. I have an aunt that has treated me as a little grown-up from the age of ten. For the last fifty five years she has been my favorite aunt on my mother's side.

The Psalmist remembered an especially trying time in his life. He called on God. The prayer of desperation was answered. The gratuitous act of God was so appreciated that the Psalmist vowed to continue praying to God as long as he had breath.

Has there been a harrowing experience in your life where you weren't sure you would live? Oh, maybe it was a rubrics cube type problem where there seemed to be no satisfactory answer. God in His infinite wisdom worked out the knotty problem or extended your life.

Would you be willing to make a promise to God because of his goodness to you, that you will serve him the rest of your life? Would it be a qualified promise? Yes, Lord if it is not overseas, nor the slums of town. I will honor you as long as the children live at home but come retirement I want my freedom to travel. Of course, I promise to pray to You as long as I live, but don't call me to teach a Sunday School class, to lead the congregational singing, or to preach.

Let us rid ourselves of fear and like the Psalmist in utter abandon promise God. With our whole heart we will serve God every minute the entire length of our lives. If you do, you'll find, like I have, that it grows sweeter as the years go by.

September 10

"The pains of death surrounded me, and the pangs of Sheol laid hold of me; I found trouble and sorrow. Then I called upon the name of the Lord; 'O Lord, I implore You, deliver my soul!' Gracious is the Lord, and righteous; yes, our God is merciful. The Lord preserves the simple; I was brought low, and He saved me." Ps. 116:3-6

Dear reader, are you now or have you ever experienced a situation where your life was crumbling down around you? Your marriage was rocky, if not on the rocks? Your credit card debt was way ahead of you with no additional money in sight. Your children or at least one of your kids was being resentful and rebellious. Maybe the stress was causing life-threatening symptoms. The Psalmist describes these symptoms as the pains of death. Everywhere he looked he found either more trouble or additional sorrow.

At this point in our lives, we ought to think of God, not be searching for a way out. When the Psalmist looked, he observed that God was good despite our breaking his rules. His manner was constantly gracious. What a relief to serendipitously discover God's kind face and all our trouble be gone! We simply need to ask for help. During our trials, God will hear our prayers. Jesus put forth the mandate that we must ask to receive (Matt. 7:7, John 16:24).

The Psalmist humbly admits that after he got himself in a fix and was at the end of his rope, God saved him. Our God is the same yesterday, today, and forever. So if we will humbly ask God, He will deliver you or me from the cauldron of trouble in which we are slowly stewing.

Come on; let's put our trust in God today. Let the power of God rescue us from disastrous personal relations, debt, unemployment, and/or marital strife. Our Savior has done it for others! Have faith that God will do it for you.

September 11

"Gracious is the Lord, and righteous; yes, our God is merciful. The Lord preserves the simple; I was brought low, and He saved me. Return to your rest, O my soul, for the Lord has dealt bountifully with you." Ps. 116:5-7

How have you been brought low? Were you happily married for many years and suddenly and unexpectedly your spouse walked out? Were you involved in an accident and spent weeks upon weeks in the hospital? Did an illness cause you to be in rehabilitation for over three years? Did an injury take away your sight or your hearing? Our Psalmist had been there and found the answer for getting out of the bottom of the barrel.

The Psalmist trusted in God with child-like faith and He lifted him up. Worries were left unworried because the Psalmist knew for certain that God was going to bring the causes for oppression to an end. With that confidence, he could keep his worry switch on 'off'. If the trouble or trial wasn't removed, God would give him strength to endure until God was ready.

After the Psalmist was back up on an even keel, he talked to himself. He said, "Soul, return to your rest." In other words, "Don't get back into the mess you were before, but continue trusting in God, who is in control. Rest comfortably in the arms of the Lord." That way you can keep your worry switch on 'off'.

As he reminisced, the Psalmist began to realize how God had his eye on him the whole time he was low. It was marvelous in hindsight that God cared that much for him. That's why he closed his thoughts for today with, "The Lord has dealt bountifully with him." I pray you can echo his words.

September 12

"The Lord preserves the simple; I was brought low, and He saved me." Ps 116:6

As you know, sheep are defenseless. They simply nibble on grass and grow hair. They can't outrun a fox, or bite the wolf nor claw the bear. The Lord provides protection for them. Similarly, we have no real defense against our spiritual enemy, Satan.

The Psalmist admits he stumbled. You can be sure we will lose against Satan. The Devil enjoys putting us between a rock and a hard place. Satan often gets on our case. At that point, God springs over the wrestling ring rope. He rips Satan off of us. In so doing, we won the match. How wonderful to have a tag team partner that is always ready to leap over the rope and help us whenever we are spiritually penned! He's never too busy playing to the crowd but always mindful of our condition.

Earlier when we were headed for Satan's hot paradise, God bounced into the ring and touched us. He said, "Be spiritually healed." Through confession, scripture reading, and prayer, let us stay on God's team with the tag team member who has never lost a match. He is the Champion of Love.

September 13

"I will pay my vows to the Lord now in the presence of all his people." Ps 116:14

Why in the world do I owe God? He let me be born into this awful existence. Doesn't He owe me? If I overuse my credit cards, He is obliged to furnish the wherewithal to pay it off. I don't remember making any promises to God I have to keep, do you?

As a born again Child of God, I owe him a lot. Among my co-workers I will work hard so they will glorify my Heavenly Father. I will not use any words that cast any negative reflection toward God. I will honor God with the first fruits of my paycheck. In front of the whole congregation I will give the first ten percent of each paycheck. Not only will that show others how to tithe, it will keep the continual temptation to be greedy or overly ambitious out of my life.

At each opportunity I will brag on my Heavenly Father, just like I complimented my earthly dad. In church, I will use my voice to say and sing, "Hallelujah to the King." What a way to praise God, like the Psalmist constantly urges us!

We surely owe God our love. We can pass along the love God gives us to others. What the world really needs now is, "Love, Sweet Love". As God has forgiven me, I should forgive others.

King David owed God faithfulness. Loyalty and faithfulness to a person or cause is a rarity these days. Hopefully, when things get tough, we will stand firm in the Lord.

If you made a vow or promise to God, like King David, you ought to keep that.

September 14

"I will pay my vows to the Lord now in the presence of all his people." Ps. 116:14

You probably are not a Korean War or Afghanistan/Iraq veteran that once made a promise to God when caught in an ambush. But did we in a time of dire circumstance make a promise to God: ...to ask forgiveness from another person? ...to tithe from this moment on? ...to read the Bible every day? ...to never break the speed limit, no matter what others do? ...to teach Sunday School class or take a job in the church? ...to never again abuse our body?

Well, the Lord can distinctly remember the circumstance and the exact words of our promise. He is still patiently waiting for us to keep our promise. If you think our promise was too rash and there is no way we can keep our word, God will graciously assist us. We must try, if we want assistance. If a baby never stands, they'll never be able to learn to walk. The same attempt applies to fulfilling our promises.

Maybe it would strengthen our determination, if we told our friends or family what we promised God and what we decided to do about it. One better, would be to tell this to our prayer meeting crowd or share group. They would not only hold us accountable, like our family, plus would intercede to God on our behalf.

God pledges to supply all our needs for strength, determination, and courage to tackle that promise. God specializes in things thought impossible and He can do what no other power can do.

The Psalmist was able to keep his vows to God in full view of the entire congregation. I pray we will be able to say the same very soon.

September 15

"Precious in the sight of the Lord is the death of his saints." Ps. 116:15

Saints of Old: Abraham, Isaac, Joseph, Joshua, David, Isaiah, John the Baptist.

Saints of the middle ages: Joan of Arc, Augustine

Saints of our time: Billy Graham, Norman V. Peale, Bishop Fulton Sheen

Saints of my time: Name the saints in your life

Precious are their lives and their deaths to the Lord. Their lives exemplified the character that God is attempting to instill in every one of his born again children. When we allow ourselves to be malleable, God molds us into persons He visualized when we were born. Reaching our maximum potential only comes when the Master Sculptor is permitted to work on us.

Once I had the honor of watching a professional artist work. He began with a wire formed in the position he wanted the final product. The process of adding began. Soon it took on the form of a human. The smaller lumps were then added for the cheeks, arms and legs. In time, it was an exact replica of a sixteen year old boy.

God starts us with some innate talent, a little fortitude for a backbone, and the core virtue of love. As trials come along, He adds patience, perseverance, and long suffering. Later tolerance and compassion are added in the right places in our character. One day our character took a direct hit from Satan and made a gaping wound. God packed it with a mixture of love and forgiveness. As we neared maturity our character began taking on a likeness of a saint. God is molding and making us because we are precious in His sight.

Jesus wept at Lazarus' grave and 'who knows' he may weep, when we die.

September 16

"Oh, give thanks to the Lord, for He is good! For his mercy endures forever '....Let those who fear the Lord now say, 'his mercy endures forever.'"
Ps 118:1, 4

God's mercy endures forever! God's forgiveness continues unabated. His pardon bears up through the years. The Lord's big-heartedness lives on and on. Yahweh's generosity fares well with use. God's liberality holds out against abuse and/or indifference. His compassion stays on and on like Vick's salve.m The Lord's patience never ceases. God's tolerance withstands changes in social morays. His tenderness lasts longer than chewing gum or car batteries. Our Savior's benevolence hangs in there through thick and thin. Our Intercessor's kindness continues to exist no matter what happens. The Lord's consideration persists despite the evil and ugliness of the world. God's thoughtfulness remains prominent.

We hurt God's feelings by rebelling and doing what we want, still He loves us. Oh, how can we be thankful enough for the mercy of the Lord, when we deliberately sin? God was generous in forgiving us when our friend talked us into doing something we were doubtful about. We felt awfully bad the Sunday we were indifferent to God's desire and slept in. God did not withhold his pardon for our lack of interest in his kingdom.

Let's thank our Creator for having mercy that endures no matter how badly it is abused. I believe we can agree with the Psalmist that his mercy does endure forever!

September 17

"I called on the Lord in distress; the Lord answered me and set me in a broad place. The Lord is on my side; I will not fear. What can man do to me? The Lord is for me among those who help me; therefore I shall see my desire on those who hate me. It is better to trust in the Lord than to put confidence in man. It is better to trust in the Lord than to put confidence in princes." Ps. 118:5-9

Are you putting your trust in the President of the United States to keep the economy rolling? Even though they may die tomorrow, you think they is what keeps our future bright. Even though they may have a multitude of sins hid in their closet that the news media has not found, you think his decisions are what will make your floundering business a success. Even though our congress is made up of frail humans, you believe their votes will keep our portfolio of stocks in a bull market.

The white haired Psalmist states that it is better to put our trust in God than feeble people. Legislators usually have their own agenda or welfare in mind, while God is always on our side. Strengthened with this confidence our worries and fears will evaporate. In the full light of God's presence the actions of people are of very little consequence to Him. Even if their actions were aimed at our destruction, God would turn these actions around for our good and for his glory.

In the midst of a scrimmage with his enemy, the Psalmist said that God lifted him out of the fray. God set him in a broad open field, like a tranquil pasture with contented cows happily grazing and our faithful dog by our side. If we keep our trust in God, He will do the same for us when our enemies on intent upon our downfall. Remember, that's a promise from the One who never breaks a promise.

September 18

"The Lord is for me among those who help me; therefore I shall see my desire on those who hate me." Ps. 118:7

There is a television station in our town whose motto is "WEHT, Channel 25 – On your side." Do you recall back in grade school at recess? We all ran to the fence and lined up. Then the two big kids chose teams. It seemed that we often wound up on the side with no good batters. We wished that so and so was 'on our side' then we were guaranteed a victory!

The Psalmist emphatically states that God is on our team. With Christ, we are more than conquerors (Romans 8:37). That means we ALWAYS win and win by a big margin. When times get tough, it not the tough that get going but the tough call on Jesus who is 'on our side.'

As you head out to work, bear in mind that the Lord is for you. There are unscrupulous co-workers who are not afraid to put you down to make themselves look good before the boss. Don't fear them, for guess Who is 'on your side'?

You will keep a fantastically positive attitude, if you could perpetually retain in the forefront of your mind the idea, "God is on my side". Nothing would be able to bowl you over emotionally. When you are emotionally up, look at what your productivity level is. With your increased productivity on a consistent basis, the boss will notice. Who knows? With "God on your side" you might get a promotion and raise in income.

As a child of God, let's start today constantly repeating "God is on my side" until it is indelibly imprinted in our subconscious. After that, we can walk worry-free because we know that finally we will win. Why? "God is on my side!"

September 19

"The voice of rejoicing and salvation is in the tents of the righteous; the right hand of the Lord does valiantly. The right hand of the Lord is exalted; the right hand of the Lord does valiantly." Ps. 118:15-16

    LEADER; God is good.
    Audience: **All the time**
    LEADER: All the time.
    Audience: **God is good**.

In our selection from Psalms 118, the repeat is for emphasis. The Lord fights valiantly. The Lord is therefore exalted. Remember the Lord fights valiantly to defend and protect us from the wiles of Satan and evil in this world.

Therefore, we should exalt the Lord. Since the Lord delivers us from many evils and keeps our feet from slipping into traps, we ought to sing praises to Jesus. Our neighbors and our friends should over hear our sounds of rejoicing. Do they hear grumbling and complaining instead?

If we would stop and think about the salvation we have accepted, we would sing and even shout. Shout? Yes, a camp meeting shout would be in order. To miss hell and all the torture should bring a song to our lips. Thinking of the ecstatic joys and fabulous comforts of heaven should be the cause for an authentic Christian shout.

For sure, those enslaved by Satan have no reason to rejoice, sing, or shout. So as a Christian, let's go out and rejoice in the rewards of the Christian life.

September 20

"Open to me the gates of righteousness; I will go through them, and I will praise the Lord. This is the gate of the Lord, through which the righteous shall enter. I will praise You, for You have answered me, and have become my salvation." Ps. 118:19-21

Do you have the privilege of remembering an old fashioned gap gate? It was a gate of a barbed wire. On one end there were two posts. On the top and bottom were two circles of barbed wire or other metal. A cowboy could stay on his horse and open and shut the gate. You lifted the ring on the top and pulled the post out of the bottom ring then draw the wire out of the way to let the herd through. After they are on the other side, he and the horse on the other side of the fence while still on the horse, he placed the post in the bottom ring and stretched the wire and put the top ring over the post.

We aren't sure what type of gate the Psalmist had in mind when he asked the Lord to open the gates of righteousness. Could it have been like your gate to the yard or garden or maybe one to the shepherd's sheep fold? In any case after entering the gate, he expected to start praising the Lord. Please recall the last time you deliberately praised God. Was it ages ago at a youth conference or was it as recent as last Sunday morning? I mean a time of praise when there is no ulterior motive other than blessing God. That sounds like a project you might want to try in the coming week.

Does the Psalmist know something we don't know about praising God? Is there serenity or an ecstasy that comes through sincerely praising God?

In summation, the Psalmist believes everyone should praise God, if for no other reason than because God had heard and answered our prayers. It is like saying thanks to your parents for all they have done for you recently or over a lifetime. Let's lift our hearts and hands in praise to the Lord!

September 21

"The stone which the builders rejected has become the chief cornerstone. This was the Lord's doing; it is marvelous in our eyes. This is the day the Lord has made; we will rejoice and be glad in it." Ps. 118: 22-24

Do you recall a time when someone made a simple remark that had an enormous affect on your lives? My grandmother said, "Dale, you are like your dad. You always finish what you start." Since then I have finished a Bachelor's degree, two Master's degrees and published a book which took thirty two year, I still marvel at how God has directed my steps.

The Psalmist was amazed, as well as baffled by such incidences. This was a foreshadowing of the time when Jesus would come and few would notice nor long remember his time on earth. God made Him the key stone in the arch of civilization. God's intervention into our lives was just marvelous to the Psalmist. It caused him to says, "This is the day the Lord has made; we will rejoice and be glad in it."

Instead of a mantra, let us take the Psalmist attitude for each and every day. Since God formed us in our mother's womb and created this day for us, let us rejoice and be glad all day long. God, who spoke the universe into existence, gave us one more day to live in. How much more personal can a God be? Could it be that if you were the only person in need of salvation, God would have still sent his Son to die to forgive you? Wow! How much more exciting or stupendous could it be? So how come we don't continuously praise and bless God throughout our day?

I challenge you to praise God one entire day. If you don't succeed, try try again. Who knows what blessings may be in store for you on the way or when you reach your goal?

September 22

"Blessed are the undefiled in the way, who walk in the law of the Lord!" Ps. 119:1

Happy are they who don't cheat on their income taxes.

Blessed are they who obey the speed limit.

Happy are they who don't yield to the pressure of their so-called friends and do what they know is wrong.

Joyous are they who keep the golden rule of doing unto others as they would have others do unto them.

Happy are those who aren't enslaved by alcohol, nicotine, or drugs.

Elated are those who try to keep the Ten Commandments

Happy are those who haven't gotten addicted to pornography.

Buoyant are those who give love to everyone and receive lots of love in return.

Happy are they who refrain from gossiping.

What a sunny disposition a person has, who loves their neighbor as themselves!

Happy are those who resist the temptation to put others down in front of the boss to make themselves look better.

A person is usually cheerful when they trust God daily. They are relaxed knowing God is in control of everything that comes into their life.

Happy are the people who don't think only of themselves but consider others better than themselves.

Content are those who love God with a dedicated love. Their main goal is to love Him more and more.

So today we can be blessed, if we keep undefiled from the sins of this world. The easiest way to a blessed life is to love God plus follow all we know of the Bible.

September 23

"Blessed are the undefiled in the way, who walk in the law of the Lord! Blessed are those who keep his testimonies, who seek him with the whole heart! They also do no iniquity; they walk in his ways. You have commanded us to keep your percepts diligently. Oh, that my ways were directed to keep your statutes! Then I would not be ashamed, when I look into all your commandments. I will praise You with up righteous of heart, when I learn your righteous judgments. I will keep your statutes; Oh, do not forsake me utterly!" Ps. 119:1-8

Why do I have to always do the right thing? Many of my friends cheat a little, lie a little, and do like the crowd a little. Why must I stay as clean as a spiritual whistle? No one ever says, "You are a good Christian." No one ever seems to notice my spiritual efforts, even my family. The Psalmist promised that God will reward you for living an undefiled life. Blessings will flow your way plus joy and peace will reside in your heart.

Another promise to those who keep the golden rule, as well as, the two great commandments is that God will shower you with good things that the wicked will never receive. These blessings will be in the physical realm, as well as, the spiritual area of your life.

There is a payday for all the care you take in walking physically in the path of God. Even though there are times you feel God has gone on a Florida vacation, keep stepping in the right way.

It is gratifying to look back over your day, week, or life and not feel ashamed of anything you have done wrong. At times like this, it is easy to thank and praise God for all his help along the way. How pleasant to sit in church and hear how God rules. We enjoy learning from God's word and the ways God mysteriously runs this world.

God promises to bless all your efforts in living for Him. Let's praise the Lord sometime today.

September 24

"Your word I have hidden in my heart, that I might not sin against You. Blessed are You, O Lord! Teach me your statutes." Ps. 119:11-12

How many scriptures can you recall that are hidden in your heart so you won't sin against God?

I will love the Lord with all my heart, mind, soul and strength. Deut. 6:4

Evil companions corrupt good morals. I Cor. 15:33

As a person thinks, so are they. Prov. 23:7

Love your neighbor as yourself. Matt. 22:39

Even though I walk though the valley of the shadow of death I will fear not evil. Ps. 23:4

Lo, I am with you always even till the end of the world. Matt 28:20

I will not worship anyone but God.   Ex. 20:3:
I will honor my father and mother.   Ex. 20:12
I will not steal.   Ex. 20:15
I will not kill nor assassinate another's character. Ex. 20:16

I do unto others as I want them to do to me. Matt 7:12

God always forgives me, when I confess my sin.   I John 1:9

Happy are the peace-makers for they will be called the children of God. Matt 5:9

Each day I try to remember it is a day You have made and try to rejoice in it. Ps. 118:24
Do not worry. Matt 6:34
God is always with me. Heb. 13:5
How many other scriptures did you think of that helps keep you in the center of God's will?

September 25

"Open my eyes, that I may see wondrous things from your law. I am a stranger in the earth; do not hide your commandments from me. My soul breaks with longing for your judgments at all times. You rebuke the proud – the cursed, who stray from your commandments. Your testimonies also are my delight and my counselors." Ps. 119:18-21, 24

O Lord, don't hide your commands from me. May I not hurry over things You want me to do such as: Transform my heart and renew my mind that I might do your perfect will (Romans12:2). Let our hearts be without covetousness and jealousy so we can be content with the things we have (Heb. 13:5). Do not let our body be saturated with wine, beer, and liquor but instead let God, the Holy Spirit be in us. Then we will sing hymns and gospel songs, praise God, and give thanks (Eph. 5:18, 19). Walk through life with our head held high as a child of the King. Don't let fear control or have a foot hold in our life. Fear comes from Satan who can put you in hell. Therefore, help us, Lord, to keep our faith in God and never fear so heaven can be our final home (Luke 12:4). Refrain from judging the actions and motives of others so we will not be judged with the same severity we judge (Matt 7:1). Let us permit God, himself to put his divine nature within us (Eph. 4:4-6).

With these truths refreshed in our mind, let's live an exemplary life for Christ. The next time we read the Bible, let us seek for truth that will keep us from sinning. When spiritual truths, rules, and commands of God are obeyed, God's wishes will not stay hidden from us.

September 26

"...Do not hide your commandments from me." Ps 119:19b

How many times have you read the Bible through and failed to see what they did with cattle rustlers (I Chronicles 7:21)? Did you notice in that same chapter of the woman who became a civil engineer? She planned and built three cities, naming one of them after herself.

Have we misinterpreted what we read? Is it the money or the love of money that is a sin? What killed Goliath of Gath, the stone or was it his own sword? Is it "Do unto others before they do to you or as you want them to do to you"? Are we born to love the same sex or is it actually a sin to lay with the same sex as you would with the opposite sex? Is it a tenth of our gross or a tenth of the net that we give to God? Are we to obey the laws of the government or can we remain a Christian and break the law as long as we don't get caught? If we get caught, then it is a sin.

Then there are some truths, and promises we may have forgotten.
Don't be lazy but copy true Christians. Heb. 6:12
Those who freely give will prosper. Prov.11:25
Do not commit adultery. Ex. 20:14
People whom you bless, God will bless.
Gen. 12:2, 3
If I sin, God will stop hearing my prayer Ps 66:18
God promises to always be near us. Heb.13:5
If we call on God, we shall be saved.
Rom. 10:9, 10

If we are pure in heart, we shall see God. Matt. 5:8
If I hide God's word in my heart, it will keep me from sinning.   Ps 119:11
God will supply all my needs.   Phil. 4:19
If we bring our tithe to church, God will bless us. Mal. 3:10
Love one another, as I have loved you. John 15:12
Confessing our faults to a true friend, helps bring healing.   James 5:16
   Lord, open my spiritual eyes that I might see the help and promises you have for me in the Bible.

September 27

"Remove from me the way of lying, and grant me your law graciously." Ps 119:29
   When we are adolescents, Satan tries to get everyone of us to lie. It seems the easy way out of a bad situation. As kids, we are not aware of nor is it apparent the punishment that comes with it. Even adults in the business world are tempted to say, "It's in the mail." We are convinced that the check has not yet been cut and won't be for three more days.
   In the 163rd verse of Psalm 119, the Lord states that he hates, even abhors lying. That's something when the Creator of the Universe states so plainly he hates something. Doesn't that show how powerful Satan is? It has been said that everyone lies each day in one form or another.
   King Solomon, the wisest man said that God loathes lying lips but delights in the words of truthful persons. Along with that pronouncement he said that we righteous persons should hate lying. If we hate this sin, we definitely will not participate in nor practice lying.
   St. Paul urges us to put away lying. Like Blind Bartimaeus we should throw off our dirty cloak of

sin, and come to Jesus. He can cleanse us of all sin. Just because God can and will forgive us of lying, does not mean we should go on lying to prove how magnanimous God is.

We know neither the day nor the hour Christ may return, so we ought not to let one lie slip through our lips today. Let's not miss heaven by lying to make a situation more convenient or avoid facing the truth of our actions.

September 28

"Remove from me the way of lying, and grant me your law graciously. I have chosen the way of truth; your judgments I have laid before me." Ps. 119:29-30

Do I have to tell the truth, the whole truth and nothing but the truth ALL THE TIME? In considering this question, let us ask one more question. How much stretching does it take for God to consider it a lie? Is it when you internally decide when it is not going to be the whole truth? When you begin to doubt whether this is the whole truth, should we then consider it a lie?

Sometimes children get in the habit of lying, thinking it is a shortcut. Sooner or later they experience the sting of their sin. If lying were of God, there would be a reward – not a punishment for lying.

Jesus personifies the way, the TRUTH, and the life. So if we want to be like Jesus and finally go where Jesus is, we need to be like Him. Jesus never sinned, and since he always spoke the truth, then we need to copy his example. The Psalmist lived long before Jesus and intuitively knew honesty was not only the best policy but the only way to live. So the ancient writer stated that he laid the scriptures out before him and absorbed the

Words of God so he would not sin. Without sin, he could enter heaven, which was his final destination. His sincere desire was for God to graciously engrave the commandments in his heart. That way he would, more or less, do God's will automatically.

Do our everyday plans coincide with the integrity of the Psalmist?

September 29

"Make me walk in the path of your commandments, for I delight in it. Incline my heart to your testimonies, and not to covetousness. Turn away my eyes from looking at worthless things," Ps. 119:35-37

To covet is to want something that belongs to someone else. Coveting is when you want your neighbor's spouse or their fancy red car. It is different to wish for another Cadillac like the one they have or wish for a girl or boy friend that has all the admirable qualities of your friend's spouse. The point is the wanting what is theirs.

A person who has gone through a tornado and instantly lost all their earthly possessions realizes how insignificant property and belongings are. Life is what is important! To God, your relationship with his Son, Jesus Christ is what is important. All the things we accumulate are worthless things. Collectors realize that their antiques or stamps are worth-less if there isn't someone who is willing to pay you or your heirs what the market says it is worth.

The Psalmist feels that it is really worthwhile to compel our self to walk in the ways of the Lord. He found it to be enjoyable, even fun; to do God's will every day. So often we are distracted by television ads and other advertisements. What we really need to do is to train our hearts and minds to listen to the subtle urges of the Holy Spirit. Let us also ask God to watch over the things we see and read, so we will not sin. Lord, also screen our wants so what we desire will be pleasing in your sight.

September 30

"Incline my heart to your testimonies, and not to covetousness." Ps 119:36

Just what does it mean to be covetous? One is greedy or grabby of what someone else owns. Covetous is being miserly, stingy or tight-fisted. At its worse, covetous people are lustful, lecherous, or have an unquenchable desire for what is not theirs. The core of that person is selfishness or an egocentric spirit.

This is the opposite attitude of the 'giving' Jesus. He gave bread to the hungry, healing to the sick, hope to the desperate, and his life for our salvation. Jesus was always thinking of others. So when we are covetous, we are doing the opposite of our Great Example.

The Psalmist realized that negative thinking does not glorify God. So his request was to have the Almighty make his thinking lean toward what is written in the scriptures. If we ask for wisdom, God will be liberal in his giving (James 1:5). With the amount of generosity we use, God will in turn pour blessings on us (Matt. 7:2). As we forgive others, God, in reciprocity, will forgive us (Matt. 6:14, 15). The promise is, if we give, it shall be given to us pressed down, shaken together, and running over (Luke 6:38). God is delighted with cheerful givers (2 Cor. 9:7).

God gives us examples of giving: He gave to the widow of Zarephath oil and meal to endure the famine. God gave King David a great and mighty nation to govern. Jesus gave life unto the son of the widow of Nain. God provided jars and jars of oil to the widow so she could pay off her dead husband's debts and keep her sons. God sent us prophets and preachers, so we could hear and respond to the message of salvation.

Let's abandon any covetous thoughts and lean always on the side of generosity.

October 1

"I remember your name in the night, O Lord, and keep your law. This has become mine, because I kept your percepts. Ps. 119:55-56.

Can you recall the number of times the Lord has awaken you in the middle of the night? As you came to, a person was laid on your mind to pray for. Has there been many times or just a few? Maybe you felt you were only awakened to see how many sheep you could count before sleep came to you again.

The Psalmist had a habit. When God awoke him, it was to pray. He recalls how he often laid on his mat and spent hours praying and conversing with God. It was a pleasure, not an unending tossing and turning.

Personally, I have learned that if one prays, Satan will personally put sleep in your eyes. For all the praying you do, will be detriment to his evil kingdom.

That takes care of the night time but the Psalmist also covers the daytime too. He says that he keeps all the commandments of God which includes: Return good for evil. Do to others as you would have them do unto you. Love others as God has loved you. Forgive as you have been forgiven. Love God with all your heart, mind, and soul. Love that cantankerous neighbor, as well as, our favorite relative. Pray without ceasing. Seek first the

Kingdom of God and his righteousness. Look always unto the Author and Finisher of your faith. As for me and my house, we will serve the Lord. Do not worry. Do not fear for God is with you even through the valley of the shadow of death. Rejoice always and again I say rejoice.

So day and night we can be in the divine presence of Almighty God, the Keeper of Our Souls.

October 2

"I entreated your favor with my whole heart; be merciful to me according to your word." Ps. 119:58

What toy was it we wanted so badly, when we were in grade school? Can we vividly recall how fervently we appealed to God on our knees by our bed? We begged, cajoled, pleaded, and almost cried to God in our prayers.

Then as a teenager, we implored God to send us the newest model car we could afford.

After high school we got a little desperate about a prospect for a husband or wife. We solicited God to send them our way. Every day they didn't show up and every night we would appeal again to God to listen to our prayers and PLEASE answer them.

When our first baby came along, we begged and called upon God to make him or her healthy. We would be eternally grateful and never complain just because it wasn't a boy or girl as we preferred.

Oh! How I remember strenuously entreating God to send money to pay the first semester of college and every semester thereafter. You know what? God did hear and answered those prayers!

God has been merciful to our family. He extends his mercy to us. The Lord loves us more than we love ourselves and for some of us that's a lot. In the Bible, it states that God promises to offer mercy and help to all who call on Him and love Him. The Psalmist was reminding God of that promise. Moses often reminded God of what He had done in the past and His promises. If a saint like that prayed this way, it behooves us to study the scriptures and be acquainted with what God promised to do.

October 3

"I am a companion of all who fear You, and of those who keep your precepts." Ps. 119:63

Summarization of the verse in today's words is, 'We run around with Christian's people, those who keep all the commands of the Savior and Lord. This crowd is always on the look out for those who claim to be Christian, not the ones who are involved in evil schemes of the Wicked One' (Matt. 7:15).

Our Christian friends guard against gossip about their friends and even their enemy. Idle talk is like poison to them. They would rather you say something good or positive about others than to ever put someone down. Seldom will Christians let slang words leave their mouth nor detrimental terms about our precious Lord (I Timothy 6:20).

Our friends are in the habit of looking for things for which to be thankful. This keeps them in a positive frame of mind, which results in a smile on their face. They are also sensitive to the urgings of the Holy Spirit (I Thess. 5:18-19).

The Psalmist also associated with those who abstained from lust and sexual perversion. Any action that doesn't bring glory to God is not practiced. Those actions that only gratify ourselves are avoided (I Peter 2:11).

Our companions consider their children as gifts from God. These gifts are to be trained and nurtured by word and example. It is 'do as I do,' not 'do as I say.' These friends are also bold to speak for the Lord (Eph. 6:4, 20).

It is much easier to live for Jesus, if we bum around with his adopted children.

October 4

"You have dealt well with your servant, O Lord, according to your word." Ps 119:65

King David was well blessed. We are well blessed. Some of us own more than one vehicle. What married person does not sport a gold ring? Every house now has an air conditioner. Many of us even cool every room in their house whether they go in there or not. Every member of the family has seven sets of clothes plus three or more pairs of shoes in the closet. Most of us can not recall the last time we missed a meal. All who are reading this have a roof over their head and comfortable bed each night. Each of us has adequate and available health and dental care. Oh, the blessings of watching our children grow and the added privilege of spoiling our grandchildren.

When troubles tumble our way, the Lord helps us through them or provides a way around them. When we have enemies at work, God sees to it that they finally get what they deserve. The difficult part is waiting on God's timing. During times of imminent danger and severe health problems, God deals wonderfully with us and stays near us. Even while we are unconscious on the operating table, God watches over us. There are times of joy: birthdays, wedding, anniversaries, and home comings. There were also wonderful church services when God's Spirit covered the service with peace.

When we stop to count our blessings, we begin

to consciously realize how wonderfully we have been blessed. At that point, we will definitely agree with the Psalmist in his admiration of God's generosity.

October 5

"Before I was afflicted I went astray, but now I keep your word.... It is good for me that I have been afflicted, that I may learn your statutes.... Let, I pray, your merciful kindness be for my comfort, according to your word to your servant. Let your tender mercies come to me, that I may live; for your law is my delight." Ps 119:67, 71, 76-77

Another version of the Bible puts it this way. "I used to wander off until you disciplined me; but now I closely follow your word." The Psalmist's desire is for God to teach him good judgment and knowledge. God's discipline or affliction always proved beneficial.

Do you recall when you were ten or younger? Mom called for us to come home. We were so interested in the game or playing with our friends that we disregarded her clarion call. The first time she reprimanded us. The second violation brought forth the board of education and we felt the heat thereof. The Psalmist said later that the paddling from God was good for him. He stated he had learned his lesson. We learned ours, right?

The Psalmist seemed concerned about the time he was wandering and away from God. Would the Lord be like the good shepherd and diligently search for him, gently lift him off the precipice of sin, and thorough cleanse him and put ointment on his spiritual wounds? Hopefully, God would take him back and forgive him of any and all transgressions. The Psalmist comprehended what God was teaching him. "Now that I am back with you, Lord, I will now study the Bible and faithfully follow what I read in it." The Psalmist openly declared that following the Lord would be a pleasure for the rest of his days.

October 6

"It is good for me that I have been afflicted, that I may learn your statutes." Ps. 119:71

Thank you, Lord, for the time I broke my leg. For through the healing process, I learned patience with myself and with my care-givers.

The Lord be blessed for the financial crunch in our family budget. This was the means for me to grasp the knack of trusting God for the next payment. God promised and supplied our needs according to all the riches in heaven.

Glory be to God for that disease that sent me to the hospital. The pain was severe. During the time of healing, I acquired a deep sense of gratitude. For years, I ran around with a healthy body and never once thanked You, Lord.

I can hardly believe I am thankful for losing my job. I was depressed and at first really angry at You, Lord and others. During that time I discovered the comfort of accepting help: dollars, food, and rides to the grocery. This important lesson was hard, for all my life I had been on the giving end.

Your name be praised for the car accident. Through the ambulance ride, the emergency room, critical care unit, hospital room, I determined to let gratitude replace my constant complaints and griping about the course my life was taking. Now I try to praise God the first thing of the morning and keep praise in the forefront of my mind while I walk life's road. Now that my knees are better I am trying to be more self-disciplined in my exercise regimen, as well as my spiritual welfare. Each day now I read my Bible and pray.

Thank You, Lord, for the troubles that have drawn me closer to You.

October 7

"It is good for me that I have been afflicted, that I may learn your statutes. The law of your mouth is better to me than thousands of coins of gold and silver." Ps. 119:71-72

How can the Psalmist say it is better to be on the bed of sickness than have thousands of dollars in pure gold or tons of fine silver? Sounds ridiculous, doesn't it? Let's check out our scripture.

The first sentence says that my sickness has been a blessing. The pain was not enjoyable. The mandatory quiet time in bed has blessed me into thinking how busy I have been making my way through life. It is so hurry-scurry that I forgot God and all that is in his Holy Word. Now I realize when and how long it was that I stopped thinking about obeying your commands in the Bible.

Next comes a reference to money and riches. After being laid on his back for a while, the Psalmist began to reread and recall all the promises of God. Take one for an instance. "If my people who are called by my name will humble themselves, and pray and seek my face, and turn from their wicked ways, then I will hear from heaven, and will forgive their sin and heal their land" (2 Chronicles 7:14). When we follow and heed promises like these, they are more valuable to us humans than piles of gold. Promises like these bring us peace and serenity not just passing pleasures mixed with strife.

It is profitable for all of us to mind the truths and promises that lie buried in the Word of God. When we follow them with a true heart, blessings beyond what riches can provide will begin flowing our way.

October 8

"Let those who fear You turn to me, those who know your testimonies. Let my heart be blameless regarding your statutes, that I may not be ashamed." Ps. 119:79-80

Blameless! How in all creation can one be blameless? Can one live without mistakes? If anyone is like me, they can be blamed without even doing any wrong.

Since we are not blameless, we must be reconciled – reconciled to the one we wronged, as well as reconciled to our Heavenly Father. That calls for us to humble ourselves and openly admit we were weak or wrong. It is so easy to blame someone else for our error.

One way to avoid blame or doing wrong is to be knowledgeable of the scriptures. Hopefully, each of us read it everyday. Often we read it to find ammunition for an argument. Other times we hurriedly skim it or have our mind locked in neutral. But we should actively look for ways to better serve God, as we read our daily devotions. It would help, if we read more than the small amount of unadulterated Word of God noted at the top of each devotion in the Upper Room, Daily Bread, or this devotion.

Our request should be to make our heart blameless. Our actions may not be blameless but our motives can be pure as the driven snow of a Nor'easter. If our motive can be pure and blameless then we can stand with a clear conscious and to be unashamed before others and our God.

October 9

"Forever, O Lord, your word is settled in heaven." Ps. 119:89

The Psalmist got bogged down in the inconsistencies of life. The economy was always fluctuating. His friends were truthful one time and the next advice was faulty and for their advantage. It is frustrating when people make you a promise to be there or to have such and such task done. When the appointed time comes, they are no where to be seen.

Haven't you had friends you thought were really your friend? Later on through the grapevine you found out they had betrayed a confidence. The Psalmist was weary of this kind of changeable behavior.

To give himself stability, the Psalmist rested on the Lord. God is settled forever and will not be changed. The Psalmist looked to the Creator, who was alive and well before our earth was formed. This old timer meditated on the God, who gave the Ten Commandments. The Psalmist looked into the future to when the Son of God would give the world the Beatitudes. Jesus would display the only example of agape love, the kind of love that gives with no expectation of return. The Psalmist liked the idea of a stable God, who existed before we were born and would continue long after we died.

This wise man urges us to lay our hope and trust on a God whose words are settled in heaven for all the eons of man's existence. Don't lean on nor steady our faith on changeable things of this world. Let's set our future only on the reliable and eternal word settled forever in heaven.

October 10

"I am yours, save me; for I have sought your precepts." Ps. 119:94

Lord, I'm about three (3) percent yours. When I am in a jam or pickle I immediately call on you, God. I remind You that You created me and You owe it to me to get me out of this crisis.

Dear God, I am fourteen (14) percent yours. Oh! Father, you know I go to church every Sunday and even stay for Sunday School. I keep your command to rest on the Sabbath. All Sunday afternoon I watch football or races in my lounge chair. When that super eager worker at work gets the boss mad at me, Lord, please rescue me.

That's not me! I pray to you four times a day. I pray over each meal and I put you in my schedule every night before I go to bed. Surely, I am thirty two (32) percent yours. So with that much commitment, Lord, protect me in that rush hour traffic.

I love you even more than the last person. On top of what they do, I am a member of the board plus practice and sing with the choir or praise group. My dedication shows and I am surely sixty four (64) percent yours. Please don't forget to save me when a heart attack hits me from overwork and stress of my getting ahead.

Lord, you and I met at an altar in my home church. There you cleansed me of all my sin, and placed your love in my tender heart. We have daily fellowship. I'm in the process of becoming one hundred (100) percent yours; I do what you tell me in the Bible. I so enjoy doing what the Holy Spirit urges me to! What a feeling of bliss to know I am in the center of your will. There are days I give only seventy-seven (77) percent of myself to You. My deepest desire is get to the point that I can say, "I am Yours" with utter abandon.

I am attempting to listen to and obey the Holy Spirit and keep every commandment I can remember because I love You.

October 11

"The wicked wait for me to destroy me, but I will consider your testimonies." Ps. 119:95

Often the bad people are out to do us in. They often think of the harmful things and scheme of ways they could hurt us. Many times people sit or stand around waiting for us to say some unchristlike thing or make a promise we can't keep. Then they confront us in front of all who will listen, how we flubbed up.

Others don't care about us. If they need to win, they begin rumors about us. Each rumor makes us look bad before the boss; but makes them appear to be an outstanding employee.

There are people who are envious of our position in life or our success. So these people are often out to make us look bad. In the process, their mediocrity looks better after their derogatory comments. Many times people in the political arena delight in trying to destroy their opponent across the aisle. We must be watchful of their mischievous and cunning ways.

We can depend on God to rescue us from the slavery of sin. Lord, your promises are great! You promised never to leave us nor forsake us (Heb. 13:5). You told your disciples You would be with them to the end of the age (Matt. 28:20). Those, who delight in the Lord God, will be given the desires of their heart (Ps. 37:4). Commit your ways unto the Lord and He will direct your path (Prov. 3:5.6). If you seek, you will find. If you ask, you will receive. If you knock, it will be opened unto you (Matt 7:8). Where two or three of God's children are gathered together, God will be in their midst (Matt 18:20). God will supply all your needs according to his riches in glory (Phil. 4:13).

Let us get our eyes off wicked people and turn them to all that God has promised us!

October 12

"You, through your commandments, make me wiser than my enemies; for they are ever with me. I have more understanding than all my teachers, for your testimonies are my meditation. I understand more than the ancients, because I keep your precepts. Your word is a lamp to my feet and a delight to my path." Ps. 119: 98-100,105

Part of the pledge of allegiance to the flag of the Holy Bible is this verse. "Your word is a lamp to my feet and a light to my path." Do you remember that from the preliminaries of Daily Vacation Bible School? Isn't this phrase so true?

Practical rules for life in the Bible are still in force today. Cast all your cares and worries upon the Lord because he loves and cares for you (I Peter 3:7). St. Paul in his letter to the Philippians states that all of us should do things in and out of the church without ANY complaining or arguing. In so doing, we can become faultless children of God in the midst of a crooked and evil generation (Phil. 2:14-15). Oh! A verse in I Thessalonians 5:18 tags on to that verse so well. In every thing give thanks for this is the will of God in Christ Jesus for you. When we follow all the commandments of God, we become wiser than the world.

I hope you had an older friend like I did. Mrs. Ballarby was the sweetest widow of a minister I have ever met. She was an encourager. Her words were filled with wisdom. As a twelve year old, I felt as though I had conversed with a sage. I prized her advice as I would have bars of silver or nuggets of gold. I kept her words close to my heart and let them lodge firmly in my young mind. Her wisdom came from her daily communion with God. Stay close to God; wisdom will finally come to you.

October 13

"You, through your commandments, make me wiser than my enemies.... I understand more than the ancients, because I keep your percepts. I have restrained my feet from every evil way, that I may keep your word. I have not departed from your judgments, for You yourself has taught me. How sweet are your words to my taste, sweeter than honey to my mouth! Through your percepts I get understanding; therefore I hate every false way. Your word is a lamp to my feet and a light to my path. I have sworn and confirmed that I will keep your righteous judgments." Ps. 119:98a, 100-106

How in the world does one get wise? Many read a lot so they can store and synthesize various materials. With a great store of knowledge, they can make valid judgments or predictions about the future. Many years before Gutenberg and his printing press, scholars realized that if they ingested and mentally assimilated the words of God, they would be wise. When one became wise, they realized they needed to begin practicing the principles they located in the Scriptures.

The Psalmist kept God's percepts. Jews were admonished from a youth to keep the Ten Commandments and the other admonitions of the prophets.

The next step requires self-discipline. He was to restrain his feet from going toward any evil. Prior to walking toward a wrong action, a mental decision must be made. So the Psalmist guarded the thoughts of his mind. His desire was to please God by keeping the Biblical rules he knew. It seems that he had done a fairly good job for he could say he had not strayed into sin. The more he knew about the Bible the more precious God's word grew to him. The more he loved the scriptures the stronger grew his hatred for any evil.

Now in his newly acquired wisdom he spoke the favorite words of many Christians. Thy word is a lamp unto my feet and a light unto my path

October 14

"You reject all those who stray from your statutes, for their deceit is falsehood. You put away all the wicked of the earth like dross; therefore I love your testimonies. My flesh trembles for fear of You, and I am afraid of your judgments." Ps. 119:118-120

Our nation seems to be in a constant state of crisis. There are drive-by shootings and school shootings. Violent crime is rampant throughout the land. Could the reason be as simple as they have been doing things that are okay in their own eyes while forgetting completely the laws of the country and the rules of social behavior that God laid down? These law breakers are only fooling themselves. The laws of retribution are still in affect. Those who break God's laws will be broken. God is not on a trip to Hawaii nor does He sleep. Our sin will find us out! In God's economy, the sinner will rise to the top and our Maker will skim them off, like a silversmith does all the impurities.

God is concerned about the urges of immature Christians. One way to change unholy actions is by internalizing God's words. The other way is the method chosen by the Psalmist. He told us that he loved to follow all the advice of the Bible. He visualized the awesomeness of God and his fairness in judging. No one squirms out of reaping exactly what they sowed. God even knows our intentions and motivations when the sin was committed.

So we all must step up, look Christ in the face, and confess any sin. Then we will be forgiven and be able to live a life in the light of the love of God instead of dwelling under the shadow of impending wrath and judgment of God.

When we meet Christ, his arms will be opened to welcome us or we will meet with rejection and sentencing to eternal punishment?

October 15

"You put away all the wicked of the earth like dross; therefore I love your testimonies." Ps 119:119

I was raised in a steel mill town. There they had iron ore and scrap iron. They dumped it into the giant furnaces lined with bricks. The impurities rose to the top and were poured off. This was called slag. This was taken to a mountain of impurities five stories high. The railway leads to the top where the little kettles were turned on their side. In the middle of the night this hot slag would light up the sky. After it cooled, it looked like a grey mountain.

God, in like manner, causes the impurities of our life to surface. Suddenly we notice: the off color vocabulary that slips out, thoughts of revenge pop up, questionable activities gnaw at our conscience, small infractions of the law nudge at us, and immodesty makes us blush whether on us or others. Lack of knowing the Bible makes us uncomfortable, flashes of temper, or the smoldering of a grudge keeps our joy at bay, or lastly selfishness slides out in front of us. If we will permit, God will skim these bad things out of our lives, leaving the pure gold of a God-filled life.

The Psalmist realized that God's word helps high-light the spiritual dross in our lives. He and we truly enjoy following God's word. It is not a heavy burden but a genuine pleasure. The feeling is similar to the time we did a chore for mom or dad and they bragged on us in front our friends. The end of life will be infinitely more enjoyable, when God speaks those memorable words, "Well done, my child, welcome into heaven."

October 16

"I have done justice and righteousness; do not leave me to my oppressors. Be surety for your servant for good; do not let the proud oppress me." Ps. 119:121-122

Were you fortunate enough to be one who gave their heart to the Lord before they reached their teenage years? Then you might be able with the Psalmist to say, "I have done justice and righteousness." You were blessed to never have strayed into willful sin whether personally or business-wise. Many of us wish we could say that we have never committed bad sins. We are now truly sorry for the times we were not true to God.

This sinful world is oppressive in the varied ways it treats people. The Psalmist was pleading for God walk with him. Lord, please keep these wicked people away, who would oppress me or my family. Have you ever been jailed? To be released, we had to have someone go our bond. If we failed in our efforts, we stayed lock-upped. At a time like that, we would join the Psalmist and call on the Lord. "Please, O Father, come be the surety for me, so I might go free. You have the resources to set me free." The price Jesus paid on the cross can cleanse every sin that got you in such a place. Only God could and would pay such a cost for people who are in sin and rebelling. For us, there is no cost except to change our lives around to living for God instead of self or Satan.

Lord, over and over you have said you hate the haughty and proud. Please, Father, keep them in their place. I beg of you do not permit this kind of people to rule over me. Thanks, Lord.

October 17

"Your testimonies are wonderful; therefore my soul keeps them. The entrance of your words gives light; it gives understanding to the simple." Ps. 119:129-130

"Son, do you remember when you almost broke your arm and daddy gingerly put you in the front seat of the car and carefully made our way to the hospital? There you timidly sat while the ex-ray machine whirred and buzzed?"

"Daughter remember when you came home broken hearted? The boy you had fallen in love with, started hanging around with another girl. You laid across the bed sobbing your heart out." Mom came into the room and sat quietly on the bed until you let up enough to talk.

The Psalmist recalls the great acts of God on his behalf. His forefather Abraham almost sacrificed Isaac but God provided a ram. God provided sustenance for the twelve tribes of Israel in Egypt. He also provided a miraculous way out through the Red Sea. He performed many mind boggling miracles in the wilderness. God sent hornets to drive people out of Canaan so no Israelite need die. The Psalmist mentioned to his Heavenly Father the wonderful acts of God that he witnessed in his short lifetime.

Remembering all these miracles, the Psalmist feels constrained to keep the laws of God. For us it would be the Sermon on the Mount, the love chapter, and the other words of Jesus. He assures those who obey them will receive inner light and understanding. Are we as smart as the Psalmist? If not, we need to follow his lead.

October 18

"Look upon me and be merciful to me, as your custom is toward those who love your name. Direct my steps by your word, and let no iniquity have dominion over me. Redeem me from the oppression of man, that I may keep your precepts. Make your face shine upon your servant and teach me your statutes." Ps. 119:132-135

Hey, Lord, look my way. I know You are out there. Come down and be kind to me and my family as your custom is. All nations know that You extend mercy to those who adore You and live a good Christian life.

The next plea in his prayer was to ask God to guide him from his arising in the morning until his lying down at night. He pleads with God to not let anything have control over him; drugs, hatred, alcohol, pornography, revenge, nicotine, jealousy, or driving ambition to succeed. It is a fact of life that if something has control of your mind and/or body, God can not be in control. The Psalmist was aware of that.

The request after that was for God to save him from forces that might have control over him. He asks God to keep him and his family from being oppressed by a nation, government, or religion that would prevent him from worshiping God. The Psalmist was committed to keeping God's word. This compliance was not from duty, but was because he loved God.

His last entreaty was a direct and personal one. Lord, look my way, not on the other side of the world. If you look directly on me, the glow of your face will send life-inspiring warmth into my heart. It is almost indescribable – the security and the complete acceptance he felt! The Psalmist was longing to experience that sublime feeling once again.

Let's pray like the Psalmist. Lord, send your mercy my way. Keep things, ideas, chemicals, or people from controlling me. Then please send a flood of love into my heart and on my life. This I ask in the name of Jesus Christ, my Lord and Savior. Amen.

October 19

"Righteous are You, O Lord, and upright are your judgments. Your testimonies, which You have commanded, are righteous and very faithful." Ps. 119:137-138

All the promises we can recall from God's word are upright and righteous. God is very faithful to keep each of them (2 Peter 3:9).

God promised that if we would willingly give our tithe first that He would open the windows of heaven. From there God would dump blessings upon us that were compacted, with all the air shaken out, and running over the rim of our container (Malachi 3:10).

God promises that if we ask, we shall receive. For everyone who asks shall receive. If we don't ask, we may not receive (John 14:14, Matthew 7:8, James 4:2).

God promises to give us strength to meet every circumstance in our life. When there is need for anything, He will fill it according to all his riches in heaven (Philippians 4:13, 19).

God promises never to leave us high and dry nor abandon us in the middle of nowhere! He vows that He would never abandon us nor forsake us (Hebrews 13:5). Our Heavenly Father would never abandon his children for any reason.

God promised to create us in his image. Even at this point in our life, God is continuing to shape us into a spit'n image of his only son (Genesis 1:26). Kindness, mercy, and love are surfacing more often.

God promised to immediately start on a building for you, a residence in heaven. The promise is that his contractors will have yours ready by the time you enter heaven (John 14:1).

Lastly, God promised that when the end of time comes, He would come like lightning from the East. He will pick up all believers and not leave a single one of us behind (Matthew 24:27). Hallelujah! What great and precious promises these are (2 Peter 1:4)! Let us rejoice in these promises throughout this day.

October 20

"Your word is very pure; therefore your servant loves it. I am small and despised, yet I do not forget your precepts." Ps. 119:140-141

Who am I? Does anyone really care about me? I never win. I'm always one of the last to be chosen. I don't have talents like others. I'm not even the oldest in our family. This is exactly how the Psalmist felt. But despite that, he said I love obeying God's laws. He did that because he loved the Lord, not to avoid a hot reception at the end of his life.

One of those rules is not to let the sun set while you are angry at someone (Eph. 4:27). God's main reason for this advice is if we keep a grudge it gives Satan a crack in our spiritual armor. The Devil will use a machine like the Jaws of Life to make the hole even wider and will finally break our relationship with God.

Another noble rule: Don't live such an evil life that it would bring sorrow and pain to the Holy Spirit (Eph 4:30). It takes less evil to hurt God's feelings than it does to hurt mom and dad's heart. St. Paul urges us to live a genuine Christian life because God was the One who chose you as one of his adopted children.

Jesus summarizes the Ten Commandments, which we dare not forget. Let us review them: Do not murder. Do not commit adultery, no matter how many others do. Do not lie about others. Honor your father and mother because they deserve it. Lastly, Jesus says love your neighbor as much as you love and take care of yourself (Matt.19:18-19).

Just like having a string around your finger not to forget to go by the store on the way home, the Psalmist says I will not forget to live a holy life that pleases God.

October 21

"I hate and abhor lying, but I love your law." Ps. 119:163

The Psalmist was vehement about his displeasure with lies. He had a downright hatred for all forms of lying. I'm sure he hated white lies. You know like recounting what happened and intentionally leaving out part of the story. The reason was that person didn't want to hurt someone's feelings. Could another case lying be when one told the whole truth but lessen the severity of one little point?

There are so called grey lies. These are told with a purpose. From the beginning, we stretch the truth. When asked if we drove the speed limit, we say, "Yes". The fact is we drove four miles an hour over the limit all the way. Sometimes, we slant the story so we won't look bad.

Then there are black lies, we call them. Black lies are out and out lies, like the used car salesman tells. These we swear is the whole truth. Sometimes we raise our right arm as a sign of our honesty. We make a promise that we will be there, but we knew at the time there was not way on God's green earth we could be there. If the truth be known, we seldom keep our word. Some lie with their actions while they talk and act like a Christian on Sunday. During the week they lie like a rug, cheat like a thief, and swear like a sailor.

The Psalmist was nauseated by lying. He knew that dire consequences came with those actions. He was aware that lies made the Lord unhappy. He was sure of that because no lies will be allowed in heaven (Revelation 21:8). The Bible doesn't distinguish between white lies, grey lies, black lies, or between big or little lies. God doesn't color code lies. The rule is neither lies nor liars in heaven.

Instead of lying, the Psalmist loved to follow all that he found in the Old Testament scriptures.

October 22

"Great peace have those who love your law, and nothing causes them to stumble." Ps. 119:165

Many accumulate unnecessary stress in their life by not following the Bible. They lied yesterday. Now they have to worry and make sure they don't contradict yesterday's lie.

Some sin on the weekend. Then all week they have to fret whether anyone saw them at that evil spot or that certain motel. They were not faithful to their spouse nor true to themselves.

Others come to work with a head feeling like a pumpkin and noise booming in their brain like the interior of a bass drum. They fail to keep their body healthy. They fail to maintain it like the house of the Lord it truly is.

Fear stalks those who embezzle. They lose sleep over the next audit or the next inventory. Simple integrity would have given continual peace.

Dread walks the hallways of people's mind that are promiscuous. Fear of aids and sexually transmitted disease stalks their mind.

Great peace have they who are genuine born-again Christians. Walking in the pathways of righteous is a great stress reliever. When decisions come, we don't have to struggle over the choice. It is the right way.

It is simple as can be. The lesser of two evils is an outright "No" not a traumatic experience. Who are the righteous and what is right? It is those who know what is right and do it. It is sin to do something when we know it is wrong (James 4:17).

If a United States citizen knows the laws of the country there is not need for them to go to jail. If a person knows God's word sufficiently, there is not need of the stumbling spiritually and going hell. If we love to please God by following His laws, we will wind up in heaven, that beautiful home of the soul.

October 23

"Great peace have those who love your law, and nothing causes them to stumble." Ps. 119:165

What occasionally causes us to tumble off the spiritual wagon? Is it a person who races away from the stop sign and leaves you in the dust? Is it when someone calls you by your pet or nick name? Could it be a picture of scantily clad girl? Could it be a grudge you can't seem to forget nor forgive? What causes you to sin?

The Psalmist found one way to keep a person from stumbling into sin. It is doing as the Bible says and living by all the principles which it presents. Stated negatively, in no way are we to do what Satan tempts us to do. Oh! This is so hard to accomplish. In other words, it is like a diet, "It is easier said than done, but it can be done."

When we surrender, God provides an inner serenity. It is worth every effort that it takes. This peace is so highly prized that everything we can do is not too high a price.

There is a secondary peace from keeping our personal relationship with God. If we should have a sudden cranial hemorrhage, a head-on crash, or a fatal heart attack before we go to bed, God will take us home to heaven. Isn't that a worthwhile reason to follow all the rules God sets down? All things are possible with God's help (Matt. 19:26).

October 24

"I keep your percepts and your testimonies, for all my ways are before You." Ps. 119:168

Can you sing, "The Eyes of Texas Are Upon You"? What a joyous song! On the other hand, having a set of ever searching eyes upon you twenty four-seven is an apprehensive thought. This is one way to visualize the roaming eyes of God. Would you feel overwhelmed by such close surveillance? In fact, God knows our thoughts as we think them. Does this idea scare you? Our thoughts are similar to a DVD; God gets to view every one.

On the other hand, how would you feel about a set of loving eyes following every step you take today and tonight? The Psalmist rejoices in the fact he is walking in the ways of the Lord. It is a real comfort to know the presence of the all powerful and sympathetic Savior is accompanying him. To experience this comfort, the Psalmist instructs us to read our Bible everyday. As we read, we need to search for ways to live more like Jesus, thereby pleasing our Heavenly Father. Dutifully covering a chapter a night doesn't make it. If we seek ways to make God happy, we will find them (Matt 7:8). When the Bible reveals some action or attitude to change that will draw us closer to God, let us not rationalize. If we are sincere in our desire, God will help us (Ps. 37:4).

Hopefully, you will soon be able to join the Psalmist and say, "I keep your percepts and your testimonies, for all my ways are before You," O Lord.

October 25

"I have gone astray like a lost sheep; seek your servant, for I do not forget your commandments." Ps. 119:176

Are there degrees of love for God? Let's ask a few questions. Do we attend church and read our Bible just to stay a Christian? Are we guilty of bragging about our accomplishments? All boasting is evil (James 4:16). When asked to pray at church, do we try to make it a long one so people will know we are a Christian (Matthew 23:14). Or do we often fail God by not praying during our devotions times? Are we jealous of the pianist, choir director, or chairman of the board? We are sure we could do it better. Could it be that we are envious of the big tither of the church? Could it be that we only give ten dollars a Sunday? If it were a tithe of our paycheck, we would have to give much more.

We are a Christian and really work in the church, but many times in board meeting we have to have our way because it is the only right way. When we don't win there, we go to several church members and tell them how wrong the church is. Sometimes our comments cause them to choose sides on the subject. When we finally give up, we hold resentment and occasionally hate.

We are a Christian but there are times the preacher is out of line. I know he says he can prove what he said in worship service, but I'm not going to do this nor stop doing that. St. Paul says that Christians who do the above are carnal. To be carnally minded is death. To put it another way, to have a carnal mind is to be an enemy of God (Romans 8:6-7).

The Psalmist really was spiritually minded and enjoyed life and peace. We can have the same light-hearted spirit through complete surrender to the Lord who loves us so.

October 26

"Deliver my soul, O Lord, from lying lips and from a deceitful tongue. What shall be given to you, or what shall be done to you, you false tongue? Sharp arrows of the warrior, with coals of the broom tree!" Ps. 120:2-4

When was the last time you took a Minneapolis Multiphasic Personality Inventory (MMPI) test to check out your personality? The test is taxing to your mental capacities and emotional integrity. It is extremely difficult to take an honest look at ourselves. How many times do we stand in front of the mirror and comb or brush our hair and fail to see two new grey hairs or one new wrinkle on our face?

Today the Psalmist courageously took a brutally

honest look at his personality. First, he noticed that between his lips lies came out. He often shaded the truth about what someone said to fit his purposes. Sometimes he failed to honestly admit to what he said or did. Other times, he out right lied that he was there or had no part in the trouble to save his own skin.

Secondly, he noticed that all these lies sprang from a deceitful heart. Oh, how in the world could he, by himself, ever change that conniving heart! He thought if he could set fire to it, the hottest coals could scorch out the evil. If that didn't work he thought of killing it. The only method he could come up with was to have an army marksman's take dead aim on that tongue and snap the bow or pull the trigger.

As you and I know now, the blood of Jesus Christ can cleanse us from all sin and any unrighteous thoughts or motives (I John 1:9). Confession is good for the soul and our submission to the hand of God is a delight to the Lord. Trust God to keep his promise, that if we do our part, He will make us entirely whole. We would then be happy with ourselves, instead of distressed like the Psalmist.

October 27

"I will lift up my eyes to the hills – from whence comes my help? My help comes from the Lord, who made heaven and earth." Ps. 121:1-2

Have you been lost in a big city? Was the question "Where in the world can I get some help?" Similarly, the Psalmist was searching for help. Hasn't there been times you called on God for help and none seemed to be forthcoming? It was a desperate situation, maybe your spouse was dying of the excruciating pain of cancer. You called for help but they continued to experience pain and died anyway.

Where do we look for help? Do we search where money will take care of us? Do we find our best friend and look for comfort and help there? Will we look within our self in search of assistance? Do we believe that our government can provide for us?

The Psalmist walked outside his goat hair tent. There he lifted his eyes to the mountain peaks in the distance. That beautiful view of landscape touched off thoughts of immediate assistance. Let's join our friend and turn to God for any real help. Who beside the Creator of Heaven and Earth can truly be our dependable source of our help?

October 28

"He will not allow your foot to be moved; He who keeps you will not slumber. Behold, He who keeps Israel shall neither slumber nor sleep.' Ps. 121:3-4

There is comfort in the motto of the state militia, "We'll guard America while you sleep, so you won't have to." There are machines that never sleep to protect us day and night such as smoke detectors, electric eyes, and video cameras. It is difficult to conceptualize a person who always guards us and never sleeps. That's our God!

This time the Psalmist is not thinking about government watching every move we make. It is not a stern God who is looking to see if we made a mistake so he can pounce on us, like a Little League baseball dad. It is not God's desire to catch us in a sin so He can sentence us to a lake of fire and brimstone. Rather God is like a new father, who is assisting his nine month old take his first memorable steps. God is like an older brother, who is there to see that the school bully does not pick on us. Maybe God is like a big sister who helps us learn integers and equations. God is there to protect us against Satan so we never have to sin nor fall prey to temptations. Our Lord doesn't plan on us ever going backwards in our Christian faith. Though devastation and disaster may come our way, God will see that spiritually we are not moved. God's adversary laughs in triumph when he sees us fall. What a radical difference!

Just remember that our gracious Father is watching us every move day and night, so we don't have to sin against God. With God we form a victorious team!

October 29

"The Lord is your keeper; the Lord is your shade at your right hand. The sun shall not strike you by day or the moon at night. The Lord shall preserve you from all evil; He shall preserve your soul. The Lord shall preserve your doing out and your coming in from this time forth and even forevermore."   Ps. 121:5-8

Of all the billions of people are earth, did you know that God gives YOU individualized special attention? This sure does stretch our our point of believability! Not only does God pull guard duty over you day and night, He really cares about and loves you intensely. Oh! Wow!

First, God keeps watch over our physical body. It is a miracle, whether God, personally cares for you or sends a guardian angel to envelope your car or clear harm from your personal space.

Second, God watches and cares whether you get a paper cut, pop a sweat, or get a sun burn. Our Lord even cares whether you see the moon and feel romantic.

Third, God will watch for thieves, robbers, and muggers whether they strike in broad daylight or under the dark cloak of night. Our Savior will preserve your body from all evil.

Fourth, one of our main concerns is for God to protect and preserve our soul. Our conscience is disturbed when we are watching the wrong shows. It is up to us to hit the remote control. When evil companions entice us to do wrong, we are given strength to say no, if we chose to. Or if pain and sickness should come our way, it will not corrupt our relationship with Jesus or change our destination of heaven.

So the very next time you step out the door of the house, remember you have a personal guard going with you. Don't let worry enter that mental picture. Oh, how much better the rest of my life can be! I'll try to remember, Lord.

October 30

"Pray for the peace of Jerusalem: 'May they prosper who love you. Peace be within your walls, prosperity within your palaces.' For the sake of my brethren and companions, I will now say, 'Peace be within you.' Because of the house of the Lord our God I will seek your good." Ps. 122:6-9

The Psalmist was praying for his church and the town in which it resided. Could we take this prayer for his church and make it a prayer for our country? After the terrorist attack on the twin towers in Manhattan, our country could use fervent prayer.

We pray for the peace of Washington, D.C. which is the capital of our country. We definitely need congressional agreement for the good of the voters. We certainty need peace in each of our cities and towns.

Lord, prosper those who love You! May the Christians of our land grow in wealth and remain in good health. That way, evil people will not make fun of us and call us poor church mice.

May peace reside within the walls of every home throughout our land. Divorce and lawlessness would then evaporate. Love, kindness, and forgiveness would flow lubricating and cooling any friction that might occur.

Because we love one another, we will pronounce a blessing upon everyone we meet especially the members of our family. May the peace of God be upon you and his Holy Spirit dwell within you.

Because we are the land of the free and the home of brave, we will seek the good of every citizen. Jealousy and envy will disappear so when others get ahead we are glad and cheer them on. When others prosper, we have peace in our heart.

Thanks Psalmist for the form of your prayer about your beloved Jerusalem.

October 31

"Behold, as the eyes of servants look to the hand of their masters, as the eyes of a maid to the hand of her mistress, so our eyes look to the Lord our God, until He has mercy on us." Ps. 123:2

In my hungrier days, I was the assistant to a friend who installed self-supporting television towers. They came in ten foot length in a triangle shape. Once he climbed the tower, it was my job to anticipate and supply every need he had. So if he was ready for a new section of tower, I was to have it tied on the rope ready to pull up. If he needed wire or an antenna, it was to be ready. I thought ahead in the process, thinking what would be needed next. The more accurately I anticipated, the faster we got the job done.

Here the Psalmist illustrates how we are to please God. When a person verbally cuts someone down in front of the office staff, we should be thinking about how to please God. It would be to return good for evil. When we have a blue Monday, we should be eager to please God by continuously praising His holy name. When we have a chance to witness for Christ, we are to be looking to God for the slightest signal of what to say or do?

As a child, we looked for things we could do to please our father. Oh, what a moment of delight when he said, "That was good job!" As a child of the Father of the World, do we consistently look for the slightest idea of what would please Him? Then without a command, do we hurry to do that deed to please our Savior? When we perpetually attempt to please the Lord, his mercy will flow our way.

November 1

"Those who trust in the Lord are like Mount Zion, which cannot be moved, but abides forever." Ps. 125:1

Those Christians who ostensibly place their faith in God are like Jerusalem. For the Jews, Mount Zion was revered and held in very high esteem. God's children will be held in high regard according to the Psalmist. Jerusalem was built on a hill so it could be more easily seen and defended. As the pilgrims journeyed to the festival, they looked up to see the Holy City. When we live genuine Christian lives, people will look up to us. They may routinely try to trip us up but when they are in a crisis, they will look us up.

Jerusalem was a holy place. The family bible camp we go to is holy ground for us. As you step on the campus a mysterious feeling sweeps over one's body and mind. As each Jew neared the temple with its holy of holies, God's presence flooded through their mind and body.

Those who put their trust in God will continue to walk with the blessings of God upon their lives. As St. John says, we will abide in Him and He shall abide in us (John 15:5). That is an awesome feeling! It is unexplainable and indescribable! It is impossible to describe the Holy Spirit living within our physical body.

The spirit of a Christian shall continue to live forever, two eternities end to end. The Child of God lives throughout the ages of infinity. Oh, how much better being with God than the alternative. How does one compare bliss to torture, thirst, and flames?

Let us keep our trust in God every minute of every day.

November 2

"Those who trust in the Lord are like Mount Zion, which cannot be moved, but abides forever. As the mountains surround Jerusalem, so the Lord surrounds His people from this time forth and forever." Ps. 125:1, 2

Stop a minute and think of a person you would call a saint. Take time to recall their personal traits. Was one of these qualities a consistent up-beat spirit? Was another attribute always thinking of others before them self?

The Psalmist noticed that people who fully rely on God never seemed ruffled, disturbed, or moved. They are the same happy Christian through financial difficulties, emotional stress, churning marital crises, or turbulent thunderstorms. These Christians victoriously endure storms. When the squall is over, they are still in their appointed place like the ever faithful buoy for the ship. Their stability comes from Christ being by their side. The divine Holy Spirit dwells within them and gives them security and strength. They seem as permanent as the Statue of Liberty on Ellis Island in New York harbor.

The reason, according to the Psalmist, is that God surrounds them like that picturesque ring of mountains that surrounds their beloved city of Jerusalem. Imagine these rugged unmoving granite mountains guarding that city. Our God is more awesome and infinitely kinder to those who trust in Him than those jagged mountains. Hills may melt into the sea, but our God is eternal. Never will your enemy overcome you, while you trust in the Lord.

We can rest comfortably in God's tranquility, calmness and peace.

November 3

"Those who trust in the Lord are like Mount Zion, which cannot be moved, but abides forever. As the mountains surrounds Jerusalem, so the Lord surrounds His people from this time forth and forever." Ps. 125:1-2

While in the U. S. Air Force, I flew into Goose Bay Air Force Base in Labrador, Canada. As we approached at a low altitude, I could not see the base. As we popped over a mountain, there it was. My immediate question was, "Could they get the plane down on the runway, and stop it before we crashed into the mountains at the other end of the runway?" The base was surrounded by mountains.

The Psalmist had a similar feeling about the mountains around Jerusalem. This was in the day before dynamite, colossal drag-lines, and huge earthmovers. The mountains around Jerusalem were as unmovable as God. You could depend on the mountain being there every time you looked, just as God was present every time you called. This fact produced a feeling of security that need not change. If the mountains will stay and protect Jerusalem, God will be unmoved when we need protection.

The one advantage of God over the mountains is that God can always be close. When Jesus came, He stated that not only can God surround you but be in you. The Holy Spirit will come to live in you. Wow!

Oh! How we should keep the thought of having God near the forefront of our mind. His presence lasts forever and ever, never to vanish or disappear. Let us go forth into life today holding tightly to that loving thought.

November 4

"For the scepter of wickedness shall not rest on the land allotted to the righteous, lest the righteous reach out their hand to iniquity." Ps 125:3

Are you the proud owner of a plot of soil of your native country? You are then entitled to vote and have a right to decide on major decisions affecting your country. Being a landowner was just coming into prominence, when the Psalmist wrote. The Bedouins or nomads just roamed and lived wherever they pitched their goat hair tent. They found that where people built houses and settled down, evil was not far behind. Thievery and prostitution immediately came to town.

There is a definite difference between anyone owning land and a child of God possessing property. The Psalmist had a special promise for God's children. When you purchased a lot, evil would not overcome you. Evil and good can not occupy the same piece of real estate. This is true whether it is a tract of earth or the territory of a soul. One recent example of this was as soon as the new church purchased the tavern, evil fled away. It was almost immediately that God's spirit was manifested in their worship services. In like manner, God guided when you bought that house. God's spirit was there. God knows that if we Christians are surrounded continually by evil, we are tempted to do evil. Could this be the reason God ordered the Israelites to drive out the Canaanites before settling in? St. Paul urges us to shun the very appearance of evil.

Be a happy landowner for you are assured that God will see to it that wickedness will not overcome you or your family.

November 5

"For the scepter of wickedness shall not rest on the land allotted to the righteous, lest the righteous reach out their hands to iniquity. Do good, O Lord, to those who are good, and to those who are upright in their hearts." Ps. 125:3-4

Do you own the house you are living in? I understand you and the mortgage company own it. That means you own the land your house sets on. According to our scripture, evil can not rest on the house and land allotted to you. Your happiness and contentment are of vital concern to God. Our Lord would like to see you spiritually and physically happy (3 John 1:2).

It is physically harmful and spiritually detrimental to do evil. If you are a happy Christian, you will not be looking across the proverbial fence wanting anything in line with what the Devil is offering. Similarly, if you are in a wonderful marriage, you won't be tempted to check out the field.

The Psalmist pleads with the Lord to direct blessings toward all the people who are trying to live a genuine Christian life. He asks God to aim the heavenly spout where the glory runs out toward his children. He asks God to back his heavenly eighteen wheeler and lift the dump bed and immerse each Christian with love and blessing. Oh! What a wonderful Savior! He continually showers us with blessings. Would you like a challenge? Take the dare of the lyricist who wrote "Showers of Blessings," and count your many blessings – name them one by one. So take a tablet or notebook with you for the day. Record each blessing as you become aware of it. See if your list is two full pages or tops one hundred different blessings. May your efforts be a total success.

November 6

"Do good, O Lord, to these who are good, and to those who are upright in their hearts." Ps. 125:4

The Psalmist was appealing to God. Similarly St. Peter said, "To whom else can we go? You have the words of life" (John 6:68). Each of us often goes to God with requests. Our appeal most of the time is for things to better our life. Sometimes God doesn't answer our requests for that very reason according to St. James. (4:3).

This time the Psalmist was requesting assistance for all children of God. Today the benefactors would be all genuine Christians. The blessings would also be sprinkled over the good moral people. Society, as well as the church has a sizable number of good people in them.

Jesus in the Sermon on the Mount laid down a principle that whatsoever a person sows that will they reap. If a person continually sows good deeds, pleasant smiles, and returns good for evil, they will be blessed. These blessings will multiply. They will be pressed down and shaken together to the point of running over. Since the Psalmist didn't get to hear the Son of God speak those words, he entreated God to bless good people and God's children.

If you are a Christian or even a good moral person begin expecting blessing. Expect them as an answer to the Psalmist's prayer or because of the principle Jesus laid down. It might even arrive before dark tonight.

November 7

"Those who sow in tears shall reap in joy. He who continually goes forth weeping, bearing seed for sowing, shall doubtless come again with rejoicing, bringing his sheaves with him." Ps. 126:5-6

To reap a harvest one has to intentionally sow seeds. In American history, Johnny Appleseed was determined to sow apple seeds. He ate apples all fall and saved the seeds. Even in the winter he started little trees. His actions were not haphazard but preplanned. His goal was to see apple trees growing from the eastern seaboard to the Pacific Coast.

If we are to see a spiritual harvest, we must plant. We must weep in prayer. This seems to be more than, 'name it and claim it' praying. Sincere weeping and fasting are only to let God know we are sincere in our request for the lost soul for whom we are praying. We are not paying a price to get the prayer answered. If our weeping gets the attention from others or fasting helps us lose weight, we are insincere with God. Our main desire should be to see our friend accept Christ as their

Lord and Savior. A divine relationship between them and God should grow.

God can plant the seed or we might when we tell others what Christ has done for us. The conversation need not always be religious or spiritual to plant seeds. If like Johnny Appleseed, we keep dropping seeds with the intention of leading persons to Jesus Christ; God will see that we reap a spiritual harvest that will last for all eternity.

November 8

"Unless the Lord builds the house, they labor in vain who build it; unless the Lord guards the city, the watchman stays awake in vain." Ps 127:1

We can plan and strategize all we want for our lives. Many of us as a kid knew exactly where we were headed in life. After one man gave his life to God, he got laid off. In the down time, he had to re-prioritize his goals. God has a delightful way of upsetting human plans. My pastor was sure all the way through college that he was going to be an architect. God changed his mind. For twenty three years now he has proclaimed the good news. Another man founded his own church. Although it was scripturally sound, the church shut down after his death. God stops things that are not his will.

The Psalmist is stating that the Lord must of necessity be consulted before we plan. The admonition is that even our work in the church needs God's approval and blessing. A human plan without God's input creates its own possible problem. Since God is all-knowing, does it not sound feasible to look to Him for direction? Knowing the future, He can help us make wise decisions. God's directions may seem wrong. When the prophet Samuel anointed the runt of

Jesse's family, it looked wrong. His older brothers looked strong and knowledgeable. God knew the strength of character and David's propensity to trust God. After we ask for God's guidance, we need to proceed with that information. Don't listen to reason over the will of God.

November 9

"It is vain for you to rise up early, to sit late, to eat the bread of sorrows; for so He gives his beloved sleep." Ps. 127:2

Some grieving persons spend years adjusting to the loss of a loved one. The Psalmist noticed people with this distress. Early every morning these distressed people headed for the cemetery. On bad weather days, they brooded over their loss. Others can't get to sleep because their mind re-runs memories of that special loved one.

Many spend hours and days saying, "If only..." If only I had told them I love them. If only I'd known I would have done this or that. If only I would have made arrangements.

Others sing the monotonous tune of I wish I had... I wish I had been more kind but I didn't know they were that sick. I wish I had made preparation.

Some sing the repetitious refrain of "Why didn't I?" Why didn't I try harder to get along? What didn't I save more money? Why didn't I show my affection instead of being distant or playing hard to get?

The Psalmist says that it is useless or futile to keep eating the bread of sorrow. These tunes with unvarying precision disrupt our digestive system and hamper interactions in our daily social life.

God's plan for you is to get a full night's sleep. When Satan pushes the replay button on that blu-ray DVD, call on God. Remind Satan that the Lord's desire for you is a good night's rest, not roll and toss.

Your spirit may be dragging bottom but the Psalmist clearly says you are God's "beloved". You are his treasure, his cherished child, and his betrothed. You, in fact, are one of the heavenly King's kids!

November 10

"Behold, children are a heritage from the Lord, the fruit of the womb is a reward. Like arrows in the hand of a warrior, so are the children of one's youth. Happy is the man who has his quiver full of them; they shall not be ashamed, but shall speak with their enemies in the gate." Ps. 127:3-5

Children are a hindrance! Kids are selfish and demand my attention! I don't know what to do when I want to go out for a quiet dinner? I wouldn't take them to a funeral home. Kids are just rug rats that keep the house messed up. They are only good as a tax deduction.

That may be the opinion of some modern couples but the Psalmist held a much different view of children. He was of the frame of mind that children were part of his legacy. For his society, they served as his social security for old age. He knew that God expected him to have children in his youth. Older adults don't possess the patience or endurance. Also since there was no National Guard, children were their protection from other hostile tribes. If you had a large family, you had status in the community.

Besides all these practical benefits, he thought the man and wife who had lots of children should be happy. It was a reward to watch them learn, become responsible youth, and finally reliable citizens. How fulfilling to see them start their own family. Lastly, you derive the pleasures from watching your grandchildren.

November 11

"When you eat the labor of your hands, you shall be happy, and it shall be well with you. Your wife shall be like a fruitful vine in the very heart of your house, your children like olive plants all around your table." Ps. 128:2-3

When a person uses their body to earn a living, the metabolism functions much more efficiently. This activity causes a person to feel much better. Have you had to wait four hours for the next airplane going to your destination? At the end of the day, didn't you say, "I'd rather been at work as to do nothing for four hours?" Since your reply was yes, it proves the scripture that says we should earn our living by the sweat of our brow. Our first parents caused that command to come into being.

When the father of the house has a regular job, his children learn from a positive role model. Children seldom do what we say, but most often do as we do. The American Lung Association found this to be true when it comes to the habit of smoking. They created their advertisement showing their four year old grabbing a pack of cigarettes that dad had lain down. When there is a regular income, the housewife can depend on the income and take care of family needs. The Psalmist said the wife is similar to the mainspring of the house. She slows things down when life is moving too fast or raises our spirits when things we are down. Being a mother is a demanding job despite what people say today. Through the nurturing of mother and the influence of a father, children grow into beautiful young adults. Like young olive trees, they bear fruit for years to come.

The Psalmist is really giving us an often forgotten secret to a healthy and happy family. The secret is, 'make a living from the labor of your hands.'

November 12

"The Lord is righteous; He has cut in pieces the cords of the wicked."   Ps. 129:4

Cords of the wicked remind me of Delilah. She fastened evil cords around Samson. At first, sin looks so tempting and so easy to do. The difficult part is to stop once you have consented to do what Satan asks (Judges 16).

The first time Samson was tempted by Delilah, she tied him up with seven (7) fresh bow strings. Our slip into sin might be lying. It is so tempting to get out of the trouble. Samson snapped those like sewing machine thread.

Samson's second dip into sin was to be tied up with brand spank'n new rope. For us it might have been watching pornography in secret or looking at someone else's husband/wife. This is harder to get out of. You are mentally hooked on what you have seen or experienced. Samson got out again.

The next slide into sin was that if they would weave his hair into the loom, he would be helpless. Our slide may have been drinking or smoking. A time or two you can drink but soon Satan has you bound. Samson shook it out of his hair easily. After sliding into sin, only Jesus can help.

Finally, Samson was neck deep in sin and couldn't get out. Remember he told her if she cut his hair he would be normal. The Philistines gouged out his eyes and put bronze shackles on him. Samson paid his physical penalty by grinding wheat like an ox. He also did something else. Samson confessed his wrong and sin. God forgave him. God broke his bondage. Later he pushed against the two supporting pillars of an arena building. He killed more in his death than he did his entire life. In other words, God used him again. When we confess and believe, God can and will use us again, even if we have sinned.

November 13

"Neither let those who pass by them say, 'The blessing of the Lord be upon you; we bless you in the name of the Lord!'"   Ps. 129:8

The Psalmist in the previous verses was describing the wicked people of his day. Some of that type are still with us today. There are hypocrites who tear down all the good that Christians do. Their words of criticism hurt like the needle hitting a nerve ending. When the church board or committee meets they are the roadblock to moving ahead for Christ. There are days or times they appear to be genuine children of God. They walk and talk as upright as the preacher. So when others go pass them, they are tempted to brag on how holy these people are. The Psalmist asks us to refrain from asking God's blessing upon them.

In America, we seldom think of the power of blessing someone. The closest we come is by pronouncing the Irish blessing on a friend. You know, may the wind always be at your back etc. The Psalmist is of the firm conviction that God truly would dump blessings on those on whom **we** bless in the name of the Lord. Even today in the Spanish tradition, the blessing pronounced by the elder of the family produces a positive impact on the recipient.

So let's meditate and possibly consider blessing our family. As I understand a blessing, it is a vocal or audible invocation of a blessing upon someone. The witnesses nearby who hear the blessing hold God accountable for what was pronounced. The Psalmist gives us authority to ask God to bless someone in the name of the Lord. Be careful whom you bless!

November 14

"Out of the depth I have cried to You, O Lord; Lord, hear my voice! Let your ears be attentive to the voice of my supplications." Ps 130:1-2

Remember the days of radio before there were push buttons. When you wanted to get a radio station like XERF, Del Rio, TX, you had to carefully turn the dial. If you didn't have it right on the frequency, you heard jazz or some talk show. When you had it right on the correct frequency, you heard Roy Acuff or Gene Audrey clearly. The Psalmist didn't know about frequency but he was familiar with cow bells, camels hissing, sheep bleating, and hawkers haggling about the price of their wares. In all this noise and blare, would God be able to hear his lone voice? So he was pleadings with God to tune in to his prayers, so He could hear.

Surely the Psalmist was familiar with kids. You know how your children tuned out your voice and are definitely tuned in to the music of their favorite vocalist or singing group. So the Psalmist is appealing to God not to tune him out but tune in to his call for help.

God, since You are God of the entire world, will You make time for me? Do You receive so many prayers that it will lock up your computer system? Maybe there will be so many different languages, that you'll forget how to translate English so You can understand my need.

Have you ever been in the pits of despair? That's the exact spot where the Psalmist found himself. It was out of the depths of despair, he desperately called on God for assistance. Hear my entreaty, O Lord. It feels so terrible at the bottom of the barrel! Isn't it frustrating to call on God and feel like He didn't hear nor have any intentions of answering? How easy to have empathy for today's Psalmist!

November 15

"Out of the depths I have cried to you, O Lord; Lord, hear my voice! Let your ears be attentive to the voice of my supplication."   Ps. 130:1-2

Out of the depths the Psalmist cried. Was his despair as deep as a fourth of a mile down as in a submarine or five miles down as in a bathyscaphe? But it could be true that his depression felt that thick! It was so far down, that he was afraid it would be too far for God to hear him. He insinuated that he wanted God to cup his hands behind his ears to hear the Psalmist slightest prayer. If He didn't, the Psalmist didn't hold out much hope of God hearing his request.

The Psalmist cried! It sounds to me like this fellow was desperate. Sometimes we ask in prayer. At other times we beg. Occasionally we really plead. How long has it been since any of us have cried in anguish to God to hear and answer our request?

The Psalmist knew on whom to call! It was the Lord Almighty, God of Abraham, Isaac, and Jacob. The rest are idols with mouths that can't talk and hands which can not help. He was well aware not to depend on mankind because their arms are too short and mind is so limited.

Even before Jesus came, the patriarchs were appealing directly to God. 'Lord, hear my voice.' We are to come boldly before the throne of grace (Heb. 4:16). Ask and you shall receive (John 16:24). We don't have many things because we don't ask (James 4:2).

November 16

"If You, Lord, should mark iniquities, O Lord, who could stand? But there is forgiveness with You, that You may be feared." Ps. 130:3-4

How would you feel, if an FBI person were assigned to follow you 24-7? This would be worse than the presidential family. This person would carry a clipboard to check every sin we committed. How would we hold up?

The Lord is even more severe. Day and night God keeps track of every thought that pops into our mind. There would be no check marks for bad thoughts, if we booted them right out and replaced them with virtuous thoughts. God is well aware that Satan makes a practice of tempting us with evil thoughts. If we fondle or harbor an evil thought, there would be a check mark on the clipboard.

The Psalmist was well aware he could not stand such close scrutiny. He was of the opinion that none of humanity, neither male nor female could handle that kind of surveillance.

The solution is that God in his kindness extends forgiveness. Even on our worst day, God will grant us forgiveness. Jesus asked Peter to forgive others seven times seventy. God will go infinitely beyond that. One can not unknowingly nor willingly sin so many times that God will not patiently hear the confession and completely forgive us. Neither is there a sin you commit so heinous or horrific that God can not or will not forgive us.

Today let us stand back in awe of the Almighty but also revel in the beneficent God we serve and whose we are!

November 17

"I wait for the Lord, my soul waits, and in his word do I hope. My soul waits for the Lord more than those who watch for the morning – yes, more than those who watch for the morning." Ps. 130:5-6

Have you ever car-pooled on a regular basis to school or work? Most mornings your ride is exactly on time, but oh, the times they run late! You stand on the curb and think, "Did I come out too late and have they already gone by?" "Are they sick and didn't call me?" "Did my clock stop during the lightning storm and not turn back on?"

Maybe the girls reading this remember a similar nauseous feeling. It wasn't their first date. It was a date with their regular boy friend. They were dilly-dallying around getting ready to be fashionably late so as not to appear too eager. But the appointed time for him to honk or knock on the door came and went. You walked back and forth starting a slow boil. Wait, you did, but not very patiently. He never did show!

The Psalmist may not have experienced any of the above but he was very well acquainted with insomnia. Sometimes three or four hours into the night, he awoke. There was no refrigerator to raid, nor any all-night QVC to watch so he continued to lie on his mat. He began the unending vigil of looking for the dawn to break under the goat-hair flap of the tent. Oh, how the rolling and tossing wears a body out! After so long, one eagerly looked forward to the daylight.

The Psalmist applies this expectant attitude to his soul. He states that he pins his hope on the Word of the Lord. He anxiously looks toward God for the next visitation to his soul. The times in between seem as long as a sleepless night. He intensely yearns for the Lord to come. Do we walk many days not thinking of God? I pray you continually keep your hope and expectation in the Lord.

November 18

"O Israel, hope in the Lord; for with the Lord there is mercy, and with him is abundant redemption. And He shall redeem Israel from all his iniquities." Ps. 130:7-8

Do you put your hope for the future in a sign of the Zodiac? Is your future locked to a bull market? Is your vehicular safety record latched to your prowess on the interstate? Do you attribute your physical health and physique to your strict regiment of diet and exercise?

The Psalmist is urging the whole nation of Israel to place their hope in the Lord. Can you even imagine how America would change, if we all put our hope for our present and our future in God? When our hope is in the Lord, the sale of headache capsules, anti-acid pills, and sleeping tablets would plummet. With the nation's hope in God, our churches could not contain all the new worshipers?

We need to place unwavering confidence in our Savior, for with him there is mercy. Most of us at one time or the other need mercy, relief from distress, or divine compassion because we have offended God. Hardly a day goes by that we do not commit a sin of omission or commission. That fact brings us to the ultimate reason for relying on God. With the Almighty, we can have cleansing from any and all sin. No earthly person nor power can forgive sin. Satan is a professional at causing us to sin but even the Devil does not have the capability to eradicate sin. God has the capacity to purify all humans now living on earth, whether it is instantaneous or gradual. Oh, what a marvelous and omnipotent God we serve! With all that power still He is touched by the feelings of our infirmities.

Let us begin right now to deliberately keep our trust in God, and not on self, others, nor things of this world.

November 19

"Lord, my heart is not haughty, nor my eyes lofty. Neither do I concern myself with great matters, nor with things too profound for me." Ps. 131:1

Lord, my desire is to simply trust You to work the details of my life out according to your divine plan. I keep forgetting to remember that the more I trust You, the less I worry. Sometimes, Lord, my stomach hurts from my worrying. Please forgive me for my lack of trust in your sovereignty.

The Psalmist stated he didn't take part in discussions like: Did the chicken or the egg come first? How can the sun continue to burn and not burn up? How does God make an artesian spring that keeps bubbling water up through the ground summer and winter, day and night without running out of water?

These questions the Psalmist left to God, who spoke them into existence. The Psalmist might forget to give God praise, if he understood it all? These great matters that confound mankind are as simple as 'a, b, and c' for God. These profound mysteries God takes care of 24-7, while we must take six to eight hours for sleep each day.

We think we are self-sufficient until we catch the flu bug. Oh, how weak we are then! Like the Psalmist, let's leave the secrets of nature to the Creator and keep our trust in his wisdom.

November 20

"Behold, how good and how pleasant it is for brethren to dwell together in unity!" Ps. 133:1

As a ten and eleven year old, I used to go down the street to my friend, George's house to play. The times that we did go inside to get a drink, his mom or dad were yelling about something. Oh, how much better it was at my house! Mother would raise her voice to show she meant business, but never at the yell or scream stage.

Was it recently you got involved in a quarrel? Your nerves tightened, your voice raised three notes and your stomach began to ache. It was an hour or two before your body got back to normal. Oh, how much better to live in peace than to quarrel!

Have you had to associate with or live with someone who was a nitpicker? They take exception with every thing you say: they paid more or less. They never remember it being exactly the way you explained it. Maybe they comment about how the dress or accessories don't really match. Oh, how much better it is to live with someone who is complimentary and one who promotes peace!

Do you have a friend who has a personal problem that causes them to constantly envy or make jealous comments? If they are picking on you, it's really that they are wishing they had this or that. At times, you were happy until they mentioned how much happier you would be, if you had what they voiced. Oh, how much more pleasant it is to be around a Christian!

Unity and peace in human relations are like lubricating oil. The friction and heat is kept to a bare minimum. What a blessing abides on these who live in unity!

November 21

"Behold, bless the Lord, all you servants of the Lord, who by night stand in the house of the Lord! Lift up your hands in the sanctuary, and bless the Lord. The Lord who made heaven and earth bless you from Zion!" Ps. 134:1-3

Have you ever wondered what position the people were in while the rabbi spoke? Were they strewn all over the sanctuary in a relaxing position? Wonder if they knelt with their hands out front and forehead on the mat? We definitely know they didn't have pews with padded cushions! The Psalmist gives us a clue. Blessed are the people who stand in the sanctuary. So during the sermon the people stood.

If the Psalmist went to church at night, did he flip on the light switch? The flaming pine torches were put in notches in the wall. The fumes from the light filled the room. So to stand in the temple sanctuary at night was not all that pleasant or healthy. The worshipers had to love the Lord. The disadvantages of standing the whole service plus the smell of the torches would keep our modern church goers home.

Are we singing or praying at the height of our worship service? Old timers in the Methodist Church shouted, when the glory of the Lord fell upon them. When Israeli worshipers got blessed, they lifted their hands to the Lord. It was easy to see when the Holy Spirit visited a service because hands were extended heavenward. What a magnificent sight!

Last, the Psalmist urges all of us to praise the Lord. Surely, we could be more demonstrative about our feelings for Christ. At the end the Psalmist entreats each of us to bless the Lord.

November 22

"Praise the Lord! Praise the name of the Lord; praise him, O you servants of the Lord!" Ps. 135:1

Everyone in every corner of the world sing and praise the Lord! The Lord is gracious to us! How healthy we are compared to all in the hospital. How wonderful it is to be able to walk without assistance! How great to have the freedom to go in and out at our pleasure and not be confined to a cell! Let us shout aloud, telling our world how blessed we are. May we not be ashamed to praise God everywhere we go. How good we feel when we think positively and praise God instead of complaining.

God is so great! He made the heavens with all the stars, planets, and galaxies. It is marvelous how he rarefies the air as we leave earth's gravity. Can we really tell when the Creator began to make our earth or when the dinosaurs began to roam the earth? Can we tell when God changed watering the earth with dew to raining upon it to keep the grass green? God in his infinite wisdom created wind to remove hot and cold spots on the earth. How great is our God!

Our God is incomparable! Who but God could know which child was the first born in the whole land of Egypt? He killed them and the first born of all the animals in one night. Besides that, only God could create all those plagues overnight or make them all die overnight! God fought for the Israelis. One night God killed an entire army while the Israelites were still in town inside the walls.

Another time the Israeli army went to battle with the chancel choir leading the fight. They won, thanks be to God.

Let us praise God for his exploits but also praise Him because He cared enough about each of us to give his only Son, Jesus to die for our sins. Hallelujah! What a Savior!

November 23

"You who stand in the house of the Lord, in the courts of the house of God, praise the Lord, for the Lord is good; sing praises to his name, for it is pleasant." Ps. 135:2-3

God is good for we were born with all our fingers and toes.

God is excellent for He gave us a good mind. Sometimes in school we wondered if God poured in enough.

God is marvelous for we so enjoyed all our aunts and uncles. At times though we could have killed a brother or sister when they tormented us.

God overwhelmed us with good times like skating parties, birthday parties, and friends at sleep-overs.

God loves us so much that we, at one time, gave our life completely to Him. Since that time, we have missed many hard knocks of life and had moments of pure joy as a Christian.

God sent his Holy Spirit to guide us in paths of righteousness. It is so exhilarating when we realize we are walking in the center of God's will.

God was so precious to send us a compatible mate. Our love has grown through the years. [Fifty-two years for us]

God touched our bodies so we had babies. We were utterly amazed at the perfectly formed little hands and feet. It was equally astounding at the volume of sound the miniature lungs could produce.

God, You didn't leave us during the difficult years of raising a family: toddler, adolescence, teenage, and young adult.

Every one, who attends church, or goes in and out of the fellowship hall, be sure to praise God. You know God is good and worthy of all the adoration we give Him. Sing lustily as to the Lord because it pleases God.

November 24

"Oh, give thanks to the Lord, for He is good! For his mercy endures forever." Ps. 136:1
We are well and not in a hospital.
Oh, give thanks to the Lord.
God woke us this morning.
The Lord is good!
We have more than enough clothes to wear.
For his mercy endures forever.
Today's sunlight brightens our spirit.
Oh, give thanks to the Lord.
Our family brings us great pleasure.
The Lord is good!
Our enemies do not overcome us.
For his mercy endures forever.
Friends enhance the quality of our life.
The Lord is good!
God graciously provides us with a vehicle not a horse, mule, nor bicycle.
For his mercy endures forever.
We enjoy so much food we have trouble keeping excess weight off.
Oh, give thanks to the Lord.
Our church and church family are such a support.
The Lord is good!
Our parents were a great influence on us.

For his mercy endures forever.
How nice to have a job to support the family.
Oh, give thanks to the Lord.
How wonderful to have the sense of touch, sight, feel, taste, and smell!
The Lord is good!
O, Lord, You cleansed us and came to live in us.
For his mercy endures forever.

November 25

"I will praise You with my whole heart; before the gods I will praise You." Ps. 138:1

The Psalmist was sold on the Lord. He didn't care who he witnessed to. He wasn't afraid to acknowledge God before idols or any of his mortal enemies. Are we afraid to tell our co-workers or acquaintances that we love Jesus? If we ask in prayer, God will give us courage and the motivation to witness even before the president of the United States.

God is worthy of being praised before unbelievers. How did the Psalmist praise God? How in the world do we praise God? We could exalt God by glorifying Him, honoring the Lord, giving devotion to the Creator, worship God, or giving reverence to Him. Other ways of praising God might be because we have a spirit of thanksgiving, give gratitude, and offer blessings. Sometimes we could admire Him, appreciate Him, respect Him, repeat a psalm to the Lord, adore, pay tribute to Him or revere the Lord.

The Psalmist says, "The Lord inhabits the praises of his people" (Ps. 22:3 KJV). Do we praise God often enough for him to provide a residence? Or just a three foot square building, a one room cottage, a bungalow, a house, or a mansion? How can God live in a house made of three 'thank you's' a week?

The way to praise God more is to love God with all our mind, soul, and strength. If He keeps number one spot in our priorities, praise will begin to flow easily from our mouth. Besides that a holy boldness will in-fill us so we feel free to witness just anywhere.

November 26

"In the day when I cried out, You answered me, and made me bold with strength in my soul." Ps. 138:3

Can you imagine General Moses' thoughts? He was doing such a good job of staying ahead of the Egyptian army. All of the sudden he came to a roadblock, the Red Sea. He called on the Lord. The Red Sea separated and a million and a half people kicked up dust as they walked through. Someone calculated that the gap was three miles wide for all of them to cross over in one night. He heard Moses' prayer and drowned an entire army in less than five minutes and not a single Israeli casualty. God found a bold spirit within Moses.

Can you imagine the mental battle of Daniel? He knew the decree was signed for the lion's den. All the way from the office to his room, he called on the Lord. God gave him strength in his soul to open the window and publicly knee down and pray to Almighty God. Sure enough, the King had to throw him in the lion's den but by now he was bold in his soul. The next morning the King called down into the den. "O Daniel!" Daniel replied "O, King live forever!" You should have seen the impromptu dancing fit of joy the king gave before those royal officials. God had answered Daniel's cry for help.

Think back over your life. Can you recall a time you were in a very dire circumstance? Did you think to call on Lord? If you did call on God, it would be interesting to hear how God answered your prayer. Many times the way the answer comes can not be explained.

Have you had a time you were being sorely tempted to commit a sin? When you called on God, He made you bold in your spirit. It was, as if God injected iron into your blood giving you the strength to overcome. Let's praise the Lord, again.

November 27

"Though I walk in the midst of trouble, You will revive me; You will stretch out your hand against the wrath of my enemies, and your right hand will save me." Ps. 138:7

Even though I walk into a roomful of people of a different nationality, or into a crowd all of the other gender, your hand will guide me. When I must walk past the tavern of drunken people or through the rough section of the neighborhood, You will divert trouble from me. During the times of financial reversal, times of rocky marital relationships, or difficult times of guiding our children through adolescence, God will guide me and give me wisdom.

The Psalmist doesn't say, "The Devil made me walk into trouble." He confesses that when he inadvertently walked into trouble, God gave him strength. Many times we see things that look enticing on the other side of the fence. We decide to go there which gets us into trouble. The Psalmist lets us know that although **we** get in trouble on our own, God always comes to our rescue or defense. That is God's nature. It is not a boring duty for Him.

The Psalmist states a fact that God will reach out his giant hand against your enemies. Where are your enemies? Are they at work, school, or at the club? Oh, you don't have an enemy but you do have someone who gets your dander up with only a few choice words. God's right hand will save you from displaying your anger and/or violence toward them. That is great, right? God will also grab the arm of your enemy to keep them from striking you. So even when your enemy is upset and angry, God will stretch his mighty hand to restrain them. You should be so grateful that God cares enough for you that He curbs the harm that might come your way.

November 28

"O Lord, You have searched me and known me. You know my sitting down and my rising up; You understand my thought afar off. You comprehend my path and my lying down, and are acquainted with all my ways"   Ps. 139:1-3

Remember as a teenager, when you tried to fake it with mom? "How are you, Honey?" "Fine, Mom." She knew you were depressed or in a bad mood. "Did you enjoy the party?" "Sure, Mom," but she instinctively knew you had broken up with your steady. "What kind of grade do you think you made on today's exam?" "I did alright." She could tell whether you bombed it or you actually did pretty well. "Do you have your room clear?" "Yeah, I picked things up." She knew you had just made a path from the door to the bed.

Some people act like teenagers with God. "Did you read my love letter today?" "Sure, God I read a chapter." God knows you speed-read it because you had somewhere to go. "Did you have conversation with Me?" "Sure, I had a prayer time today." You know that you just listed all your needs and to show your dedication you mentioned the needs of your friends. God couldn't label that conversation because you didn't wait long enough for God to answer. "Did you witness for Me today?" "Well, I did mention how much fun I had at church Sunday." You did not say anything about the change in your life, since He saved your soul. Were you courageous enough to ask them if they knew Jesus personally?

God knows how you feel. He knows what you are thinking. He knows if you are really trying to live for Him. He knows your favorite fast food place and hanging out place where you just talk. The Psalmist warns us not to fake with God!

November 29

"O Lord, You have searched me and known me. You know my sitting down and my rising up; You understand my thought afar off. You comprehend my path and my lying down, and are acquainted with all my ways. For there is not a word on my tongue, but behold, O Lord, You know it altogether."   Ps. 139:1-4

The Lord knew us when we were two cells. He vividly recalls what we thought at six, at twenty-two and last night. God watched while we made those stupid mistakes. It is mind boggling that God registers every thought of every living person on earth. He searches us inside and out.

God is knowledgeable of all your daily habits. He is aware of how we treat the family early in the morning or late at night whichever is our bad time. We need to be careful how we say things. He also knows when we intentionally snub someone.

How awesome that God knows our dreams and our plans! God watched as we handled that crisis in the office or the discipline problem at home. Oh, yeah, God was noticing when we quit and gave up. Yes, He felt for us when we were so confused we didn't know that to do. God was beside us when we inadvertently put our foot in your mouth. Believe it or not, He knew the words on the tip of our tongue that we successfully kept on the inside our lips. God was proud of us.

If God knows each thought we think, we should guard our mind from bad thoughts. Having the bad thought is not bad, but harboring it and mulling it over is sinful. We are to boot out every evil thought and replace it with what is honest and just.

It is astonishing that You, Lord, know all about us and love us enough to die to save us!

November 30

"You have hedged me behind and before, and laid your hand upon me. Such knowledge is too wonderful for me; it is high, I cannot attain it." Ps. 139:5-6

God guards us before we get there, plus watches out behind us. A military patrol does the same thing. There is the point man out front looking for booby traps or enemy. Next comes the navigator with a compass to keep the group correctly headed for their destination. Behind him is the lieutenant who is in charge. Next is the radio man who can call for additional support. Finally, at the end of the patrol is the rearguard. He must be adept at walking backwards for his eyes are continually checking for ambush or snipers.

God can see where we are going and knows what is ahead for each of us. We need not fear the future. God's sense of direction is out of this world. He has a layout for every human upon earth. Unfailingly, He has predestined each of us to fulfill his magnificent plan. The lieutenant stays with his patrol. God stays with us throughout our entire lives. We may leave the patrol but not at the insistence of the lieutenant but over his protest. Last, God is our rearguard. He leaves no vulnerable area of our life open for Satan to harm. The Psalmist was amazed that God could be ahead of us, as well as, behind us. This all was too much for him to comprehend.

The final request of the Psalmist was for God to lay his majestic hand upon him. How marvelous to have such an omnipresent God! What a tremendous God we serve!

December 1

"Where can I go from your Spirit? Or where can I flee from your presence? If I ascend into heaven, You are there; if I make my bed in hell, behold, You are there. If I take the wings of the morning, and dwell in the uttermost parts of the sea, even there your hand shall lead me, and your right hand shall hold me." Ps. 139:7-10

Can one fly fast enough or far enough to get away from God? The Psalmist was asking if he could quickly skirt to the other side of the earth, and get where God is not. Take our modern satellite capsules for instance. They orbit at 24,000 miles an hour. In one week they cover half a million miles. That is not fast enough! Our astronauts have confirmed God was still with them. If we took the Concord Jet to London and flew twice the speed of sound, we could not go fast enough to get ahead of where God is? If we pulled a Jonah and took that space craft straight out in space at 24,000 mph, we could not escape the presence of God?

Where can one go where God is not? Is there a spot where we can be without God? Is there a possibility that we can drop down to hell and be away from God? Could we go straight up to heaven and find God not there? Can we fly the speed of a bullet and skip out of God's presence for a split second? The Psalmist shouts an astounding, "No!" to all the above questions.

He does say yes to the fact that God will take us by the hand and lead us wherever we go. We definitely are not left on our own to wander throughout life. He also says when we trip, stumble, or are about to fall, God will use his strong hand to hold us up. With that kind of assistance, we need never fall to sin. God's ubiquitous presence will always be near us.

December 2

"If I say, 'Surely the darkness shall fall on me,' even the night shall be light about me; indeed, the darkness shall not hide from You, but the night shines as the day; the darkness and the light are both alike to You." Ps. 139:11-12

Some people might say that modern society doesn't do one thing in the daylight and something else when it is dark. The Psalmist was ashamed of his actions and wished it was dark so God and the world couldn't see.

We are prone to do evil in the dark. When one is out-of-town and people we know can not see us, we slip into a bar or even an adult movie. They can't see us. When mom was not around, we would let swear words slip out. Or when dad was gone, we sneaked out behind the barn and smoked. Wonder why lover's lane is used only after dark? Do lovers go too far because no one can see? Robbers, muggers, and rapist work mostly at night. CEO's and corporate board members steal from the company because they think the investor will never know. Or the clergy in their small office permit counseling to go too far.

Tell me why policeman say the average driver increases their speed by 10 mph after dark. Is the answer because they can't see the law – so the policeman can't see them? It seems that when night comes or the shades are pulled, we lose our inhibitions and break the laws of society and God.

The moral of the devotion is, "Remember daylight and dark are alike to God." Therefore, walk like a Christian all the time.

December 3

"For You formed my inward parts; You covered me in my mother's womb. I will praise You, for I am fearfully and wonderfully made; marvelous are your works, and that my soul knows very well."
Ps. 139:13-14

Does it amaze you, as it does me, to know that each of us have a DNA map in every cell? When mom and dad got together how did those cells know how to multiply and divide? After all there were many different kinds of cells in our body. How did this cell know to be an involuntary heart muscle cell, or be a hard toe nail, or be the vitreous humor in the eyeball? The simple answer is God formed our parts in our mother's womb.

If you agree with that last statement, we can say we are marvelously made. This is true whether you are five foot or seven foot tall. You are a master piece even if your nose or stomach sticks out a too far in front for you. God created some skinny as a rail and some like a snowman.

If we are a child of God, we all could agree that our soul was created beautiful. In this area, we don't argue with God. It is now cleansed and attractive enough to be permitted past the Gate of Pearl into heaven. The reason we agree that our soul is wonderfully and fearfully made is because no one can compare our soul with others. Therefore, my soul is as beautiful as yours.

Lord, I will praise You for You made me. I am so glad to be alive. Many of my school friends are with You already as are some of my enemies. I prefer walking and talking with you oh, Savior, day in and day out. Thanks again, Lord, for creating me!

December 4

"How precious also are your thoughts to me, O God! How great is the sum of them! If I should count them, they would be more in number than the sand; when I awake, I am still with You." Ps. 139:17-18

Do you know God never thinks a bad thought about you? He keeps saying, "You can do it; I know you can." God wants us to get better and better. He forgives us when we flub. He picks us up when we fall. He looks beyond our faults and sees our needs. His thoughts are always good toward us.

God watches out for us when critics analyze and vocalize their appraisal. He sees to it that we have moderate weather most of the time. The Lord sends persons to share our love and/or share our mental load. God is touched by our physical pain and emotional stress.

The Psalmist was overwhelmed at the true concern God has for each of us. The more he meditated on God, the more truly he was astonished. God's consideration for all the people of the earth was amazing. Thoughts tumbled one upon one another until the Psalmist said these thoughts would be as many as the sand in all Palestine. What a God who cares so much about us!

Even when the Psalmist fell asleep thinking about how God cares for him and his thoughts about God, he woke up in the presence of God. Not matter how often he drifted in and out of meditation, God was there to greet him.

It was staggering to contemplate the number of thoughts that God has toward us. Would it be staggering to God, when he thinks how few thoughts we have about Him? Our indifference does not lessen the number of good thoughts He has for you or me. Thank you, Lord!

December 5

"Search me, O God, and know my heart; try me, and know my anxieties; and see if there is any wicked way in me, and lead me in the way everlasting." Ps. 139:23-24

When you first fell in love, did you love them so much that you were willing to tell them every detail of your past? Instead in falling madly in love with a man/woman, the Psalmist fell completely in love with God. Here he gave God permission to search every area of his life as much as He pleases. He handed over his entire being, past, present, and future to God. All keys were available for every room in his life. No places were exempt from His scrutiny. There is no false piety or undue pride here. See, O Lord, if you can find any wicked way in me.

How deeply are we in love with Jesus? Oh, I dearly love to go to church on Sunday and sing that lively music, but during the week I can take Him or leave Him. Now I do believe in Jesus and read my Bible and say my prayers although I wouldn't ask Him to search my past. Some might say, "I've been born again." I love him and sometimes I feel his love but I have a secret I don't want him to know about. Very few of us would be like the Psalmist. If it will help me be more like Jesus – let it be! The feeling of oneness with Jesus is so enjoyable. I wouldn't have it any other way. I know when I give Christ my all. He takes better care of it than I ever could. He not only is good but the best.

Now that the Psalmist is at this point, he wants to remain surrendered. His closing request is have God lead him in the way everlasting. Joy continues in this close relationship Jesus Christ through conversation with Him and reading his letter to us. This joy endures even through any physical, emotional, or the mental storm in my life.

If you don't have this joy, let God search your life and lead you in the paths of righteousness.

December 6

"Search me, O God, and know my heart; try me, and know my anxieties; and see if there be any wicked way in me, and lead me in the way everlasting."   Ps. 139:23-24

The Psalmist and King David were brave souls! They were truly courageous to ask God to search their lives for sin and/or evil. I would even be leery of asking my dear mother to point out any sin in my life. She was finite and could only judge on what she saw. Even that would probably be more than I wanted to confess.

When we ask God to look in the dark corners of our heart, He would find lots more than mom ever saw. The scary part of asking God to bring his clipboard, is that He knows and can run the video tape of every thought that ever run through our mind. That area would be one gigantic floating mine field that could blow us plumb out of the water. Our confessions might be unending.

Would it be okay, if God knew every desire you ever had? It's overwhelming to think that all these would be brought up for inspection and consideration and then judged as to purity or evil!

Can you believe the Psalmist asked God to bring upon God's monitor every worry and fret? I can hardly believe that. How would we fair in this area of our life? The Psalmist must have trusted God for most everything. My mother-in-law, bless her heart was a worry-wart. God would put in overtime bringing up the archives in her "C" drive. Come to think of it, I am not much ahead of her.

The Psalmist gave up the goal of being worry-free and ask God to lead him in the way everlasting. Let's join him and humbly plead to God to keep us from any more sin, evil thoughts, wrong desires, or worries. God, I believe You will help and support us, starting right now!

December 7

"I know that the Lord will maintain the cause of the afflicted, and justice for the poor." Ps. 140:12

Surely you have heard the saying, "The squeaky wheel gets the grease"? The principle is plainly seen in the New Testament story about the widow and the unjust judge. She knocked on the lawyer's door every day of the world. Finally, because of her persistence, he granted her request.

In many countries the poor are not represented, so therefore does not have a voice against the injustice. When the population walks en mass, the Governor or President listens at that moment. They may or may not do a thing to alleviate their poverty.

The way to get something done is to continuously bring pressure to bear on the elected officials. I'm not sure threatening to kill them as they are doing in Columbia is the correct way.

The Psalmist knew of One who could keep the pressure on the oppressor! It was the Lord. He could maintain the pressure for the cause of those being unjustly burdened. God can load the oppressors with feelings of guilt. He can provide an antagonist, who is consistently at oppressor's very elbow.

God is strong! He is strong enough to see that justice comes to the poor. The time will come when the laborer will get paid a good day's pay for a good day's work. When equality and justice rolls down, the poor will rejoice.

December 8

"Set a guard, O Lord, over my mouth; keep watch over the door of my lips." Ps. 141:3

While this is being written there are National Guardsmen at the entrance of every airplane. They stand guard and are ever vigilant for terrorists. They never leave as long as there is a plane to be loaded.

Would you, like the Psalmist, be willing to ask Almighty God to place someone, maybe an angel, to sit or stand guard over our lips? Their job would be to watch each word that exits our mouth. If any outrageous promises, little words of revenge, ugly statements of gossip, or nasty curse words left your lips, they would take their sword and touch our conscience. Their hours of duty would be very minute we are awake. On their off hours they could go back to heaven to rest.

How busy would our guard be? Would they have to be ever ready with their sword? Or has our level of Christianity matured to where they could stand at parade rest most of the time?

How much do we strain out bad and evil thoughts and let the good ones past the doorway of our mouth? St. Matthew (15:18) says that evil words come from the heart. In other words, the mind has to think about the evil before it can be verbalized. If we boot out each evil thought immediately, only good will remain. Then with only good thoughts in our heart or head, only wholesome words will depart our lips.

If we have trouble with kicking bad thoughts out of our mind, we can always call on God. While we are still requesting help, God can be on the way to assisting us with our problem. Lord, help us to give the guard over our mouth a rest today.

December 9

"Set a guard, O Lord, over my mouth; keep watch over the door of my lips." Ps. 141:3

How many of us have a problem of saying the wrong words at the wrong time? Were we telling a friend about the co-worker's bad traits and they over heard? Were we telling the truth but we realized later that we didn't have all the facts? Was there a time when you said the right thing but in the wrong tone of voice? These got us in trouble up to about our chin.

King Solomon advises us to listen more and talk less. If we use a multitude of words, we are more apt to slip and say something we don't mean. So we might do our part by not having to voice our opinion on every subject. We could wait until we are asked to speak.

The son of King David also mentions that what we think is what comes out of our mouth (Prov. 23:7). So another area that would help what exits our mouth is to keep guard over any evil, bad, or jealous thoughts. These thoughts need to be crowded out. Like a tree can not bear both good and bad fruit, so our mind can not think good and bad thoughts at the same time.

We might ask God to break down the strongholds of our mind. Let God into the depository of all the bad memories and smoldering thoughts of the past. It is our Fort Knox where old hurts cause us to lash out or get even at an unprotected moment.

If we do our part, we can pray to God to sit just outside our mouth. May our lips not be our downfall nor embarrass You, Lord. Let our mouth build your kingdom. Please Oh, Lord, please keep watch over the door of our lips. Thanks You, God.

December 10

"Let the righteous strike me; it shall be a kindness. And let him rebuke me; it shall be as excellent oil; let my head not refuse it." Ps. 141:5

The Psalmist found a group of people that could really help him. This group gives sound advice and solid suggestions. They are never vindictive. They are never arrogant with their help. The advice is always constructive. Without exception, they are kind in how they present it because their suggestion is guided by the rule, "Do unto others as you would have them do unto you." Their suggestions are always for our good and not for any advantage for them. Their concern is for **our** welfare. This group of people is the righteous. In today's world, they would be genuine Christians.

How hard is it to listen to a close friend, sometimes our spouse, who is only concerned about our advancement? If constructive criticism were internalized and instituted, it would make us far more valuable to the company. Being more beneficial to the company would enhance our chances for a pay increase. Getting a monetary raise would inflate our self-esteem, thereby, making us a better citizen.

With these advantages, wouldn't it be wise to listen to what Christian co-workers. All of what they say should be placed against the big picture of what the goals of the company are and common sense. The Psalmist got to that point. We hold the Psalmist up as a wise and intelligent person. It surely would be profitable to follow his example!

December 11

"But my eyes are upon You, O God the Lord; in You I take refuge; do not leave my soul destitute. Keep me from the snares they have laid for me, and from the traps of the workers of iniquity. Let the wicked fall into their own nets, while I escape safely." Ps. 141:8-10

The Psalmist knew where his bread was buttered. He kept his eyes looking toward God. It was Almighty God who gave him breath, kept his heart pumping, and provided his daily bread. When his spiritual enemy or social enemies came around, he looked to the One who could without exception deliver him.

Not only did the Psalmist look to God as protector but as his Lord. For the Psalmist, the word lord meant that he obeyed Him as the Master of his life. God was to be honored but also obeyed.

The Psalmist had a true view of himself. He said that his soul was destitute. He could do nothing of any real consequence to rescue himself. It was God who was omnipotent. God, please guide my feet so they won't step into the traps set by the people who want my position at work. Lord, direct me around snares made by people who are jealous of my Christian lifestyle.

Let these tempters get caught in their own

devices. When they get caught, help me not to delight in their receiving their just desserts. May I extend grace to them as You have so often done for me when I truly deserved punishment. May I not feel glad at their getting caught in their own evil schemes.

My heavenly Father, assist me today to shift my attention from my problems to You, my Problem Solver. When trouble comes, I will run to You. Attempting to solve them myself will no longer be an option for me.

December 12

"I cry out to the Lord with my voice; with my voice to the Lord I make my supplication. I pour out my complaint before him; I declare before Him my trouble." Ps. 142:1-2

You can dump each and every emotional problem before the Lord in prayer. It's okay! Really! Not only is it permissible but advisable! When things get to be too much, the Lord wants his children to call on him. After you have had a heated discussion with your child, you are encouraged to take your burden to the Lord. Tell Him all about it – vent it. If you can, leave that stress or burden with the Lord, as you arise to go on with your life.

Many of us after a horrific crisis must orally relate all the sordid details three to six different times to get any relief. Our Lord never sleeps and is always available for these recitals. God never tires of our coming to Him with our problems. They can be the same trouble over and over. Personally, I went to God with the same weakness for fifty two years. He never tired but slowly gave me strength to overcome. He was teaching me dependence on Him.

The Psalmist has the antidote to negativity. He gave every complaint he had to God in prayer. His complaints were not heaped on his friends, neighbors, or enemies. God is glad to hear what is hurting or upsetting us. Then what the Psalmist spoke to others was pleasant.

As we reread the scripture, we notice that he vocalized his requests and complaints. Sometimes it helps us to release our burden, when we actually hear ourselves say it. It has been proven to help alleviate emotional and neutralize stress. Hopefully, we aren't ashamed for our family or others to hear us talking to our Savior. If you haven't audibly prayed lately, I challenged you to try it soon.

December 13

"I pour out my complaint before Him; I declare before him my trouble. ...Answer me speedily, O Lord; my spirit fails! Do not hide your face from me, lest I be like those who go down into the pit. Cause me to hear your loving-kindness in the morning, for in You do I trust; cause me to know the way in which I should walk, for I lift up my soul to You." Ps. 142:2, Ps. 143:7, 8

Is your craw stretched to the limit with hurts, others cutting remarks, lots of revenge thoughts, some hatreds and a few grudges? All of these are creating emotional indigestion. This psychological heartburn is painful.

The Psalmist over his many years of life learned the remedy to this malady. He deliberately one by one regurgitated each hurt. Then he vervally rehashed his complaint before God. It seems the Lord patiently listened to each and every problem and never refused to hear one.

The pain of psychological indigestion is so severe the Psalmist cried, 'Please, oh, please Lord, hurry and heal me. This may be the death of me. Lord, don't turn and walk away or I'll lose all hope. If You do, my end will be like the vilest sinner.'

My heart yearns to hear your kind words of forgiveness. Brighten my life before I faint under this load of anxiety. I trust entirely in You. Only You can clean out my craw and give me the urge to crow about your goodness.'

The Psalmist ends with one more request. 'Lord, guide my feet in the right way. My desire is to be an excellent model for the younger people, who are watching my life. May your Holy Spirit direct each of my actions so I will never get my craw full ever again.'

December 14

"Look on my right hand and see, for there is no one who acknowledges me; refuge has failed me; no one cares for my soul." Ps. 142:4

Have you ever been in a jam? When you looked for a friend, they were all elsewhere. When you searched for someone to help you, there was no one in sight. You know, like the last time you needed a policeman – they were on a call. Can't you just feel the pathos in the voice of our Palmist? He asks if anyone might help! No one, literally no one was around to help. After a careful look for assistance, he said that no one paid a bit of attention. Have you been there?

The Psalmist looked for a hiding place. The sand dunes offered no defense from the elements or the enemy. Have you been in a position where everybody could take a pot shot of criticism about you or at your work? When you looked for support no one would stand up. It is, oh, so lonely when you are there!

Are there times your children ever say, "No one

cares about whether I go to heaven or not"? Have you in your table grace blessed their brother or sister and they just knew their name is included when they are absent? Have you ever checked on whether they were: reading their bible? Praying? Attending church somewhere? Remembering to call on God when decisions pressure them? Mentioned that you are praying each night for them? Hopefully, you have shown your concern for their soul in someway or you have decided to demonstrate your love for their soul. Hopefully your children will never get to say, "No one cares about my soul."

December 15
"I remember the days of old; I meditate on all your works; I muse on the works of your hands. I spread out my hands to You; my soul longs for You like a thirsty land." Ps. 143:5-6

How old are you? Are you old enough to remember some good old days? Remember the days when all you had to do was play – no housework, no daily job, nor bills to pay! Maybe you can hearken back to: Duz soap, P-F Flyers, Whiz candy bars, Butch Wax, Cloverine salve, kerosene lamps or even Model "T"s.

The Psalmist remembers back when times were slower. He had found time to just sit and meditate on things. He had time to think on things of God like: power of the moon, why trees reach for God, how man has an internal urge to know God, and how things go well when man thinks continually about God.

The Psalmist stretched his hands heavenward with the palms up. He thought all I have, Lord, I give to You. You have been so gracious to me! I present to You my praise for all the blessings, both spiritual and physical.

While his arms were extended upward, he thought about his small niche in such a mammoth plan. Since the palms are turned upward, he let the longings in his heart roll up his sleeve to his hand. There the longings lay like a dry sponge before the Lord. How it longed to soak up its fill of the majesty of God. His heart cried in thirst for more of God in his life, as a dry cornfield craves a shower. If and when God rains on the Psalmist's soul, nothing could be better or more satisfying.

As our minds recall the old times and remember God's love, we praise God for his presence in our life!

December 16

"Cause me to hear your loving kindness in the morning, for in You do I trust; cause me to know the way in which I should walk, for I lift up my soul to You."   Ps. 143:8

Do you ever wake up in a bad mood? You know, one of those days when everything tees you off, or anything said tips your saucer, and nothing satisfies. Surely the Psalmist hated those days as much as we do. He pleads with God to direct him. Instead of the Psalmist scanning his packed schedule for problems or the discouraging prospect of meeting with a wrangling board, he yearns to hear the tender and soothing voice of God. He dearly longs to feel the loving-kindness of God. Having this love is so much better than a piping hot mug of coffee and a lip-licking delicious fresh donut or an ice-cold coke to start the day.

Whether it was a good or bad day, the Psalmist was dependant on God. He put his trust in the Lord. He did this consistently. Seldom, if ever did he start the day trusting in his own wisdom or preparation. Each step he took throughout the day was in compliance with the will of God. Oh, if we could only say we trusted the guidance of God throughout each day. There are days we begin like the Psalmist, but soon we feel we know better than God and make decisions on our own.

The Psalmist was so close to God that he was willing to present his soul to God. He was comfortable with giving God his heart. In his imagination, he scooped his soul out of his body, presented it to God. What courage! Oh, but it didn't take courage for the Psalmist. He was sure God would touch his soul with his loving-kindness and bless it. Never did he feel a hint of fear.

Could we make a decision similar to the Psalmist? He states that **every** morning he asked Almighty God to touch his soul with heavenly loving-kindness. From that moment on throughout that day, he would trust in God to guide his steps in the way everlasting. Do you think we can do it? I hope! Let's try it.

December 17

"Teach me to do your will, for You are my God; your Spirit is good. Lead me in the land of uprightness." Ps. 143:10

"Teach me to do your will." The Psalmist was willing to learn. I have a seven year old granddaughter who knows all the answers! If you don't believe me, ask her how anything works and she'll tell you. Oh, don't tell me you were one of those teenagers, who didn't need to be instructed!

The attitude of learning starts with being humble enough to listen. We need to open our ears to the words and our mind to their meaning. The next step is assimilating or absorbing what was declared. Many listen but let the vibrations go in one ear and out the other. To be useful the knowledge needs to be stored so later you can add it to other information and come with valid conclusions.

The Psalmist was open to learning the will of God. God wants each person to submit themselves back to Him, the Creator. We are then adopted into the family of God out of the Devil's family. As we continue our personal relationship of Father and child, we have fellowship one with the other. It is similar to God in us and us in God.

The closer we stay to God, the easier it is to find the will of God for specific situations in our lives. In our daily devotions of reading God's word and conversation with God, we are enlightened as to God's wishes for our daily life. The leading of the Holy Spirit will be less like a bridle and more like verbal commands. It is no longer a pain but a joy to fulfill the desire of God. Walking in the steps of our Savior will be the way of the upright. Oh, how pleased God will be and how contented we will feel!

December 18

"My loving kindness and my fortress, my high tower and my deliverer, my shield and the One in whom I take refuge, who subdues my people under me." Ps. 144:2

Surely King David had discontents and rowdies under him as he ruled all Israel. Some of these people were in his court, his advisors, and/or his generals. The Psalmist here is appealing to God to keep his omnipotent hand on all under him.

All of you who are in leadership positions can follow the example of our wise Psalmist. You can call on God to watch the actions of those under your supervision. God can stay ever near that negative person in your unit. He can be at the water cooler, when the faultfinding person makes those critical comments about your decisions or leadership style. God's eyes never shut but keeps watch over that insubordinate person. He watches the schemes they initiate. Nothing passes the Almighty's gaze. There are times when you are not sure when a worker is trying to deceive you. God knows their heart and can mete out just punishment. God knows the hiding place of the lazy.

Another group under you that God watches is the aggressively ambitious. God also watches those who are conniving to get your job. God is not asleep. So when we call on God to subdue the people under us, God understands and will take care of them. He will do this to keep you from worrying. (Matthew 6:34). In the time of trouble, God will deliver us and permit the disaster to fall on the troublemakers (Jeremiah 14:8-9).

Lord, please be my fortress, my high tower, my refuge, and my shield. Your loving kindness is the joy of my life. I firmly believe, now help me keep in mind that you will subdue all the workers under my supervision.

December 19

"Lord, what is man, that You take knowledge of him? Or the son of man, that You are mindful of him? Man is like a breath; his days are like a passing shadow." Ps. 144:3-4

Humans are really something! We can discover, invent, and organize. As women, we can become a loving mother or we can be a business woman and became an executive or possibly a WEO. The men can begin as a laborer and move up to crew chief. From there they become boss or manager on a monthly salary. On up the ladder they can go to vice-president or CEO. Some may attain political power and have substantial clout in Washington, DC. Possibly one could gain the stature of a top executive in a corporation pulling down a million dollars a year. Perchance one might become a mogul with several homes, multiple holding and ride in a limousine and on a Lear Jet.

With all these successes, what is man? We are born penniless and grow to the mature age of 60 or 70 and die. Whose will all this success be then? God was here when the earth was born. Who do we consider ourselves to be, when most of us will not live one hundred years? A century is a blink in the whole scope of time. Our lives are to God are like the shadow of a tree on the grassy pasture on one sunny summer day.

But Glory! God, Creator of all the universes that are in existence, is mindful of us! The One without beginning or end cares when we are hurting physically or emotionally. He is vitally interested that we accept the cleansing blood of his only Son. He is concerned that we miss hell and that we enjoy heaven. His supreme desire is that none should perish but all should inherit eternal life in heaven (II Peter 3:9).

December 20

"I will extol You, my God, O King; and I will bless your name forever and ever. Every day I will bless You, and I will praise your name forever and ever. Great is the Lord, and greatly to be praised; and his greatness is unsearchable." Ps. 145:1-3

I promise to extol the Lord. I will exalt, magnify and applaud, pay tribute to, honor, acclaim, and enthusiastically approve of God. You notice the

Psalmist was self-motivated. God did not coerce him to sing these praises.

Could we, like the Psalmist, deliberately say, "I will highly extol or praise my Lord?" That would mean that we would brag on Jesus ever chance we got. When we whistled or hummed, it would be about Him. When at church or in the choir, we would lift our voice in praise to Him. If out of the blue the pastor or Sunday School teacher should ask if anyone had a testimony or a good word for Jesus, we would stand.

The vow of the Psalmist was to praise God everyday. If we made the same pledge, would we need reminders along the way like: a cross in our pocket, the sight of a hymn book, or hear a key word? Surely God would not want us to do punishments, if we missed a day, but would keep encouraging us.

Praising God everyday would be great practice for praising God throughout eternity. The end goal of the Psalmist was to praise God forever. What a dream!

His objective was to be in continual praise to God. Oh, how great God is! He is so wonderful and enormous that his greatness is unsearchable. Our effort would accomplish as much as if we placed a tablespoon of praise into a tall elevator silo. Even though it might take us a lifetime to fill that silo, we must continue praising God.

December 21

"One generation shall praise your works to another, and shall declare your mighty acts." Ps. 145:4

How many stories can you repeat that your grandparents told you? How many tales can you repeat from your parents? Americans aren't inclined to tell stories to their children.

These are stories of your family tree. Other stories are from experiences where you learned a lesson of life. These could help your children avoid some hard knocks in their lives. There are events in history you witnessed, which would be exciting to your offspring. In my life, I personally saw President Harry S. Truman. The U. S. President that had a plaque on his desk that read, "The Buck Stops Here".

The Psalmist knew that current events march down the halls of history, but the omnipotence of Lord is the same yesterday, today, and forever. God is the strength that is always present in our time of need.

Can you recall a time when the Spirit of God was so close the hair on your arms stood at attention? That would be wonderful to tell your children. Was there a time that by a miracle of God you are still here? Think about the details and recite that to your grandchildren. Don't be surprised, if they ask you to tell it again. Parents reading all the Bible stories each night with expression can lay a wonderfully secure foundation for the future decisions of your children.

See how exiting your family will be, when you start reading the Bible stories and recounting God's miracles in your life!

December 22

"The Lord is gracious and full of compassion, slow to anger and great in mercy. The Lord is good to all, and his tender mercies are over all his works."
Ps. 145:8-9

Who do you know that has a super-short fuse? They can get angry in less than a minute. The cause could be the least little thing. The Psalmist must have known someone like that too, when he wrote this Psalm. He contrasted God's almost imperturbable patience with your short-fused friend.

God did get angry. One time just outside Canaan He sentenced the Israelites to walk in the Wilderness for forty years. During that trip, they made a golden calf and made God angry. Another time King David insisted on taking a census after God said, "No." That is why the Psalmist stated that God is slow to anger. We could say God has an extra long fuse.

The next part of the scripture changes to the positive and constructive. God's mercy is great! When we get our self in trouble, the Lord in his mercy reaches down from heaven and gets us out. Even when we knowingly commit the sin, God forgives. After we try to get revenge, which is God's job, He still forgives if we will confess and ask to be cleansed.

Some will say, "I've been so bad, God will not forgive me!" The Psalmist gives the comforting statement, "His tender mercies are over all his works." God made you. You are entitled to full redemption! His desire is to pay the price to redeem you from the bondage of sin. You are a prime candidate for full salvation in God's eyes. Just sincerely say, "Lord, I'm sorry for the sins I have committed. Please forgive me (redeem me) and adopt me as hour child." Believe that Jesus is the Son of God and that he will keep his word and save you (I John 1:9, Rom. 10:9-10). God always patiently forgives us!

December 23

"All your works shall praise You, O Lord, and your saints shall bless You."   Ps. 145:10

Earlier the Psalmist stated that nature would praise God before humans would? Could his reasoning be that nature does not rebel against God's intended purpose? The blade of grass holds a drop of dew so the morning sun can split the rays and show us a rainbow thus glorifying the Creator. The majestic mountains stand firm against the azure sky dotted with cotton ball clouds beneath high wispy cirrus clouds thus declaring God's omnipotence. Nature consistently displays and honors God.

Humankind seems intent on themselves. So often we are driven to fulfill the Day-Timer schedule that we forget about God until bedtime. Other times we are so focused on getting and having, that we neglect any thoughts of blessing God. Many days we are so occupied with earning a living that we don't give a fleeting thought to God. The Psalmist wanted us to do more than think about Him but to actively bless the Lord.

When we do find time to bless the Lord, often all God hears is our supplications and requests. Oh, how often I have been guilty of only having "gimme" prayers. Every phrase we pray starts with "I want!" A good remedy to that sort of prayer is to begin with blessing the Lord. In other words, relate all the virtues of God and describe how you have been blessed by them. Next, in the line of prayer, would be to get on a thanksgiving spree. Count those blessings name them one by one. Then if you have time, you might confess any sin and then humbly ask God to fill any needs you may have.

Let's decide today to praise God like nature.

December 24

"The Lord is righteous in all his ways, gracious in all his works. The Lord is near to all who call upon Him, to all who call upon Him in truth. He will fulfill the desire of those who fear Him; He also will hear their cry and save them." Ps. 145:17-19

The Lord is righteous in all his ways. Wouldn't it be good to never sin! God without exception always thinks and performs good and constructive things. People will always be helped by God's actions. The future is in the hands of our righteous God, who dearly loves and tenderly cares about each of us.

The Lord is gracious in all his works. How lenient and compassionate He is, when we flub up! God is compassionate and warm-hearted even after we leave him and return. Our Lord continues to be gentle and benevolent, when we treat his commands with indifference.

The Lord is near those who humbly entreat God in prayer. Insincere prayers and preposterous requests are not honored by God. Do you think God hears prayers prayed out of duty? Does he consider them vain babbling, like the Pharisees of his day did on the street corners?

The Lord will fulfill the desires of his children who hold God in awe. Those, who honor and obey his commands, are entitled to having their longings satisfied. In our scripture, did you catch that "fulfill your desires" part? Can we actually believe that? God spoke though the Psalmist, right? I am sure we can believe God!

The Lord will hear our prayer of confession and save our soul from spending eternity with Lucifer. Oh! What a wonderful bargain. He takes all there is of me and gives me all there is of Him. Since there is more of God than there is of me, that is a greatest bargain in the world!

The words of the Psalmist give me such a hope and exhilaration! What a magnanimous God we serve!

December 25

"Do not put your trust in princes, nor in a son of man, in whom there is no help. His spirit departs, he returns to his earth; in that day his plans perish. Happy is he who has the God of Jacob for his help, whose hope is in the Lord his God," Ps. 146:3-5

Do you rely on Social Security for all your retirement? Do you trust the President to keep the economy going so your stocks will grow? Does your boy-girl friend or spouse bring you all your happiness? Do you trust your intuition to make you wealthy?

The Psalmist says it unwise even detrimental to trust in the President of United States or any human being. At any minute they could die. There would go your hopes and dreams as well as, any confidence we had put in them to help. All that hope vanished in a second.

Happy is the person who trusts in God. In our Savior we find eternal continuity. When we are ready to sink, our God extends compassion and mercy, when we are ready to sink. The Almighty never sleeps or is on break. God's Holy Spirit is ever with us. God is closer than hands or feet. Since we have trust in Christ as Savior, a piece of divine nature has been placed within us. How much better than trusting a Senator or Governor!

Humans have a spirit that departs, when they die. The physical body begins to decay immediately but the spirit never dies. The crucial question is, "Where will your spirit depart to?" If you want to be sure it goes to heaven, make preparations now. Believe that Jesus, the babe of Bethlehem truly is the Son of Almighty God. Confess any sin the Holy Spirit lays on our mind, and then God will cleanse you of all sin and unrighteousness. If you did that, you are ready to walk right through that gate into heaven at this very moment.

December 26

"The Lord builds up Jerusalem; He gathers together the outcast of Israel." Ps. 147:2

There is no other religion that welcomes outcasts and rejects of society. Even before Jesus came to earth, God was looking for those who had messed up their life.

Moses was one who had the best of everything as an adopted child of the king of Egypt. He was standing up for one of slaves and killed the foreman but God still used him.

King David had it good, too. He accidentally fell in love with Bathsheba. Having her husband killed made him a murderer. The scriptures say David was a son after God's own heart.

Esther had the opposite: She was an orphan and was raised by her Uncle Mordecai. Poor as she was, God made her a queen.

Zacchaeus was a hated man by all his neighbors. This leader was rejected by his countrymen because he helped the conquering country. Jesus came by and saw the good in him and forgave him.

The woman at the well was literally married five times. She could not keep a husband. Jesus totally rearranged her life. Immediately thereafter she led an entire town to the Lord.

Legion was rejected by his family, his neighbors, and the entire country. Jesus didn't fear him but loved him and changed his life. He became a missionary to ten cities for Christ.

The two thieves on the crosses next to Jesus were not only rejected but crucified by the government. The one asked God and was forgiven and went to heaven.

Today God is looking for outcasts and rejects. Why don't you say, "Lord, take me with all my faults? Use me to be a trophy of what You can do through your almighty power."

December 27

"Who covers the heavens with clouds, who prepares rain for the earth, who makes grass to grow on the mountains. He gives to the beast its food, and to the young ravens that cry.' Ps. 147:8-9

Oh, have you ever stopped to think how the wild mustangs in the west, the bobcats in the mountains and sea gull get fed? Or have you wondered how the hobos, runaway kids, and children who live under bridges eat? God can look down into the dark alley and see exactly how hungry he/she is? Invisibly God guides them to where food is available. Some attribute this to fate or good luck, but only God can arrange such things.

It is marvelous how God can manage when his children need fed. When the children of Israel had walked up out of the Red Sea, they had to be fed. There were 600,000 men by count. If you added a wife for each and only one child, you now have 1.8 million to feed. Can you imagine how many railroad tank cars of water each day? Oh, don't forget the water for the cows and goats that produced milk and the camels that served as trucks. Now figure how many boxcars of wheat and refrigerator cars of meat to feed the million plus mouths. Check this out! God did it 365 days a year for forty years. He accomplished it without a railroad or a fleet of semi-trailers. Let's give God a hand for faithfully providing for our ancestors.

God is still supplying food for the flocks of birds,

herds of antelope, gaggles of geese, hordes of elephants, and nations of people. So tonight let's remember to thank and praise God for his provision.

December 28

"He does not delight in the strength of the horse; He takes no pleasure in the legs of a man. The Lord takes pleasure in those who fear Him, in those who hope in his mercy." Ps. 147:10-11

Have you ever taken the time to carefully look at a well groomed stallion or mare? The hair on their back shimmers like silk. They are so graceful as they trot, cantor, gallop, and run. Their muscles ripple as they call on strength to run. They are strong. Some horses of medieval times carried a knight in full armor. In early America, teams of Clydesdale (Budweiser horses) horses pulled tons of logs to the saw mill. The Psalmist admired both the strength and beauty of horses. He watched some people put their trust in the speed or strength of their horse. God is not pleased when we delight in the power of a horse to the neglect of the Lord.

Have you known a marathon runner? Their legs carry them 26.5 miles without a rest. It makes me tired just thinking about running that far. My friend was nearing sixty five and has run in 49 or 50 marathons. He could have bragged about his legs. The opposite was true for my friend. He was most delighted when a person brought up the subject of Jesus. He loved to tell anyone how he accepted Jesus Christ as his Savior. His trust was in the Lord, not in the strength of his legs.

Let us follow the admonition of the Psalmist. Each moment, let's hold God in holy awe. As we start each day, humbly entreat God to protect us from evil, and guide us past traps of Satan. When we walk in the light of Jesus' word, God, himself is very pleased. How wonderful it feels to please God! The feeling, like we experienced as a child when we pleased Dad or Mom, but multiplied. Happy are you, if you enjoy pleasing God.

December 29

"For the Lord takes pleasure in his people; He will beautify the humble with salvation." Ps. 149:4

The Lord takes pleasure in causing your efforts to be successful. God listens to and glad to answer many of your prayers in a positive way. The Almighty delights in assisting your children in growing into mature Christians. The Lord revels in touching the sick person you are praying for. Our Creator glories in causing the love between a husband and wife to be strong. Rejoicing occurs in heaven, when the heavenly Father forgives a sinner.

God loves pleasing us but when was the last time we pleased Him? God likes it, when we stop telling Him what we want done in our prayers and just show up for duty.

When we admit we are nothing without Him, God is pleased with us. When we get to that point, God promises to beautify us. That doesn't mean a perm or haircut, lift off some wrinkles or delete some crow's feet, nor melt off some fat. This beauty gives a glow from the inside out. It is the results of salvation, which is, being saved from all our sin. Your smile then will always be genuine, never false or phony. Your personality will be winsome and charming because of the clear conscience and the spark of divine nature inside. God is always successful in personality make-overs. Let's go to Him.

December 30

"Praise the Lord! Praise God in his sanctuary; Praise Him in his mighty firmament." Ps. 150:1

Should we have to be urged to praise the Lord, who saved us from sin and eternal punishment? We should continually thank and praise the One, who saw that we lived at birth. Our motivation ought to be internal. External motivation is only good as long as the pressure is on. As an example, take the moments preceding and during a final exam. As soon as, it is turned in, we go into a relaxed state. The motivation to be attentive and remember is gone.

The Psalmist realized that even saints need to be reminded to praise the Lord. The last five or so Psalms are chucked full of admonitions to praise the Lord.

First, he urges us to praise God at church. Have we gone many Sundays and worshiped but didn't praise the Lord? Isn't praise a frame of mind, as well as saying words like: hallelujah, glory, and amen? Our attitude switches from duty to a form of thanksgiving. In other words, we change from thinking about what we are doing to what God has been doing for us.

Second, the Psalmist admonishes us to praise God everywhere, not just when we come out from under the roof of the church. St. Paul urges us to rejoice at all times (I Thess. 5:16). Similarly, the Psalmist wants us to praise the Lord continually. That would replace every syllable of negativity out of our speech? What a world we would live in, if all Christians unceasing praised the Lord! That lifestyle might intimidate our co-workers, who are forever griping or putting someone down.

So let's praise God in church and everywhere on the earth!

December 31

"Let everything that has breath praise the Lord. Praise the Lord!" Ps. 150:6

Oh, how magnificent is our God! Who can calculate when God began? His knowledge makes our Library of Congress seem almost insignificant. God's wisdom exceeds the outer limits of our imagination. The authority of God covers every action of man and beast. Nothing, not even Satan, has a shadow of the power God possesses. Our Lord knows our thoughts before we think them. He knows and guides our actions with his divine providence. Who but God guides the lioness to the antelope, the ant to a crumb left from a picnic, or our children away from sin? The Almighty knows how many hairs are on our head and which ones will turn white this week. The power of Jesus in his short lifetime gives us a glimpse of the Almighty One. We can only imagine the purity of God. We have all sinned and fallen way short, like my trial shot-put I gave in an effort to get on the team. How faithful and trustworthy is God to keep every promise! He has never failed to keep one of his promises. We often see things from one point of view. Our all-wise God always renders a just verdict. God continues to be patient with us after we habitually say, "I don't want to give You my all, yet." His desire is that none should perish in the flames of the Lake of Fire.

God's love is like a 100% pure chocolate. No matter where you might look in that chunk of chocolate all you find is chocolate. No matter how you look at God, you always see love and mercy. Let's praise him all next year as the Psalmist urges us.